Anthropology
at the Front Lines
of Gender-Based Violence

Anthropology
at the Front Lines
of Gender-Based Violence

Edited by Jennifer R. Wies
and Hillary J. Haldane

Vanderbilt University Press
Nashville

© 2011 by Vanderbilt University Press
Nashville, Tennessee 37235
All rights reserved
First printing 2011

This book is printed on acid-free paper made
from 30% post-consumer recycled content.
Manufactured in the United States of America

Library of Congress Cataloging-in-Publication Data

Anthropology at the front lines of gender-based violence/
Jennifer R. Wies and Hillary J. Haldane, editors.
p. cm.
Includes bibliographical references and index.
ISBN 978-0-8265-1780-7 (cloth edition : alk. paper)
ISBN 978-0-8265-1781-4 (pbk. edition : alk. paper)
1. Violence—Cross-cultural studies. 2. Women—Violence
against—Cross-cultural studies. 3. Abused women—Cross-
cultural studies. 4. Domestic violence—Cross-cultural
studies. I. Wies, Jennifer R. II. Haldane, Hillary J.
GN495.2.A567 2011
303.6'2—dc22
2010040505

*This book is dedicated to all frontline workers
who respond to and prevent gender-based violence:
Your tireless efforts transform thousands of lives.*

Contents

Acknowledgments

This volume grew from a conversation in a hotel coffee shop in Vancouver, British Columbia, in 2006 during the Society for Applied Anthropology meetings. We were both finishing our dissertations and felt fortunate to connect with another anthropologist committed to the issue of gender-based violence. While the field has grown rapidly in the past few years, our own literature reviews were constructed largely of accounts by sociologists, psychologists, and social workers. We believe that anthropology has much to contribute to this important field of study, and this book is a result of our shared passion to ultimately eliminate gender-based violence. We came to this topic from our own experiences on the front lines, working in emergency shelters as victim advocates and hotline volunteers. We have personally felt the adrenaline rush and nausea that can overwhelm one when driving to a hospital emergency room or police station in the middle of the night to assist a survivor of violence. In that coffee shop we commiserated over our common frustrations with a safety net of care that sometimes appeared to have more holes than thread, and how our prevention efforts seemed to fall short. But we were energized by the spirit of humanity and compassion that cuts across the various sectors of the front line, across communities, and even nation-states. We convinced each other that *Anthropology at the Front Lines of Gender-Based Violence* was the much-needed next step to the contributions in anthropology focusing on gender-based violence.

The workers whose stories are presented in this book deserve attention, support, and appreciation. We cannot thank all the workers by name, but we hope that you find the stories told here to be a faithful rendition of your thoughts and work. On behalf of our colleagues, and the survivors to whom you devote your energies, thank you for your labor, devotion, and care.

Many colleagues have supported our efforts through the years. Three fellow travelers in the field of gender-based violence deserve special mention. Melissa Beske and Karin Friederic have joined us on panels at conferences over the years and their work has helped us to think about the diversity of experiences that the anthropologists, as well as the workers have in this field. Sarah Orndorff organized a panel for the 2008 Society for Applied Anthropology meetings entitled Experiences of Violence, Sites of Recovery: Understanding the Complexities of Intimate Partner Violence that led to a special issue of *Global Public Health*. The papers from that panel provided clarity on what issues we wanted to tackle here.

Madelaine Adelman's work on political economy and domestic violence provided the theoretical framework from which this volume developed. Her feedback on early drafts and her comments from a working session at a conference on gender-based violence in 2009 helped us see the promise in this project. Sarah Hautzinger agreed to serve as a discussant for a panel we held in 2010, and her comments from that session reminded us of the importance of this project and the unique perspective it brings to the field.

We are especially appreciative of the feedback from our two anonymous reviewers, who identified lacunae in the original draft, and their critiques have lead to a much stronger final text. While we incorporated feedback and suggestions from our reviewers, colleagues, and friends, we alone are responsible for any mistakes, errors, or disagreeable arguments found in the book.

Individually, Jennifer would like to thank her colleagues at Eastern Kentucky University and Xavier University for supporting her efforts. In addition, she sends thanks to her family for their inspiration, passion, and support. Hillary would like to thank her family for patiently living with this project for the past four years. Her colleagues at Quinnipiac University provided the humor and support necessary to keep everything in perspective.

Anthropology
at the Front Lines
of Gender-Based Violence

1

Ethnographic Notes from the Front Lines of Gender-Based Violence

Jennifer R. Wies and Hillary J. Haldane

> My work is a part of empowering the whole community. When there is violence it is the community's soul that is injured. . . . As a community, we need to ask, "Are you safe at home? Are you OK? Is there anyone you fear?" Because it is not OK if you live in fear, it is not OK that this is happening, and this can change. So it comes out of the shame, the silence, and we as a total community are releasing people from the shame of abuse. That's my ideal world.
> —Frontline worker, New Zealand

Anthropology at the Front Lines of Gender-Based Violence presents anthropologically informed ethnographies of frontline workers in the field of gender-based violence. It explores how hotline counselors, emergency shelter advocates, court advocates, child protection workers, police officers, lawyers, shelter directors, psychologists, and other direct services workers comfort, advocate for, and assist victims and survivors of gender-based violence and why these workers perform their labor. It examines the models of care and compassion they employ and tells their personal and professional stories. The chapters address the delivery of services, the struggle for legal recognition, the effort to improve the lives of victims and survivors, and the challenges of ending violence. By focusing on the front line, the "small spaces of interaction" (Merry 2008, 520), this collection illustrates the ways that workers create meaning, frameworks, and identities in a local context. At the same time, it exposes the ways that frontline workers shape and are influenced by global institutions dedicated to addressing and preventing gender-based violence.

Frontline workers offer a unique perspective to our understanding of violence. While the perspectives of the policy makers, victims, and survivors are critically important to how we conceptualize adequate responses to gender-based violence, they have only one story to tell: their own story of violence and survival or the story of the institution or organization they direct. Frontline workers can tell hundreds of stories of victimhood and survival. They can map the scope and scale of violence in their communities, and they are attuned to the ways shifts in policy affect the day-to-day decision-making of the very people such policy is intended to help. They are the barometer of violence, and understanding their stories is a necessary part of any effective effort to end the global pandemic of gender-based violence.

Gender-Based Violence

We define gender-based violence as violence against an individual or population based on gender identity or expression. We understand gender-based violence to be violence occurring in the family or the general community that is perpetrated or condoned by the state (United Nations 1993). Gender-based violence includes multiple forms of violence and reflects the political-economic structures that perpetuate gender-based inequalities among people and populations. Gender-based violence includes violence against women, defined by the United Nations High Commissioner for Human Rights (1993) as

> any act of gender-based violence that results in, or is likely to result in, physical, sexual or psychological harm or suffering to women, including threats of such acts, coercion or arbitrary deprivation of liberty, whether occurring in public or in private life, and including domestic violence, crimes committed in the name of honour, crimes committed in the name of passion, trafficking in women and girls, traditional practices harmful to women, including female genital mutilation, early and forced marriages, female infanticide, dowry-related violence and deaths, acid attacks and violence related to commercial sexual exploitation as well as economic exploitation.

Gender-based violence also includes acts of violence perpetrated toward individuals and populations as a result of gender positionality. It includes acts of pedophilia, sexual assault of female and male prostitutes, human trafficking, and violence perpetrated toward people because of their gender expression, including individuals and populations that self-identify as gay, lesbian, bisexual, transgender, or queer.

To situate gender-based violence within global political-economic structures and processes, our analysis of gender-based violence also takes into account the structural violence that contributes to macro-level patterns of oppression and exploitation. Structural violence refers to the processes, policies, and polities that systemically produce or reproduce "social and economic inequities that determine who will be at risk for assaults and who will be shielded from them" (Farmer 2005, 17–18). Anthropologists have employed a structural-violence framework to examine how "various social processes and events come to be translated into personal distress and disease" and how "political and economic forces have structured risk for forms of extreme suffering, from hunger to torture and rape" (30).

Situating gender-based violence as structural violence has allowed scholars to move from individual pathology to social responsibility. While researchers of structural violence assert a relationship between intimate partner violence (as a form of gender-based violence) and structural violence, they do not explicitly interrogate local-level violence. The study of violence within intimate settings requires a framework that allows analytical attention to some of the hidden "sites" of violence (Scheper-Hughes 1992). The public/private dichotomy masks many forms of gender-based violence, particularly such acts as rape, incest, sexual assault, and domestic violence. Exposing the hidden sites of violence allows us to reflect on the structural factors that produce, reproduce, and exacerbate the suffering of the victim, and far too often, protect the perpetrator.

This conceptualization of gender-based violence and its relationship to structural violence is further reflected in the United Nations High Commissioner for Human Rights (1993) resolution pertaining to the elimination of violence against women, where it is recognized that

> racism, racial discrimination, xenophobia and related intolerance reveal themselves in a differentiated manner for women and girls, and can be among the factors leading to a deterioration in their living conditions, poverty, violence, multiple forms of discrimination and the limitation or denial of their human rights, and recognizing the need to integrate a

gender perspective into relevant policies, strategies and programmes of action, including effective implementation of national legislation, against racism, racial discrimination, xenophobia and related intolerance in order to address multiple forms of discrimination against women.

All acts of violence considered in this book result from culturally specific ideologies of gender roles and norms. In each case of violence, an individual person is driven to act by the victim's gender and expectations of that gender. No case in this book presents violence that could be classified as "random" or "accidental." A focus on gender-based violence allows us to consider multiple forms of violence, such as rape, child abuse, sexual assault, family violence, and domestic violence, as well as structural violence, such as poverty, homelessness, sexual exploitation, and other socioeconomic inequalities, while drawing on the same foundational works in anthropology. The term *gender-based violence* allows the reader to consider various structural dynamics producing domestic violence that heretofore have rarely been brought into the same conversation. In our own society, the United States, the specialization of labor and the professionalization of social services have prompted policy responses to various forms of violence that treat problems in isolation (Wies 2008). With this collection we seek to weave together the disparate pieces of the issue of gender-based violence, thereby demonstrating the holistic relationship between problems, and advocating for a comprehensive response to gender-based violence by our communities and our governments.

The Anthropology of Gender-Based Violence

Anthropologists have a long history of studying violence and conflict (Fortune 1939; Gillin 1934; Gluckman 1955, 1963; Hadlock 1947; Malinowski 1959; Skinner 1911; Williams 1941). Early scholars examined acts of violence as defined by warfare, cultural ethos, conflicts over material resources, or cultural rituals related to rites of passage, such as genital cutting, nosebleeding, and forced scarification (Boddy 1982; Harrington 1968; Hayes 1975; Herdt 1982; Otterbein 1999; Rafti 1979; Singer and Desole 1967). Acts of gender-based violence, however, such as rape, domestic violence, and human trafficking were left largely undertheorized. Thus, forms of gender-based violence were not identified as cultural phenomena in most societies until the 1970s. Another reason for the limited engagement by early anthropologists with gender-based violence as we define it here is the discipline's investment in cultural relativity (Harvey and Gow 1994; Helliwell 2000). Anthropology is premised on the idea that emic understandings are what we strive to study and present to our audience.

The 1989 text *Family Violence in Cross-Cultural Perspective* by David Levinson and the 1990 special issue of *Pacific Studies*, Domestic Violence in Oceania, edited by Dorothy Counts, were the first major anthropological treatments of domestic violence. These writings initiated an anthropological focus on gender-based violence at the same time that many societies began to pay greater attention to the problem (Counts 1990, 248). Levinson and the authors in the *Pacific Studies* special issue challenged the established practice among anthropologists of writing about violence in culturally specific terms by beginning to interrogate in universal terms the violence they witnessed as part of their fieldwork. These two publications were also significant for creating new categories of analysis for anthropology to engage, for identifying and classifying victimhood, and for attempting to explain why violence was present or absent in a given social context. The authors addressed such issues as alcohol consumption, gender equality between women and men, changing political-economic stressors and contexts, and the effects of "modernity" on people who were rapidly being incorporated into a wage-labor mode of production.

Following the publication of the 1990 special issue of *Pacific Studies*, Counts established the study of violence against women as a legitimate research domain within the discipline with the publication of two major works, *Sanctions and Sanctuary: Cultural Perspectives on the Beating of Wives* (with Judith Brown and Jacquelyn Campbell) in 1992 and the second edition of the book in 1999, *To Have and to Hit: Cultural Perspectives on Wife Beating*. These two books inspired a new generation of anthropologists to study gender-based violence as the main object of inquiry. Several significant monographs and influential works soon appeared in the anthropological literature that dealt with domestic violence and other forms of violence against women. As gender-based violence cut across niche specializations, anthropologists from various subdisciplinary backgrounds turned their ethnographic lens on the topic. Medical, legal, and political anthropologists addressed such issues as the problems shelter workers face, the role of the police, and the way policies often fall short of victims' needs.

Laura McClusky's (2001) *"Here Our Culture Is Hard": Stories of Domestic Violence from a Mayan Community in Belize* chronicles the experiences of violence through first-person narratives and addresses the problem of attempting to study a "closed" and "private" topic. Donna Goldstein's (2003) ethnography *Laughter Out of Place: Race, Class, Violence, and Sexuality in a Rio Shantytown* explores interpersonal and state-level violence through a political-economic lens, examining acts of battery and rape within the structures of inequality that obliterate poor black women's experiences from view. Goldstein shows how women use laughter to make sense of the violence that the state simultaneously ignores and promotes. In *Sheltering Women: Negotiating Gender and Violence in Northern Italy*, Sonja Plesset (2006) brings us closer to the lived experiences of victimhood by exploring the inner-workings of two women's shelters. Plesset's work is important for its consideration of how diverse the local can be, as she explores two very different shelter programs: one run by communists, the other by the Catholic Church.

Ethnographically informed journal articles have also broadened our qualitative understanding of how violence affects everyday lives. Nia Parson's (2010) "Transformative Ties: Gendered Violence, Forms of Recovery, and Shifting Subjectivities in Chile" examines the way a woman's experience with a nongovernmental organization (NGO) created what Parson terms "transformative ties," relationships that radically alter the way survivors see themselves in the world and those around them, as well as how these ties create avenues for them to enact positive change in the world. And Maureen Hearn's (2009) "A Journey through Ashes: One Woman's Story of Surviving Domestic Violence" provides an uplifting account of one woman's journey from victimhood to survival. Such pieces are an important reminder of the humanity that often gets lost in the analysis and dissection of gender-based violence.

While anthropologists address the issue of gender-based violence in multiple locales, political and legal arenas have proved to be especially rich sites for exploring how individual actors define, negotiate, and respond to various categorizations of gender-based violence. Sarah Hautzinger's (2007) *Violence in the City of Women: Police and Batterers in Bahia, Brazil*; Cecilia MacDowell Santos's (2005) *Women's Police Stations: Gender, Violence, and Justice in Sao Paulo, Brazil*; Elizabeth Shrader and Montserrat Sagot's (2000) *Domestic Violence: Women's Way Out*; and Margaret Abraham's (2000) *Speaking the Unspeakable: Marital Violence among South Asian Immigrants in the United States* draw on legal frameworks that complement cross-cultural, ethnographic research that examines how women obtain protection from abuse. Ethnographies such as Mindie Lazarus-Black's (2007) *Everyday Harm: Domestic Violence, Court Rites, and Cultures of Reconciliation*, Fiona Macaulay's (2006) *Gender Politics in Brazil and Chile*, and Ziba Mir-Hosseini's (2001) *Marriage on Trial: A Study of Islamic Family Law* highlight cracks in the system, including court procedures that are out of reach for many victims, the disjuncture between laws on the books and victims' lived experiences, the economic barriers that prevent victims from obtaining their rights, and the state agents who unknowingly or unwittingly perpetuate systemic violence.

As this review indicates, much of the contemporary anthropological literature on gender-based violence shares two concerns. First, employing a structural-violence framework, anthropologists consider the relationship between the individual and structures of power. The anthropological literature moves our understanding of gender-based violence from individual characteristics (batterer profiling, victim characteristics, etc.) to the more complex topic of how individual actors make sense of their own behaviors, the behavior of others, and the institutions and ideologies that contextualize an experience of gender-based violence. This approach does not deny the lived experience of violence; rather, it foregrounds the ways that individuals and institutions make sense of the cultural world in which a person's trauma takes shape. Second, while anthropologists who work with these issues strongly believe in the value of maintaining cultural relativity, no one excuses the violence. The acts of abuse are treated as human rights violations with grave health consequences. These anthropologists still attempt to make sense of the violence in emic terms, as they demonstrate how individuals around the world are working to prevent and end violence in their homes, their communities, and their countries.

Local Workers in the Global Political Economy

Sally Engle Merry has persuasively made the case that transnational discourses of gender violence are translated into local vernaculars in distinct and inventive ways. Her 2006 book *Human Rights and Gender Violence* examines gender-based violence from a structural violence perspective, demonstrating the way institutions and well-intentioned efforts to end violence also create and maintain systems of inequality. Her work provides a strong foundation for scholars wishing to connect frontline or local ethnographic perspectives with larger political-economic structures that contribute to micro-level violence.

Merry acknowledges, however, that gaps are left in the wake of deterritorialized ethnography. In responding to reviewers of her 2006 book, Merry (2008, 520) states:

> In seeking to understand the complex and vast world of human rights law, I worked with NGOs, rather than the lawyers, governments, or victims. This means that there are important dimensions of this process I did not study. . . . Moreover, there are areas of resistance and refusal that are critically important to understand, as well as obstacles and barriers to the movement of these ideas and practices. Local systems of justice may merge with the more transnational ones but may also context or reject them. These issues cannot be examined without attention to economic and political inequalities as well as those based on gender.

Anthropology at the Front Lines of Gender-Based Violence fills these lacunae by highlighting how local-level or indigenously produced frameworks for care and advocacy operate and how frontline workers engage "universal" models of preventing and responding to gender-based violence. The case studies illustrate the ways international institutions shape local places and practices and how local or indigenously crafted knowledge and practices filter back up to the transnational discourse.

Furthermore, the contributors to this book offer frameworks for situating micro-level interactions within the context of structural violence. Their approach is similar to Madelaine Adelman's (2004) in "The Battering State." In this timely work, Adelman describes the role of the state as a force for maintaining and producing the violence that individuals experience in their "private" lives. She asserts that the state, through various policies that are premised on conservative and neoliberal ideologies, promotes an idealized family that is self-sufficient, free from dependency on the state, and responsible for its own economic and social well-being. She shows that in the United States, policies such as the 1996 Personal Responsibility and Work Opportunity Act and the subsequent implementation of the Temporary Aid to Needy Families legislation further complicate a single woman's ability to raise and care for her children independent of state or extrafamilial support. According to Adelman, the dynamic resulting from these laws is punishment of single women, because they encourage women, despite the abuse they receive regularly, to remain in the care and support of men who can economically provide for them. Adelman posits that this is just one of the many instances in which victims of violence are forced because of state policy to choose between economic survival and psychological and physical torture.

Adelman's work illustrates that a political-economic analysis is central to analyses of gender-based violence. The chapters in this book demonstrate the usefulness of viewing the frontline workers as caught between the unintended consequences of state policy and individual cries for help. By approaching gender-based violence from a political-economic perspective, rather than individualizing the behavior, these chapters demonstrate that global discourses of gender-based violence circulate in local settings and are occasionally translated into culturally appropriate frameworks (Merry 2006b) while highlighting each setting's distinct and culturally specific approach to, and understanding of, the problem of gender-based violence. Through rich ethnographic examples, the pieces in this collection highlight local efforts of gender-based violence intervention, identify the lessons frontline workers offer to others engaged with gender-based violence at any scale, and provide accounts of the labor at the front line, a site undertheorized yet critical to any effort to end gender-based violence.

Ethnographic Notes from the Front Lines

Social and behavioral science researchers use ethnography to gain an in-depth understanding of the relationships between a study population, the power structures that may impact a study population, and the daily behaviors of a study population (Babbie 2001; Bernard 1994; Emerson, Fretz, and Shaw 1995). Sometimes referred to and paired with "participant observation," ethnography is the process of describing a study population through daily interaction and recording the activities that appear exotic and mundane, explicit and tacit, to the researcher (DeWalt and DeWalt 2002; Fetterman 1998). The process of ethnography also lends itself to informal conversations with the research population in the course of normal, everyday activities. By participating in the everyday activities of a population in their geographic and cultural space, the researcher can expose practices that may not be visible to the casual observer (Burawoy 1991).

Sherry Ortner (1995, 173) says of ethnography, "It has always meant the attempt to understand another life world using the self—as much of it as possible—as the instrument of knowing." The chapters in this book illustrate the intersecting roles of participant and observer as the authors are simultaneously positioned as advocate, activist, ally, counselor, and friend. The ethnographic combination of active participation and research observation yields chapters rich in descriptions, anecdotes, and reflections. The ethnographic case studies presented in this book provide a context for scholars who collect, analyze, and share the stories of survivors, frontline workers, and themselves as they pursue scholarship, advocacy, and activism to end gender-based violence.

Explorations of how frontline workers make sense of their daily experiences, and how this sense-making constructs new narratives about gender-based violence, exemplify the power of ethnography. It is not enough to document the policy changes, the decision making, and the sites of contestation and compromise. Ethnography allows us to put ourselves in the mindset and worldview of the people whose stories it tells. Attempting to view the world of gender-based violence from the perspectives of those dedicated most passionately to decreasing its prevalence allows us to bear witness to the pain and suffering, the hope and determination of the frontline workers and victims and survivors of gender-based violence.

The authors who have contributed to this volume cover a range of theoretical and geographical territory. It includes four chapters by frontline workers (Babior, Bargach, Jacobs, and Richter) and travels across Peru, Japan, Russia, Turkey, Canada, Morocco, Vietnam, and the United States. The chapters explore the constraints of state policy and the workers' acts of resistance, the insider/outsider status that complicates an ethnographer's attempt to remain apart from events, and the vicarious trauma experienced by workers and ethnographers alike who attempt to document acts of structural and interpersonal violence that defy simplistic explanations or formulaic solutions (Farmer 2005).

The authors use terminology that is appropriate to each case study, and thus the terminology is different in each chapter. Rather than fitting their collaborators' words into a disciplinary-specific language, the anthropologists who carried out the studies they report here use language that reflects the local conceptualizations of the problems. We hope the reader appreciates the unique standpoint within each chapter, recognizing that all the pieces lead us to a greater understanding of the complexity and nuance within the broad term *gender-based violence*.

We open the book with a powerful reminder of the connection between structural violence and suffering by Roxane Richter. In "Disparity in Disasters: A Frontline View of Gender-Based Inequities in Emergency Aid and Health Care," she discusses how after working as an emergency medical technician (EMT) and Red Cross volunteer assisting victims in the aftermath of Hurricane Katrina, she found herself on the receiving end of "disaster relief" as a victim of Hurricane Ike a few years later. Richter examines the complexities that unfold within organizational efforts to assist victims from the perspective that state-level structural violence produces and contextualizes the violence that frontline workers hope to prevent. She analyzes how "natural" occurrences become "human-made" disasters, particularly through the glaring omission of a gender perspective in disaster preparedness and relief planning.

Ethnography as the practice of simultaneously learning about others and about oneself is the foundation of Sharman L. Babior's chapter, "Participant and Observer: Reflections on Fieldwork in a Women's Shelter in Tokyo, Japan." Babior explores her insider/outsider status, as researcher and shelter advocate, and the impact this dual role, distinct from Richter's roles as an advocate and victim, has on her study outcomes. Through her analysis of frontline workers in a shelter for victims and survivors of domestic violence and human trafficking, we learn about the deep and intimate relationships among advocates and shelter residents.

In "Crafting Community through Narratives, Images, and Shared Experience," Stephanie J. Brommer uses thick description combined with participant observation and qualitative interviews to explore the emergence of organizations in California in response to violence experienced by women from India and illustrates the multiple levels of violence that advocates must respond to through organizations. She stresses the value of recognizing "culture" in the development of separate and specialized responses to gender-based violence, particularly for communities uniquely affected by global shifts in political-economic resources. Brommer's piece adds to the growing anthropological literature examining the complexities of providing domestic violence services within heterogeneous, multicultural contexts. It also provides a critical intervention in the study of the transmission of theories of gender-based violence from one context to another.[1]

While Brommer's piece emphasizes domestic violence as the key locus of experience for frontline workers in California, Kim Shively's experience in Turkey demonstrates the explicitly local definition of domestic violence. Shively's chapter, "'We Couldn't Just Throw Her in the Street': Gendered Violence and Women's Shelters in Turkey," questions the notion that domestic violence shelters are the ideal state-level response to gender-based violence. In Turkey, the past two decades have witnessed a strengthening of laws criminalizing batterers and the development of public and private institutions that offer assistance to victims and survivors of domestic violence. Shively investigates how the processes of transplantation, appropriation, and translation of international gender-based violence doctrines, identified by Sally Engle Merry, have influenced the creation of domestic violence shelters in Turkey. She exposes the dissonance between the local and the global in defining and responding to gender-based violence.

Complementing research focused on voluntary or paid work at a non-profit organization or an NGO, M. Cristina Alcalde explores the role of police officers as frontline workers in "Institutional Resources (Un)Available: The Effects of Police Attitudes and Actions on Battered Women in Peru." The ethnographic interviews and participant observation she conducted in women's police stations reveal the indifference, hostility, and discrimination often at work in the intersection of victim and police officer. As a result, this chapter illuminates a necessary shift in our understanding of frontline workers, from advocate to possible secondary perpetrator.

While Babior, Brommer, Shively, and Alcalde focus on various institutional responses to violence, the next chapter, "Child Welfare and Domestic Violence Workers' Cultural Models of Domestic Violence: An Ethnographic Examination" by Cyleste C. Collins, explores the cultural frameworks that guide the labor of the front line. Collins employs participant observation and ethnographic interviews to examine U.S.-based domestic violence and child welfare workers' beliefs about domestic violence and how these beliefs shape their everyday work with victims and survivors of violence. Collins's chapter reminds us that while frontline workers are mechanisms in society that reproduce ideologies of domestic violence and victimhood, they are also active agents in producing the very ideologies the mainstream public holds about domestic violence.

To demonstrate the decision-making process and logic of working daily with victims and survivors of violence, we include another piece by a frontline worker, Uwe Jacobs. In "Gender-Based Violence: Perspectives from the Male European Front Line," Jacobs confronts his own location as a white, European, heterosexual man counseling refugees who have experienced suffering and acts of violence. Jacobs also considers the role of men in ending gender-based violence by both ceasing interpersonal violence and acknowledging structural-level privilege and violence. Jacobs suggests that to achieve this goal we must examine our own biases, our gendered identities, our translations of local and global ideologies, and the manifestations of structural power inequalities in the relationships we engage in as frontline workers.

Lynn Kwiatkowski moves us from the perspective of an insider counselor to that of an ethnographer in "Cultural Politics of a Global/Local Health Program for Battered Women in Vietnam." Kwiatkowski focuses on an international health program in Vietnam and how the local frontline workers seek to address and redress gender-based violence in conjunction with the international health program. In Vietnam, as discussions of wife battering and domestic violence have become more public, they are increasingly understood through local cultural logics as well as transnational discourses of wife battering. The result is the development of new approaches to local practices that are infused with local and culture-based ideologies as well as global theories about gender-based violence that exist in Vietnamese society.

Julie Hemment's "Global Civil Society and the Local Costs of Belonging: Defining Violence against Women in Russia" also focuses on local/global dynamics. Hemment connects the local advocacy of frontline workers to the global neoliberal political economy. By tracing the connections between the global North and global South, feminists and corresponding sponsoring agencies, Hemment exposes the "tensions of transnational women's activism" through a study of emergent violence against women campaigns and crisis centers in Russia.

Kwiatkowski and Hemment position frontline workers within the nations, states, or other macrostructural entities within which they organize, advocate, and pursue activism. In "Memorializing Murder, Speaking Back to the State," Belinda Leach directs our attention to the state. Focusing on the creation of memorials to murdered women, Leach describes the techniques employed by frontline antiviolence workers as they organize their efforts to bring awareness of gender-based violence into the public sphere. At the nexus of these activisms is Leach's exploration of how the Canadian state defines and recognizes violence against women and in turn the frontline workers who work with victims and survivors.

We conclude this book in the same way that it begins—with a raw, intimate, and emotional frontline reflection. In "Laliti, Compassionate Savior: The Hidden Archeology of the Founding of a Shelter," Jamila Bargach recounts her experiences establishing a domestic violence shelter in Morocco. In doing so she exposes the humanity of the people managing organizations dedicated to responding to gender-based violence. Like Richter and Jacobs, Bargach uses brutal honesty to expose the fraught and fragile world of working with and for survivors of violence. Her piece continues the deep ethnographic work found throughout the book, analyzing frontline workers from the perspective of a researcher or practitioner who is simultaneously "doing the work." It also provides an account of how international donor funds influence local efforts to end violence, and how they affect the relationships between workers and between the workers and the survivors themselves. Bargach brings us closer to the important task of seeing frontline work not solely as global to local but also as local to local.

Conclusions and Beginnings

Anthropology at the Front Lines of Gender-Based Violence explores how we define and respond to gender-based violence locally and globally by emphasizing the experiences and production of frameworks at the local level. Through its ethnographic focus, this book is meant to compel those concerned with the issue of gender-based violence to incorporate the locally crafted and continuously shifting frameworks of prevention, treatment, and care into our analyses. As such, it speaks simultaneously to those working at local scales and those working at international scales in an effort to contribute to a transnational discussion of gender-based violence.

What needs to be done is staggering. The global movement against violence has existed for over thirty years, and each year new statistics reveal the growing number of cases in every part of the world. The authors in this book and our colleagues who serve as our interlocutors marshal personal and professional resources to address this epidemic. Gender-based violence is a difficult issue to fund, for both research and program delivery. Thus, anthropologists who research this topic have great empathy for frontline workers and their attempts to maintain the resources they need to continue their important efforts. We hope our work here gives voice to those struggles and highlights how important the labor of the front line is for maintaining hope and dignity in people's lives. The majority of workers presented in this book will never be famous. Their efforts receive little attention and rarely admiration. Yet their stories hold important lessons for us all. Their work is a part of our collective effort to make the world a safer and more peaceful and equitable place for all women, children, and men.

NOTE

1. See Hodžić 2009 for a critical assessment of the culture/rights dichotomy and how this dichotomy has generated problematic assumptions about local contexts as static and about transnational discourses on human rights as dynamic and modern.

WORKS CITED

Abraham, Margaret. 2000. *Speaking the Unspeakable: Marital Violence among South Asian Immigrants in the United States*. New Brunswick, NJ: Rutgers University Press.

Adelman, Madelaine. 2004. The Battering State: Towards a Political Economy of Domestic Violence. *Journal of Poverty* 8 (3): 45–64.

Babbie, Earl. 2001. *The Practice of Social Research*. 9th ed. Belmont, CA: Wadsworth.

Bernard, H. Russell. 1994. *Research Methods in Anthropology: Qualitative and Quantitative Approaches*. 2nd ed. Walnut Creek, CA: AltaMira Press.

Boddy, Janice. 1982. Womb as Oasis: The Symbolic Context of Pharaonic Circumcision in Rural Northern Sudan. *American Ethnologist* 9 (4): 682–98.

Burawoy, Michael, ed. 1991. *Ethnography Unbound: Power and Resistance in the Modern Metropolis*. Berkeley: University of California Press.

Counts, Dorothy, ed. 1990. Domestic Violence in Oceania. Special issue, *Pacific Studies* 13 (3).

Counts, Dorothy, Judith Brown, and Jacquelyn Campbell, eds. 1992. *Sanctions and Sanctuary: Cultural Perspectives on the Beating of Wives*. Boulder, CO: Westview.

———. 1999. *To Have and to Hit: Cultural Perspectives on Wife Beating*. Urbana: University of Illinois Press.

DeWalt, Kathleen, and Billie DeWalt. 2002. *Participant Observation: A Guide for Fieldworkers*. Walnut Creek, CA: AltaMira Press.

Emerson, Robert M., Rachel I. Fretz, and Linda L. Shaw. 1995. *Writing Ethnographic Fieldnotes*. Chicago: University of Chicago Press.

Farmer, Paul. 2005. *Pathologies of Power: Health, Human Rights, and the New War on the Poor*. Berkeley: University of California Press.

Fetterman, David M. 1998. Ethnography. In *Handbook of Applied Social Research Methods*, ed. L. Bickman and D. J. Rog, 473–504. Thousand Oaks, CA: Sage.

Fortune, Reo. 1939. Arapesh Warfare. *American Anthropologist* 41 (1): 22–41.

Gillin, John. 1934. Crime and Punishment among the Barama River Carib of British Guiana. *American Anthropologist* 36 (3): 331–44.

Gluckman, Max. 1955. *Custom and Conflict in Africa*. Oxford: Blackwell.

———. 1963. *Order and Rebellion in Tribal Africa*. New York: Free Press of Glencoe.

Goldstein, Donna M. 2003. *Laughter Out of Place: Race, Class, Violence, and Sexuality in a Rio Shantytown*. Berkeley: University of California Press.

Hadlock, Wendell. 1947. War among the Northeastern Woodland Indians. *American Anthropologist* 49 (2): 204–21.

Harrington, Charles. 1968. Sexual Differentiation in Socialization and Some Male Genital Mutilations. *American Anthropologist* 70 (5): 951–56.

Harvey, Penelope, and Peter Gow, eds. 1994. *Sex and Violence: Issues in Representation and Experience*. New York: Routledge.

Hautzinger, Sarah J. 2007. *Violence in the City of Women: Police and Batterers in Bahia, Brazil*. Berkeley: University of California Press.

Hayes, Rose Oldfield. 1975. Female Genital Mutilation, Fertility Control, Women's Roles and the Patrilineage in Modern Sudan: A Functional Analysis. *American Ethnologist* 2 (4): 617–33.

Hearn, Maureen. 2009. A Journey through Ashes: One Woman's Story of Surviving Domestic Violence. *Anthropology of Consciousness* 20 (2): 111–29.

Helliwell, Christine. 2000. "It's Only a Penis": Rape, Feminism, and Difference. *Signs* 25 (3): 789–816.

Herdt, Gilbert. 1982. Sambia Nosebleeding Rites and Male Proximity to Women. *Ethos* 10 (3): 189–231.

Hodžić, Saida. 2009. Unsettling Power: Domestic Violence, Gender Politics, and Struggles over Sovereignty in Ghana. *Ethnos* 74 (3): 331–60.

Lazarus-Black, Mindie. 2007. *Everyday Harm: Domestic Violence, Court Rites, and Cultures of Reconciliation.* Urbana: University of Illinois Press.

Levinson, David. 1989. *Family Violence in Cross-Cultural Perspective.* Thousand Oaks, CA: Sage.

Macaulay, Fiona. 2006. *Gender Politics in Brazil and Chile.* New York: Palgrave Macmillan.

Malinowski, Bronislaw. 1959. *Crime and Custom in Savage Society.* Paterson, NJ: Littlefield.

McClusky, Laura J. 2001. *"Here, Our Culture Is Hard": Stories of Domestic Violence from a Mayan Community in Belize.* Austin: University of Texas Press.

Merry, Sally Engle. 2006a. *Human Rights and Gender Violence: Translating International Law into Local Justice.* Chicago: University of Chicago Press.

———. 2006b. Transnational Human Rights and Local Activism: Mapping the Middle. *American Anthropologist* 108 (1):3: 38–51.

———. 2008. Commentary on Reviews of Human Rights and Gender Violence. *American Anthropologist* 110 (4): 520–22.

Mir-Hosseini, Ziba. 2001. *Marriage on Trial: A Study of Islamic Family Law.* London: I. B. Tauris.

Ortner, Sherry. 1995. Resistance and the Problem of Ethnographic Refusal. *Comparative Studies in Society and History* 37 (1): 173–93.

Otterbein, Keith. 1999. A History of Research on Warfare in Anthropology. *American Anthropologist* 101 (4): 794–805.

Parson, Nia. 2010. Transformative Ties: Gendered Violence, Forms of Recovery, and Shifting Subjectivities in Chile. *Medical Anthropology Quarterly* 24 (1): 64–84.

Plesset, Sonja. 2006. *Sheltering Women: Negotiating Gender and Violence in Northern Italy.* Stanford, CA: Stanford University Press.

Rafti, Phyllis. 1979. Review of *The Hosken Report* by Fran P. Hosken. *Medical Anthropology Quarterly* 11 (1): 19–20.

Santos, Cecília MacDowell. 2005. *Women's Police Stations: Gender, Violence, and Justice in São Paulo, Brazil.* New York: Palgrave Macmillan.

Scheper-Hughes, Nancy. 1992. *Death without Weeping: The Violence of Everyday Life in Brazil.* Berkeley: University of California Press.

Shrader, Elizabeth, and Montserrat Sagot. 2000. *Domestic Violence: Women's Way Out.* Washington, DC: Pan American Health Organization.

Singer, Philip, and Daniel Desole. 1967. The Australian Subincision Ceremony Reconsidered: Vaginal Envy or Kangaroo Bifid Penis Envy. *American Anthropologist* 69 (3): 355–58.

Skinner, Alanson. 1911. War Customs of the Menomini Indians. *American Anthropologist* 13 (2): 299–312.

United Nations. 1993. *Declaration on the Elimination of Violence against Women.* New York: United Nations General Assembly.

United Nations High Commissioner for Human Rights. 1993. Elimination of Violence against Women. In *Commission on Human Rights Resolution 2003/45.* Geneva: Office of the United Nations High Commissioner for Human Rights.

Wies, Jennifer R. 2008. Professionalizing Human Services: A Case of Domestic Violence Shelter Advocates. *Human Organization* 67 (2): 221–33.

Williams, Francis. 1941. Group Sentiment and Primitive Justice. *American Anthropologist* 43 (4): 523–39.

2

Disparity in Disasters: A Frontline View of Gender-Based Inequities in Emergency Aid and Health Care

Roxane Richter

It seemed as though all of Houston was on high alert, anxiously glued to the round-the-clock TV coverage of busloads of Hurricane Katrina evacuees pulling into our convention center in the wee morning hours in early September 2005. As an emergency medical technician (EMT) and an American Red Cross Disaster Health Services volunteer, I drove down to the convention center on the first morning of the evacuees' arrival. What greeted me was a fast-congealing mayhem of Houston's emergency medical, police, and fire services all struggling to handle an unprecedented influx of over two hundred thousand evacuees.

I immediately started to triage and assist evacuees who were lying on sidewalks and being carried out of buses. One of the first evacuees I cared for was a thirty-old African American woman with three small children in tow. She was three months pregnant and complaining of heavy vaginal bleeding over the previous three days—a potential miscarriage. In the early stages of this Herculean relief effort, there were no ambulances available. Yet to my surprise, the woman refused any transport to a local hospital. She explained to me that as a single mother, she would rather risk losing "this one" (pointing to her belly) than run the risk of losing her three other children in the evacuee chaos. There was nothing to be done; there were no child-care or support facilities to assist her at that time. I had witnessed such stark life-and-death realities in developing areas of Africa, Latin America, and Asia, but I could not grasp that such a scenario was possible here in the United States of America. It seemed both impossible and surreal.

While that particular mother's story was heart wrenching, many more followed: women who were pregnant and overwrought with concern for their fetus's health (yet there were no immediate obstetrics/gynecological [OB/GYN] services or prenatal medicines or vitamins); women who thought they might be pregnant (there were no testing supplies); women who could not seek out job or financial assistance because of their now twenty-four-hour child-/dependent-care responsibilities; one woman who had to undergo an invasive vaginal exam and treatment lying on the floor of a pastor's office at a shelter (whose large window I attempted to tape shut with scraps of paper)—and so on. In triage I lost count of the number of times women began their patient intake by leaning in and whispering to me, "I don't sleep around" or "I'm not unclean"—grappling to comprehend the onset of a vaginal infection or rash brought on by postdisaster stress or a walk through water contaminated by chemicals, debris, and corpses.

These extraordinary moments working with female evacuees forever altered my perception of disasters—as an EMT, international aid worker, and social scientist, and as a woman. At that moment, it was clear to me that we had to more effectively meet the needs of women and address the missed opportunities in gender-based care in disaster management, relief planning, and emergency health care.

I am no rookie. As a frontline worker, or first responder, in national and international disaster and emergency medical services (EMS), I have witnessed firsthand how gender-based violence (GBV) and inequities directly affect disparities in disaster and aid programs. Through my decade-long work in international humanitarian aid projects, I have witnessed glaring gender inequities and GBV in Ghana, Nigeria, India, South Africa, and Zimbabwe. But this, my "postdisaster epiphany," inextricably tied the third world to my world. It was like rerunning the glaring GBV from developing nations on a widescreen color TV, and now watching the same program here in the United States—just playing out on a much smaller, black-and-white set.

After those fateful months aiding Hurricane Katrina evacuees, I spent the next three years interviewing female victims of Katrina and researching gender-based disaster issues. In 2008, yet another disaster, Hurricane Ike, altered my perception, this time by devastating many neighborhoods and cities surrounding my own hometown of Seabrook, Texas. So it was now my turn; I was to have a firsthand evacuee experience packed with all of the fear, trauma, and frustration that comes with a rapid-onset disaster. My home sat in the direct path and mandatory evacuation zone of a hurricane the size of Texas, packing a category 4 storm surge and wind speeds of 96 to 130 miles an hour. As a single mother, I struggled with the difficult manual labor of boarding up windows, disconnecting live gas lines, packing "everything" into a Toyota Camry, and driving four hundred miles before I found a hotel to shelter me with my frightened son and often carsick 110-pound dog. We were among the lucky in that we had a house to come home to and a structure that was repairable, sustaining some $25,000 in damages. But after a few weeks without electricity, long waits in line for bagged ice and boxed government food rations, my views on disaster were again transformed. No longer did I see staid and static postdisaster statistics of 195 deaths, $32 billion in damages, and so on. Now those numbers morphed into living representations of my distraught neighbors, my struggling neighborhood, and my now homeless friends. It seems that no matter what manmade geographic, political, or cultural line I traverse, this much holds true: Wherever I work in disaster aid, the poor receive inequitable access to available resources in aid, health care, and mitigation skills, and, in general, the poorest of the poor are women.

By describing my own personal disaster aid and frontline emergency health care experiences, I have sought to illustrate, humanize, and personalize how women are disproportionately affected and disadvantaged when faced with natural and manmade disasters. Many women are at high risk to succumb to social, physical, financial, and psychological postdisaster hardships and post-traumatic stress, and specific areas of inequitable and ineffective aid and services often include EMS, OB/GYN care, triage, and supplies and services. And while it is important to identify gender-based (socially constructed) and sex-based (physiological) issues and structural violence in disasters, I prefer to highlight interventions that define gender equity as a social justice, health care, and human rights issue, and to illustrate how women are an overlooked and underutilized yet vital part of disaster mitigation and response efforts—whether they act in their traditional roles or transcend them.

Gender Does Matter

When a natural disaster strikes, its path of destruction may be indiscriminate, but the collateral damage is not. Disaster preparedness, research, and relief involve sociological variables, such as gender, race, and class, as well as cross-cultural comparisons between the responses of developed and developing nations. Social injustices and structural violence create inequities, and those already denied an equitable share of resources and benefits find themselves disproportionately affected by a disaster's devastation. Current World Health Organization (2002) studies point to a pattern of gender differentiation throughout the disaster process—in preparedness, response, physical and psychological impact, risk perception and exposure, and recovery and reconstruction.

Thus does a disaster, as a "natural" occurrence, erupt into an "unnatural" catastrophe as a consequence of the sudden interface of socially constructed roles, vulnerabilities, and imbalances of power. It is vital, therefore, that we address women's gender-specific issues, power struggles, needs (such as protection from sexual and domestic violence), rights (such as fair resource distribution), vulnerabilities (such as social isolation and lack of personal autonomy), and strengths and opportunities in these arenas. But we cannot view women's disaster risks, rights, and opportunities solely through women's physiological makeup. Rather, we must view them within their psychosocial framework. We should adopt a more holistic "Social + Biological = Whole Woman" approach so we can more effectively allow frontline workers to engage and eradicate GBV and inequities across artificially set social, cultural, and political barriers and divisions.

Two points should be emphasized. First, gender-based disaster aid research and advocacy are not zero-sum games in which every word written about female suffering means one less word is written about male suffering or vice versa. We must all seek to expose and examine gender-based disaster issues and take actions that can potentially lead to reductions in human suffering and loss. Second, I am not suggesting that men are unaffected by disasters, nor do I condone such thinking. Rather, I hope to serve as a filtered "gender lens," showing how men and women are (both) constrained by their socialization and disproportionately impacted by disasters.

Majority Population, Minority Access

Perhaps the most frustrating part of my disaster relief work and research in the United States has been watching the painstaking and meticulous disaster preparations and planning that go into meeting the needs of every "special population" group—infants, the elderly, the disabled, drug addicts, those who are deaf, and so on—yet somehow women remain largely underserved and their needs overlooked. This is despite the fact that women (along with their children) usually make up the majority population in most postdisaster shelters!

After my experience in EMS with Hurricane Katrina evacuees, I spent the next three years interviewing female victims of Katrina, researching several gender-based disaster issues: women's role, active or passive, as a decision maker in the disaster evacuation and aid processes; barriers to evacuation; women's ability (or lack thereof) to seek financial/health/child care assistance based on any increased postdisaster caregiver role due to dependents; and women's assessment of equitable and fair treatment *considering their gender* in the evacuation process, aid distribution, health services, counseling, employment assistance, and child/dependent care help. Here is what a few evacuees had to say, in their own words:

> I felt like they didn't want to hear me. If I had been a man I could command someone to hear me. . . . I had difficulty in getting people to listen to me.
>> —Forty-seven-year-old African American woman who stated that she needed (but did not have access to) a gynecological exam

> There were wild, drunken men. I was scared for my kids. I was scared. There were no separate places for women to shower or sleep.
>> —Forty-three-year-old Hispanic woman from New Orleans

> There was no birth control, so I had to go and pay for it out of my own pocket.
>> —Thirty-one-year-old African American woman

> I was on my period two blocks from the beach in a dress and I had to climb a tree during the storm. I was bleeding. The men who helped me didn't think about "sanitary items" even though my shirt and my legs were bloody. Maybe I was too embarrassed to ask. They were too.
>> —Forty-eight-year-old single Caucasian female who stated that, after her rescue, there were no sanitary items available at her shelter

> As a woman, you feel helpless.
>> —Thirty-one-year-old single African American mother of seven

In the days after Hurricane Katrina, mini tent-cities of EMS crews and hospitals sprang up all over downtown Houston. Without the timely intervention and round-the-clock work of local churches, EMS/fire units,

Houston mayor Bill White, nongovernment organizations (NGOs) such as the American Red Cross, and Houston-area hospitals including the University of Texas Medical Branch and Memorial Hermann, I think many more lives would have been lost. I remember one evacuee in her fifties that I drove to a Red Cross shelter in my car who had just been plucked off her roof after four days without food and medical care for her diabetes. She wept when I hugged her and she apologized for how bad she smelled. She said, "I would still be on my roof" waiting for help if it weren't for the compassion of volunteers and NGOs. I think she was right. What I saw time and again was the kindness of volunteers, civic workers, and ordinary people who were strangers to one another that moved Katrina aid along. State-sponsored aid was lean, hopelessly disorganized, and mired in bureaucratic indecision. But every day, I had local people come up and ask me (I was wearing an EMS or Red Cross shirt) whether there was anything we needed at the shelters, hand me checks for hundreds of dollars for the Red Cross, and give me their telephone numbers because they wanted to take evacuees into their homes. And while New York is known as the "Big Apple" and New Orleans as the "Big Easy," Houston became known as the "Big Heart" because of our post-Katrina aid.

During those days, we had warehouses overrun in infant formula, diapers, and clothing—so much so that incoming donations were halted—but what I could not find were boxes of tampons or sanitary pads for my female patients. In triage and at local Red Cross shelters, I was able to access (on behalf of our patients) free over-the-counter medications of every conceivable kind: antacids, sunscreen, cough syrup, nasal spray, antidiarrheals, contact lens solution, allergy tablets and liquids, day- and nighttime moisturizers—you name it. But not one box of vaginal yeast/antifungal cream was offered, even though many of my female patients suffered from genital rashes and infections caused by stress and wading in unclean water. I personally collected carloads of tampons, sanitary pads, antifungal cream, and new women's underwear from my own network of friends and colleagues so that the shelters I volunteered in would have some "female" supplies. Months later, one of the pastors who ran a large Methodist church shelter in New Orleans joked with me about his staffers' making "midnight Tampax runs" in the large church van to the city's outskirts to buy as many feminine hygiene products as they could get their hands on. Apparently, these were disaster planning items that no one seemed to plan on.

My postdisaster interviews of female Hurricane Katrina evacuees found that a majority (53 percent) of the 105 women surveyed felt that their female health care needs went unmet (they cited inadequate OB/GYN care, prenatal nutrition, sanitary supplies, birth control, etc.), and a majority (54 percent) felt that their access to aid and resources was inequitable compared with that of their male counterparts (Richter 2007). Perhaps the most intriguing finding from my interviews was that among the majority (51 percent) who reported that they had been the primary decision-maker in the evacuation process, the key determinant was their level of education, which proved to be a more significant factor than race or even marital status. This is a pivotal finding, in that several disaster researchers have reported significant differences in evacuation behaviors between men and women, noting that women weigh risk more heavily than men and therefore are likely to evacuate earlier and more rapidly than men. This is a gender-based disaster behavior that should be positively exploited by targeting women in disaster preparedness training and evacuation notification—an effort that could facilitate more timely evacuations and potentially save lives.

"I'm Not Disabled—I'm Female"

Several months after completing my interviews with female Katrina evacuees, I gave a talk on gender issues in disasters at the Partners in Emergency Preparedness Conference in Seattle, Washington. I saw this conference as an opportunity to get my message to every Federal Emergency Management Association (FEMA) representative I could locate. Two FEMA staffers attended my session and asked how other foreign nations and NGOs handle female-specific relief efforts. I explained that most large NGOs and government aid outreaches have gender officers and gender-awareness programs, adding that the position of gender officer was not my ingenious idea but that gender mainstreaming has long been considered a necessity in developing nations. These officers are responsible for implementing "gender awareness" across a program's framework. I then suggested that it would be wonderful to see FEMA implement gender awareness throughout their policies and procedures. One of the staffers, a man, said, with determined look, that yes, FEMA should consider gender-based policies and he would put me in touch with the national disability coordinator of FEMA. To which I could only reply, "But I'm not disabled—I'm female."

According to the agency's inexplicable system of categorization, "female" issues fell under special populations' needs, which was under the umbrella of "disabilities." Brilliant. Of course I then had to wonder whether we would have had the same conversation if I were male. Although I have since met with my nation's disability coordinator (whom I found to be a compassionate, though overworked, woman with a disability), I am not aware of any substantive gender-specific disaster aid efforts that developed from our encounters.

In retrospect, I suspect it is all too easy for disaster aid workers (especially those of us in EMS) to focus narrowly on women's physiological, reproductive, and maternal functions during a disaster, without considering gender-based biology and engendered aid and health issues. Yet as frontline workers and emergency care providers, we have a duty to assist all patients, and this duty includes fighting against the marginalization of women in disaster planning and relief programs. There should be no distinction between the systematic planning and provision of supplies and services for special-population needs (such as geriatric supplies, infant formula, deaf translation services, mental health services, drug addiction counseling, and foreign language translation) and planning and provision for the imminent needs of women.

For gender-based policies to work, we need to offer a locally based, gender-aware "rapid assessment checklist" of supplies and services. To adequately support OB/GYN services and supplies, the checklist would include pregnancy testing supplies, a (triage) pregnancy registry, daily prenatal nutritional advocacy, prenatal vitamins, ultrasound machines, sterile delivery kits, infant formula, breastfeeding supplies, breastfeeding areas, and "fact sheets" about the potential effects of vaccines, environmental toxins, and exposures on pregnancies. Providers should ensure that female physicians, including gynecologists, are available in areas where social, religious, or patriarchal traditions limit or prohibit nonfemale physical and pelvic exams for women. Other supplies and services should include the provision of antifungal yeast-infection products, new female undergarments, a variety of contraceptives, feminine hygiene kits, rape intake, sexual and domestic violence counselors, and crisis "meeting places" for community women to network and offer other women child/dependent care and support. Most of the female Hurricane Katrina evacuees I surveyed stated that they desired and would have participated in female-led postdisaster initiatives and female emotional care support groups, including groups for those with post-traumatic stress disorder.

As I witnessed in my post-Katrina service, many gender-aware supplies and services are inadequate or nonexistent. Yet the provision of these relatively inexpensive short-term interventions could mitigate suffering and even prevent acute illnesses, mortalities, and long-term health care costs. These relatively low-cost, short-term interventions speak to the adage, "An ounce of prevention is worth a pound of cure." Or I'll coin a new one: "Take care of a mother's need now, or see the mother *and* her ill infant in the emergency room later." When opportunities for early proactive patient interventions and treatments, such as providing basic nutrition for an infant, are disregarded, the resulting medical issues can prove much more acute and costly in their latter stages—including, in the example of a poorly fed infant, the addition of one more patient to the patient-care scenario.

Conclusion

Women have unique and gender-distinctive social, physical, economic, and psychological needs, vulnerabilities, and opportunities in disasters. The current glaring absence of gender-disaggregated data (due to inherent difficulties in interviews in postdisaster settings and data collection methodologies, and a lack of widespread interest in gender-specific data) continues to keep women "invisible" among special interest group initiatives and to keep women's rights excluded in planning and aid.

Gender equity in disasters and EMS is a health care issue and a social justice and human rights issue, because women's rights are human rights. A human-rights approach to disaster planning would move the impetus for change from its tidy, vacuum-packed academic research arena into the more comprehensive sphere of individualized and localized frontline worker methodologies. Yet we must strive to focus on women's unique experiences, risks, and opportunities in disasters and healthcare aid because they remain largely undocumented, unexamined, and unharnessed. As a society we must have women remain healthy and fully engaged because understanding their unique challenges and opportunities in a disaster and in medical services is a prerequisite to justice. But if the truth of women's lives remains hidden, unaccounted for, and unexamined, change is unlikely.

Disaster and emergency health care planning that takes into consideration less than half of a community (i.e., men only) can only lead to misconceptions about how to most effectively meet women's needs. When disaster health care and aid programs fail to empower women, they fail to empower the entire community. Clearly, in disaster and emergency health care, it is better to plan *with* women—rather than *for* them. The struggle for women's equitable share of health care is about empowering women in planning, mitigation, and recovery efforts, stopping discrimination and violence, and ultimately, making women's lives count equally with men's.

WORKS CITED

Richter, Roxane. 2007. Gender Matters: Female Specific Relief Efforts during Disasters Are Key. *Journal of Emergency Medical Services* 32 (2): 58–63.
World Health Organization. 2002. *Gender and Health in Disasters*. Geneva: World Health Organization.

3

Participant and Observer: Reflections on Fieldwork in a Women's Shelter in Tokyo, Japan

Sharman L. Babior

This chapter describes the methodology of participant observation and explores how these two aspects of anthropological fieldwork—"participant" and "observer"—become blurred by the stresses of a field setting. I address the premise that one can remain removed and objective as an impartial observer while confronting the everyday issues of fieldwork. I argue that as a participant observer residing in a women's shelter, I unavoidably developed subjective views of the shelter setting and the larger social environment. My view of shelter life is based on personal interactions and self-identification with the shelter clients and their frames of mind, informed by their narratives and case studies. The themes of fear and helplessness that appear repeatedly in their narratives are consistent with the documentation and literature on gender-based violence and the victimization of women. With the passage of time, my subjective views came to reflect a perspective similar to that expressed by shelter clients—a sense of powerlessness and lack of control over my immediate circumstances.

As a live-in staff member on the front line, advocating for clients at a shelter for abused and exploited Japanese and non-Japanese women in Tokyo, Japan, I confronted the immediacy of women's daily experiences with gender-based violence and sexual exploitation. Ironically, while intimacy fueled the violence and exploitation the shelter clients reported suffering at the hands of their abusers, intimacy later inspired these women to expose, reject, and escape such abuse by allowing them to tell their stories and share their fears and aspirations within the safety of the local shelter environment (Merry 2008, 522). When I joined the shelter staff as a participant observer in Tokyo, I also became part of a local community of women who served as my support system. The staff and volunteers became a surrogate family for me, and the clients became my shelter mates and friends. The intimacy the shelter provided formed a bridge between the subjective, participatory aspects of my shelter life, and the observational, objective elements of my fieldwork.

Ethnography, Reflexivity, and Participant Observation

Reflexivity, or self-reflection in the construction of ethnography, and ethnography as a constructed object concerns a large audience of anthropologists and scholars from other disciplines who employ participant observation as a methodological tool (Abramson 1992; Callaway 1992; Clifford and Marcus 1986; Crapanzano 1977; Golde 1970; Harding 1987; Jongmans and Gutkind 1967; Marcus and Cushman 1982; Rabinow 1977). Exposing the vulnerable, self-conscious side of the researcher in ethnography lies in the arena of reflexivity, and the goal I find the most difficult to achieve because it is the most personal. Reflexivity includes aspects of introspection and relationships between the "self" and the "other." For example, retrospectives of anthropological fieldwork frequently dwell on the anthropologist's anxiety about access to information, appropriate data collection, methodology, and the daily interactions with informants (Bowen 1964; Cesara 1982; Lunsing 1999; Moeran 1985; Nader 1970; Pelto and Pelto 1978; Pettigrew 1981; Rabinow 1977). These features may influence the overall description and interpretation of fieldwork, leading to enigmatic and ambiguous conclusions. Crapanzano (1977) contends that when a self-conscious effort is made to "confront" the ethnography, these anxiety-provoking and stressful encounters of fieldwork can be turned into sensitive and insightful analyses.

Rosaldo (1989, 19) points out the need to recognize each ethnographer's "angle of vision" and to view each ethnographer as a "positioned subject, who grasps certain human phenomena better than others" and who can be objective only within the framework of his or her own life experiences and social positioning. In this sense, ethnography contains a complex mixture of self-reflection, descriptive narrative, and interpretation. As Cesara (1982, 3) points out in her discussion of the fieldwork experience, the impact of research on the researcher and the researcher's response are equally important considerations.

The researcher must maintain a balance between observing and participating (Behar 1996; Bolton 1992). Some researchers are so detached, however, they are present merely to observe some occurrence. Some even purport to become invisible or unknown to those they observe. At the other extreme are researchers who reject their observer status and "go native" as full participants (Bolton 1992, 130; Tedlock 1991, 69–71). As Bolton states, "Most anthropological research falls between these two extremes, but, in general, it would appear that the emphasis is placed on observation rather than participation" (130).

Participant observation is problematic when used as a methodology in intimate or sensitive situations. In my own fieldwork, I examine incidents of domestic violence that occur most often in private, as well as aspects of intimate sexual encounters that take place under conditions of exploitation and duress. Anthropology, for example, has traditionally taken an indirect approach to conflict and violence, viewing them as aberrations from the norm (Firth 1954; Gluckman 1963; Leach 1954). More recently, anthropological theories of human violence have debated and evaluated biological, ecological, and social structural factors as contributors to violence in simple egalitarian and stratified human societies (Chagnon 1977; Denton 1979; Knauft 1987, 1991). Similarly, most anthropologists interested in sexuality "have opted to concentrate on issues of gender, identity, roles, rituals, and symbolism almost to the exclusion of sexual behavior" (Bolton 1992, 132). When sexual behavior is addressed, it is most often romanticized or justified as an individual action apart from the larger society (Lunsing 1999, 176).

For the most part, research concerned with violence and sex is limited by the difficulty of collecting data on these often concealed acts. The data are indirect, since researchers rarely observe these behaviors directly. Participant observation, however, can yield extremely rich data. In my research, through shelter interviews, informal conversations, and daily interactions with shelter clients and staff, I collected numerous stories of shelter clients with similar scenarios of abuse, violence, and exploitation. Despite the obvious limitations of participant observation as a methodological tool for sensitive and private situations, the commonalities inherent in these women's experiences suggest patterns that can be used as part of an overall approach to the research process and analysis.

Overlapping with anthropological modes of inquiry are feminist methods of doing research within the social sciences. To situate my analysis, I turn to Harding's (1987, 7) three features of feminist research: (1) designing research for women that women want and need, (2) "locating the researcher in the same critical plane as the overt subject matter," and (3) using the experiences of women "as a significant indicator of the 'reality' against which hypotheses are tested." My research meets these criteria by my addressing issues pertinent to women, placing myself as an overtly visible and consciously biased individual within the scope of the fieldwork, and presenting the local experiences and voices of the women I lived and worked with as the foundation of my hypotheses and data.

The effects of living in the shelter environment are in many ways comparable to the effects referred to in the fieldwork literature as "culture shock" or the "dysadaptation syndrome." The notion of "culture shock," originally described by Cora DuBois in 1951 as "a syndrome 'precipitated by the anxiety that results from losing all your familiar cues'" (quoted in Golde 1970, 10–11), in many ways mirrors the reflexive experience of shelter life and perceptions of life beyond the shelter. Pettigrew (1981, 76) describes her own "culture shock" and her feeling of desperation that she would never be able to return to her own people and culture after having internalized the values of the Punjabi village in India where she conducted anthropological fieldwork.

The "dysadaptation syndrome" (Wintrob 1969, 65) refers to the stresses generated by the field experience. In a description applicable to shelter life, Wintrob details how anxiety leads to repressed hostility that is intensified by unaccustomed dependence and helplessness in the new environment (67–69). Many researchers have had reactions like this to fieldwork experiences. For example, Raymond Firth's (1967) description of his very personal reaction to fieldwork contrasts sharply to his report of his impersonal ethnographic studies of Tikopian social structure and social organization. He states, "The feeling of confinement, the obsessional longing to be back even if for the briefest while in one's own cultural surroundings, the dejection and doubts about the validity of what one is doing, the desire to escape into a fantasy world of novels or daydreams, the moral compulsion to drag oneself back to the task of field observation— many sensitive fieldworkers have experienced these feelings on occasion" (xv).

In the women's shelter in Tokyo I experienced similar doubts, longings, compulsions, and daydreams. I see the shelter environment as contributing even more intensely to these common reactions because of the strains, tensions, and traumas in the everyday lives of women at the shelter. The perspectives of the shelter clients became my own internalized view. The distancing and isolation that the shelter necessarily maintains from the surrounding society compounded the situation. During the course of my fieldwork, I felt more and more alienated from Japanese society by virtue of the type and place of my research. The continual crises, threats, uncertainties, and horrific accounts of the clients tainted my view of the larger Japanese society, which I began to see as treacherous and cruel.

My ethnographic account begins with a brief description of how I located and gained entrance to HELP (House of Emergency Love and Peace) Asian Women's Shelter and continues with a description of the shelter environment, case studies, and the larger political-economic context of gender-based violence.

Field Site and the Shelter Environment

The HELP shelter is situated on the fringes of downtown Tokyo's entertainment district, Kabuki-cho, set among flashing neon lights, massage parlors, cabarets, nightclubs, and the merging train lines of one of Tokyo's largest train and subway terminals, Shinjuku. Approached down a narrow alley crowded with pedestrians, lined by parked cars and motor scooters, a hamburger shop, a noodle shop, and piles of neatly bagged garbage, the five-story concrete shelter building is inconspicuous among the other structures crammed into the densely populated area. When I first entered the building, I saw no evidence of a shelter. I followed the instructions a staff member had given to me on the telephone the previous day and climbed the stairs to the third floor. A small, wooden fence blocked the third-floor landing, the reception area for those entering the shelter. Doorways off the landing led to the shelter's dining room, community rooms, kitchen, and staff offices.

I was met by an American caseworker with whom I had spoken on the telephone about my interest in doing research at the shelter. She arranged for me to interview one of the Japanese caseworkers about wife abuse and the exploitation of women in Japan. She gave me a brief tour of the shelter's facilities and described the staff, volunteers, and clients. She also described the history of the shelter and its founding agency, Nihon Kirisutokyo Fujin Kyofukai, the Japan Woman's Christian Temperance Union (JWCTU), established in 1886 (Babior 1993; Oshima and Francis 1989).

In 1986, to mark the one-hundred-year anniversary of JWCTU, the shelter was founded as a means of recognizing the organization's history of coordinating and advocating for women's issues. As initially conceived, the shelter was to serve trafficked and exploited non-Japanese women, but soon it expanded to serve abused Japanese women as well (Mackie 2000, 190). Within six months, the shelter was housing both Japanese and non-

Japanese women and their children, a demonstration of the flexibility of the JWCTU founders and shelter staff.

The shelter staff consisted of a full-time director, three part-time caseworkers, one full-time treasurer, and one full-time housekeeper and cook. Only the housekeeper and cook, known as the "daily care staff person," lived at the shelter full-time. All other staff members commuted every day to the shelter, along with volunteers of various nationalities who came to do office work, provide translation services, or assist clients and staff.

The shelter occasionally broke into separate units of operation based on the languages and cultures of its volunteers, staff, and clients. Counseling was regularly conducted in both Japanese and English with the appropriate caseworker and translator, if needed. Food was also served according to cultural preference. Both Japanese and non-Japanese meals were prepared by either the cook or the clients. Differences in culture and personality created tensions among clients. Women often refused to dine together, and accusations of lying, stealing, or being unclean were common.

On the fourth floor of the building, one level above the offices and the main dining and community rooms of the shelter, were four single rooms and six double or family rooms reserved for the shelter's clients. Above this, on the fifth floor, was a laundry and bathing area, adjacent to a large rooftop with an outdoor area for hanging laundry and bedding on sunny days. The rooftop area also had an emergency stairway leading down the outside of the building to ground level that clients at the shelter used as an alternative entrance and exit.

My initial encounter in 1987 with the shelter clients and personnel marked the starting point for my participant observation research and the beginning of an ongoing, twenty-three-year association with the shelter. I made daily visits to talk with clients and staff, as well as help out by doing some typing and filing. After only a few days of volunteering, I was escorting apprehensive and frightened new clients to their rooms and supplying them with bedding, clothing, and a brief introduction to the shelter. When groups of visiting students and concerned citizens came to learn about the *kakekomi* (a place to run into for refuge), as the shelter was commonly called, I ran a narrated slide show that preceded a question-and-answer period with the staff. Within a few weeks, I was asked to wait for the evening arrival of a new client, after the daytime staff had gone home for the day. I was told that this particular incoming woman was a Filipina who spoke English. When she arrived, I did a brief intake interview and got her settled for the night. Welcoming and helping new clients get settled soon became one of my regular assignments as a volunteer. In this capacity, I emerged as a frontline worker who engaged face-to-face with clients, volunteers and staff.

A look at the shelter's first six months of operation, from April 1, 1986, through September 30, 1986, reveals that in its twenty-three-year history there has been little change in the basic categories of the clients' needs and problems and the solutions to their problems. In 2007, HELP clients comprised 97 adults: 34 non-Japanese women and 63 Japanese women. Among the 34 non-Japanese women, 17 were accompanied by 25 young children, 60 percent under the age of five years, from countries around the world (see Table 3.1).

The length of each woman's stay was based on her situation and could be as short as one night or as long as several months. In 2007, the average length of stay was 22.93 days, down 9 days from 31.93 days in 2006. The age range for non-Japanese women was fourteen to sixty-eight years. The overwhelming majority of shelter admissions among non-Japanese women—close to 75 percent—were related to domestic violence or violence inflicted by a partner. Violence from a different family member, such

Table 3.1. HELP Residents by Country of Origin, April 2007–March 2008

Country of Origin	Adults	Children
Philippines	12	15
Thailand	6	0
China	4	1
Brazil	3	4
Myanmar	2	1
Colombia	1	1
Mexico	1	1
India	1	0
Sri Lanka	1	1
Romania	1	0
United States	1	1
South Korea	1	0
Subtotal	34	25
Japan	63	13
Total	**97**	**38**

Source: HELP Asian Women's Shelter 2008.

as an in-law or child, affected about 2 percent, putting the total number of non-Japanese women clients citing violence as their reason for seeking help at nearly 80 percent.

Other reasons cited by non-Japanese women for seeking shelter were homelessness, human trafficking, and pregnancy. According to HELP staff, while the numbers of trafficked women dropped significantly from previous years, information gathered by telephone counseling and other groups' sources establish a clear increase in the severity and magnitude of trafficking situations.

In 2007, the HELP hotline received 603 calls from Japanese women and 1,321 calls from non-Japanese women representing thirty different countries (see Table 3.2). The reasons for the calls for help from the non-Japanese women included injury, illness, divorce, homelessness, mental illness, domestic violence, immigration issues, nonpayment of child support, cultural adjustment problems, forced prostitution and sexual slavery, threats and acts of violence by employers, a need for safety after escaping from an employer, confiscated passports and airplane tickets taken by employers, and nonpayment of wages and other employment promises not fulfilled. These patterns have remained consistent during the years of the shelter's operation for non-Japanese women, though the categories and the numbers of women in each category have varied.

Among the 63 Japanese clients in 2007, 9 brought children with them. Their reasons for seeking shelter assistance were homelessness, domestic violence from an intimate partner, violence from a different family member, and pregnancy (see Table 3.3). The ages of the clients and their children ranged from a few months to eighty years. The average residency was 15.88 days, somewhat shorter than the average for non-Japanese women. The number of homeless women and children among the Japanese shelter clients rose dramatically in 2007–2008, reflecting widespread unemployment caused by the dire global economic situation. Many of the homeless came from among the increasing numbers of men and women in temporary and part-time labor niches who were the first to face worker lay-offs with few economic or legal protections (Glionna 2009; Mackie 2000).

Although the locus of this study is the urban metropolis of Tokyo, I believe that incidents of domestic violence and sexual exploitation much like those documented in Tokyo occur throughout Japan. Current HELP shelter data suggest that the women who receive assistance and accommodation at the various Japanese women's shelters in the Tokyo area come from both urban and rural settings (HELP Asian Women's Shelter 2008, 4). These data correspond to the cross-cultural domestic violence literature that suggests that wife abuse is not confined to any one socioeconomic class or ethnic group (Gelles and Pedrick-Cornell 1983; Martin 1976; Pagelow 1981; Schechter 1982; Walker 1979). Increased awareness regarding domestic violence throughout Japan resulted in the passage of anti–domestic violence legislation in April 2001, known as the Law for the Prevention of Spousal Violence and the Protection of Victims (Allen 2006). In 2002, Japan signed the United Nations Trafficking Protocol to Prevent, Suppress

Table 3.2. Hotline Calls by Caller's Country of Origin, April 2007–March 2008

Caller's country of origin	Number of calls
Japan	603
Philippines	727
Thailand	403
China	38
Myanmar	17
South Korea	15
North Korea	12
Russia	11
Colombia	9
Mexico	8
Sri Lanka	8
United States	7
Brazil	7
Romania	7
Peru	6
India	5
Ghana	4
Serbia and Montenegro	3
Ukraine	2
Vietnam	2
Morocco	2
Taiwan	2
Venezuela	2
Indonesia	1
Australia	1
Bangladesh	1
Tunisia	1
Uzbekistan	1
Canada	1
Chile	1
Pakistan	1
Unknown	16
Total	**1,924**

**Table 3.3. Reasons for Coming to HELP,
April 2007–March 2008**

Japanese clients	
Homelessness	63.2%
Partner violence	27.6%
Family violence	5.3%
Pregnancy	3.9%
Non-Japanese clients	
Partner violence	74.6%
Homelessness	8.5%
Trafficking	3.4%
Pregnancy	1.7%
Family violence	1.7%
Other	
Immigration, children, divorce, visa problems	10.1%

and Punish Trafficking in Persons (United Nations 2000). Estimates suggest that approximately 100,000 women enter Japan each year legally and illegally for sex-related work, and at least 150,000 to 200,000 are in Japan illegally, having arrived through trafficking or because of immigration irregularities (Douglass 2003, 111). The destination of many of the women leaving HELP suggest their marginal status in society. Most end up in a residence facility until they can find alternative live-and-work situations. The majority of the illegal HELP clients are eventually deported to their country of origin.

Against this background, after I had worked for six weeks as a volunteer at the shelter, the HELP director asked me to become the night-duty staff person. The position included room and board, plus a small stipend. With a substantial amount of hesitation, I decided to accept the offer. Whether or not this was a wise decision is debatable, but the experience went far beyond my expectations both professionally and personally.

Adjustments to Shelter Life

I had agreed to live in the shelter for an indefinite period as the English-speaking night-duty staff person. This was to be my home, place of work, and site of research for the duration of my fieldwork. The shelter staff was aware of my intent as a researcher to ask questions, conduct interviews, and gather information, though my role as both participant and observer became blurred during the course of my stay at the shelter. The tension I felt between my commitment to the clients and staff I worked with and my intention to gather data for academic purposes was similar to the tension between activism and academia found in the battered women's movement (Campbell 1998; Incite! Women of Color Against Violence 2006; Sokoloff and Pratt 2005).

My job description was quite vague but ideally included nightly availability from five in the evening until nine the next morning, Monday through Friday, and around the clock on weekends. In practice, my weekday hours generally extended later into the morning and resumed whenever I returned to the shelter. My primary responsibility was to attend to the needs and welfare of the non-Japanese clients. My many and diverse tasks included giving intake interviews, arranging for airline tickets, answering hotline telephone calls from English speakers, and escorting women to doctors and hospitals for health care appointments, to their appropriate embassies for travel affidavits to replace their confiscated passports, to the Tokyo Immigration Bureau for immigration and deportation documents, and to the airport bus and Tokyo's Narita airport for departure to their home countries. Although I was not directly addressing the original topic of my research proposal, I became increasingly absorbed in my role as an advocate for non-Japanese women at the shelter. As Billings (1990) argues, meaningful discoveries may be those that are unanticipated and that we are unprepared for rather than those that result from preconceived research designs and procedures. Nevertheless, I was confronted daily with self-doubt, mistrust, and skepticism about my own roles and feelings.

One of the biggest adjustments I had to make was living in an environment that lacked privacy. I traded time alone and solitude for total immersion and access to information. Feeling what Firth (1967, xv) describes as "the desire to escape into a fantasy world of novels or daydreams," I found myself daydreaming to create a sense of personal space. It was the only way to separate myself from the intrusion and problems of others. But the blocking out of those around me only intensified my alienation, for when I returned to my daily tasks, I found myself especially resistant and hostile to the intrusions. Sometimes I would return to my room only to hear a knock on the door moments later. I felt guilty for sequestering myself, so whenever I felt the need for solitude I made a point of seeking it outside the shelter in neighborhood coffee shops, libraries, and parks. When I was in the shelter, regardless of the time designated as my "work" hours, I was incorporated into the activities of the moment. From a methodological perspective, my subjective participant role took precedence over my objective observer role. As Harding (1987, 9) suggests, "Introducing this 'subjective' element into the analysis in fact increases the objectivity of the research and decreases the 'objectivism' which hides this kind of evidence from the public."

Coping with my lack of privacy was only one problem. With the passage of time, I internalized many of the shelter clients' experiences and their fearfulness, their sense of being exploited, and their feeling of powerlessness. This kind of reaction has been identified as "vicarious traumatization" (McCann and Pearlman 1990). Vicarious traumatization describes a condition of persons who may experience profound psychological effects, including feelings of fright, numbness, ambivalence, and negative or moral/judgmental feelings as a result of working with survivors of violence. In my case, living at the shelter and working with clients shifted my attitude about the world outside the shelter to one of anger, alienation, and trepidation, and a sense of violation. When I ventured beyond the shelter I felt hostility, particularly toward men, because men were the perpetrators of so much of the suffering and violence I witnessed every day. Therapists emphasize the importance of confronting and sharing one's own feelings of rage, grief, horror, loss of control, aggression, and vulnerability as a means of coping with vicarious traumatization. But I had no place to go where I felt totally secure and I had no specific person with whom I could share my innermost fears.

Similar reactions were noticeable among the clients of HELP. Their initial fears and anxiety over their location and safety, followed by concern over finances, children, personal belongings, and future living arrangements were expressed as rage, shame, guilt, doubt, resentment, and depression. Even the mere adjustment to shelter life involved passing through various mental stages. Schechter (1982, 59) describes one of these stages in her account of shelter life in the United States as clients grapple with their new predicaments: "At first they are frightened and nervous, both about the decisions they have made and about their new environment. . . . After the initial flurry of activities . . . they may feel intense doubts, fear, and pain. Women struggle with ambivalence, self-blame and guilt as they . . . attempt to make sense of what happened." Regardless of the cultural setting, the emotions and experiences of shelter clients are similar in theme and pattern.

The case studies that follow describe the experiences of two women from two different cultures, Japanese and non-Japanese, in terms of their perceptions of safety and security and their personal sense of power and powerlessness within and beyond the shelter environment. These case studies provide a sample of the shelter clients' points of view and reveal how their narratives influence the perspective of the participant observer. The notions of participant/observer and objective/subjective identities are embedded in the practice of fieldwork and the writing of ethnography. The degree to which one is a participant or observer, subjective or objective, is highly individualized, yet these categories commonly overlap. The two case studies demonstrate the gamut of emotions that affect both the shelter clients and the participant observer.

Case Studies

Isabel de la Cruz, Age Twenty-Three, Citizen of the Philippines

Isabel de la Cruz was abducted from a train station while a resident at the shelter. Her case demonstrates the fragility of supposedly safe and secure surroundings. Her former employer, who had ostensibly hired her as a waitress, demanded that she work as a prostitute. He sent two men to survey the shelter environs, subsequently luring her into a nearby train station by telephone, where they kidnapped her. My field notes from that day describe the unfolding of events surrounding Isabel de la Cruz.

> Isabel had completed her day at the Tokyo Immigration Office, securing a visa extension and an Embassy travel document in lieu of her passport. She was residing at HELP while preparing to return to the Philippines. At 5:00 a.m., the shelter's public phone rang. One of the clients answered it and summoned Isabel to the phone. After speaking and hanging up the phone, Isabel borrowed a pair of slippers from the shelter's housekeeper and told her she was going to meet a friend at the nearby train station. No one heard from her again until the following day.
>
> When the phone rang at HELP at 2:00 a.m. the next day, Isabel was on the other end speaking in a whisper. She said she didn't know where she was and she didn't feel safe. She hung up the telephone.
>
> Early the next morning she called again, this time from the safety of a police station. She told me that two men had grabbed her when she originally went to the train station to meet her friend. She explained that she and a friend had been forcibly taken back to the night club where

they had originally been working. After their abductors interrogated, hit, and threatened to kill them both if they tried to flee, they were left alone while their abductors prepared to move them to a different location. It was at this point that they escaped.

They hid in the farming fields outside of town all night. Early in the morning they went to a park and asked a jogger to help them. He took them to a nearby police station, where the women called HELP. Isabel returned to HELP that evening escorted by one of the HELP caseworkers who went to meet her at the rural police station.

The days following Isabel's abduction kept everyone at HELP on alert for suspicious-looking men lurking outside the shelter. Isabel remained secluded and withdrawn at the shelter until she eventually returned to the Philippines escorted by a HELP guest from the Philippines. Periodic dramas like this one undermined my already weak sense of security.

As this incident illustrates, the security of the shelter as a place of refuge was limited and only temporary. On numerous occasions, abductors, recruiters, promoters, employers, and batterers came to the shelter or contacted it by telephone. Within the walls of the shelter, women could take time to think about their situation and perhaps make effective future plans. But there remained a sense of danger and uncertainty beyond the boundaries of the shelter. In 2008, a family's location was divulged to their batterer, forcing them to return to HELP. The source of the information leak about their location was a government municipal office that helped locate housing for women in need. The municipal office had promised previously to "absolutely never" give away these details and risk exposure of a family's whereabouts. "Such experiences," the shelter administration recognizes, "remind us of the gravity of the problem of continued stalking for survivors of domestic violence" (HELP Asian Women's Shelter 2008, 2).

Many of the unavoidable interactions outside the shelter were with police officers, male officials at the Tokyo Immigration Office, and men encountered at close range on very crowded subways and trains. It was jarring for women who have been in the all-female environment of the shelter to step into a world where men seem to be everywhere. As McCann and Pearlman (1990, 141) note, trauma survivors often experience a sense of alienation from other people and from the world in general, and for many of the shelter clients, these men symbolize exploitation and violation.

After long days of preparing for deportation, many of the women relaxed at the shelter and distanced themselves from the outside world by joking about their past experiences. Being able to share with others similar circumstances helped to relieve their sense of guilt, shame, and isolation. Laughing about their situations was a common practice after dinner in the dining room or clients' rooms as noted in the following field note observation:

> Commonly after dinner everyone relaxed. There were lots of jokes about Japanese men. This was followed by the acting out of men walking with their pelvises protruding and feet wide apart. There was a lot of laughing. The women acted out the lighting of cigarettes and pouring of drinks for men. Occasionally they demonstrated how the men would kick them in their groins or faces "just for fun." "Can you imagine they wanted me to swallow their sperm? They are like animals," said Maria Perez as she imitated how the men pushed her head down while forcing her to perform oral sex.

Toyota Keiko, Age Fifty-Three, Citizen of Japan

Security and safety issues were concerns of everyone at the HELP shelter. For Toyota Keiko, who finally left her physically and emotionally abusive husband after twenty-five years of marriage, the prospects of living on her own were terrifying. When the shelter caseworker encouraged her to find housing, she expressed the very real fear that her husband might locate her and harm her. She eventually rented a small room close to the shelter and spent her evenings and weekends visiting the staff and clients at HELP.

As a sojourn, the shelter acted both as a sanctuary and a place of confinement. In contrast to the many women who remained at the shelter while seeking assistance, some felt compelled to flee. One woman from Thailand decided to leave secretly in the middle of the night. A woman from the Philippines stayed at HELP for only two days before vanishing. And a homeless Japanese woman spent three days washing, bathing, eating, and sleeping at the shelter, and then she simply walked out the door, once again onto the streets. Cases such as these, which were not unusual, triggered a reassessment by the staff and volunteers about shelter structure. The shelter stood out as unusual, because, in contrast to the general regimentation of Japanese society, it functioned without rigid organization and without strictly enforced rules or timetables.

One evening when Toyota-san stopped by the shelter after work, she looked particularly upset. We had just finished dinner and offered her a cup of green tea. She began by telling us that during the night she had heard someone trying to open the lock on her door. She feared it was her husband, though it turned out to have been merely someone at the wrong door. Over the course of the next few weeks she expressed continual anxiety about being harmed. At the urging of a shelter caseworker, Toyota-san rented a larger room in an area farther away from the shelter and brought her daughter to live with her. Her shelter visits became less frequent, though she continued to keep in daily telephone contact for the duration of my six months of research at the shelter.

The shelter staff and volunteers maintained a philosophy originating in the Japanese feminist movement of the 1970s and 1980s, wherein they acted in solidarity with women rather than seeing them as "victim" and looking upon them with pity (Mackie 2000, 190). At the time of the founding of the shelter, the shelter supporters and organizers articulated the links between the current oppression and exploitation of women in Japanese society and the oppression perpetrated by Japan in Asia and Southeast Asia under systems of dominance and subordination throughout the nineteenth and twentieth centuries. Japanese feminists recognized that the production of food, clothes, and goods in daily use in Japan were manufactured primarily by Asian women under appalling conditions within a system of economic imperialism. Additional links were made between prostitution tourism and the history of Japan's sexual exploitation of women in Asia and Southeast Asia during the 1930s and 1940s. The shelter staff now sees systems of inequality based on gender, class, and ethnicity directed at migrant women who come to Japan to work and are often tricked into sex work and prostitution (Sellek 1997). Because of its improved economy, Japan now attracts increasing numbers of workers from around the world (Mackie 2000, 190), rather than exporting Japanese women workers to do the dirty, difficult, and dangerous jobs in other parts of the world once relegated to economically destitute women.

With the passage of time, my status as a staff/participant and researcher/observer evolved into a blur of roles and feelings. I identified with many of the shelter clients' experiences and their current dilemmas. I felt hostility and helplessness within the shelter environment, compounded by fear, insecurity, and violation outside its boundaries. I worried that I would need to confront antagonistic and potentially dangerous men at any time, and I was nervous about my personal safety and security. I was depressed about shelter life and worried about whether I would be able to function outside of it ever again. Both the shelter itself and how I perceived it trapped me. I directed my anger at the world outside that appeared to sanction violence and abuse through what seemed to be apathy, denial, and insensitivity. The constant needs of other people, compounded by the erratic hours, interruptions, and endless curiosity about me as a foreigner, were exhausting me. But I recognized that experiences like mine, as McCann and Pearlman (1990, 147) point out, can create greater sensitivity and empathy for the suffering of others, resulting in a deeper sense of connection and hopefulness about the capacity of humans to endure, overcome, and transform their lives.

Conclusion

This analysis is based on personal and professional experience. It examines the methodology of participant observation in shaping the views of anthropological research. It addresses the struggle to maintain a balance between the supposed objective, neutral, value-free scientific observer and the personal, experiential, and subjective participant. It draws on the importance of using women's personal experiences as resources for social analysis (Harding 1987, 7), and it reveals the interplay of "self" and "other" through ethnographic narrative (Tedlock 1991, 69).

As a shelter staff member, I engaged in both participation and observation to fulfill my dual roles as a frontline worker and an anthropologist. As I increasingly internalized the experiences of other women, I put aside my role as detached observer and became a full-fledged participant. This shift in focus forms the basis of my reflexive ethnographic narrative. Presenting myself as receptive, truthful, and innately biased about who I am and how I see others frames the ethnography and informs the reader. As Okely (1992, 24) states, "Reflexivity forces one to think through the consequences of our relations with others, whether it be conditions of reciprocity, asymmetry or potential exploitation, . . . we are obliged to confront the moral and political responsibility of our actions." I took personal responsibility for my interpretation and analysis by sharing my completed text with the shelter staff and volunteers. The HELP shelter members reacted pragmatically. They initiated a monthly women's study group to translate, discuss, and critique the finished ethnography in an effort to view the shelter from another perspective. Most recently, the issue of staff "burnout" became the focus of shelter concern. Training activities, workshops, lectures, retreats, and exchange of information between facilities highlighted an eight-month project in 2007 concluding with the development of the notion of "habitual consciousness," or maintaining preventative structures for future risk of staff burnout.

Shelter philosophy and projects like these are rooted in a historical context that encourages open dialogue, negotiation, unity, and action among staff, volunteers, and clients. For the founders of the HELP shelter, "the concept of helping was not that of standing at a distance, viewing the situation and criticizing it, but rather being involved directly in action" (Oshima and Francis 1989, 90). This model provided the ideal environment for a participant observation study. In the end, the merging of my living space and my fieldwork site enriched the overall research experience.

The construction of ethnography is framed by the experiences and boundaries of the researcher. As Clifford notes in the introduction to Clifford and Marcus 1986, ethnographies are merely "partial truths" or "true fictions" in that "all constructed truths are made possible by powerful 'lies' of exclusion and rhetoric," through selective withholding, exclusion, translation, and editing (7). I have compensated for some of the inevitable pitfalls of ethnographic writing by inserting myself as a positioned subject into the text. The interplay between my own experiences and the experiences of the women I lived and worked with is ultimately a matter of personal perception and interpretation.

ACKNOWLEDGMENTS

The research and writing of this article would not have been possible without the encouragement, advice, and support of numerous people and institutions. I wish to thank all the many courageous women who shared their lives and stories with me. I also owe enormous thanks to the Japan Woman's Christian Temperance Union, Tokyo, whose generous support and commitment allowed me to live and work in the shelter. My many thanks go out to Oshima Shizuko, the first director of the HELP shelter, for her steadfast advice, mentoring, and friendship. Her activism and unwavering belief in universal human rights continues to serve as a lofty model for us all. And finally, my mother, Lynne Babior, who has given me more feedback and editorial input than I care to admit. I am forever grateful to her for her love and guidance.

WORKS CITED

Abramson, Paul R. 1992. Sex, Lies, and Ethnography. In *The Time of AIDS*, ed. G. Herdt and S. Lindenbaum. 101–23. Thousand Oaks, CA: Sage.

Allen, Rachel. 2006. Shelter Reaches Out to Abuse Victims. *Japan Times*. Dec. 5. *search.japantimes.co.jp/cgi-bin/fl20061205zg.html.*

Babior, Sharman L. 1993. Women of a Tokyo Shelter: Domestic Violence and Sexual Exploitation in Japan. PhD diss., University of California.

Behar, Ruth. 1996. *The Vulnerable Observer: Anthropology That Breaks Your Heart.* Boston: Beacon Press.

Billings, Dorothy K. 1990. Is Fieldwork Art or Science? In *The Humbled Anthropologist: Tales from the Pacific*, ed. P. R. DeVita, 1–7. Belmont, CA: Wadsworth.

Bolton, Ralph. 1992. Mapping Terra Incognita: Sex Research for AIDS Prevention; An Urgent Agenda for the 1990s. In *The Time of AIDS*, ed. G. Herdt and S. Lindenbaum, 124–58. Thousand Oaks, CA: Sage.

Bowen, Elenore Smith. 1964. *Return to Laughter.* Garden City, NY: Doubleday.

Callaway, Helen. 1992. Ethnography and Experience: Gender Implications in Fieldwork and Texts. In *Anthropology and Autobiography*, ed. J. Okely and H. Callaway, 28–49. New York: Routledge.

Campbell, Jacquelyn C. 1998. Interdisciplinarity in Research on Wife Abuse: Can Academics and Activists Work Together? In *Women's Studies in Transition: The Pursuit of Interdisciplinarity*, ed. K. Conway-Turner, S. Cherrin, J. Schiffman, K. Turkel, 308–19. Newark: University of Delaware Press.

Cesara, Manda. 1982. *Reflections of a Woman Anthropologist: No Hiding Place.* New York: Academic Press.

Chagnon, Napoleon A. 1977. *Yanomamo: The Fierce People.* New York: Holt, Rinehart, and Winston.

Clifford, James, and George E. Marcus, eds. 1986. *Writing Culture: The Poetics and Politics of Ethnography.* Berkeley: University of California Press.

Crapanzano, Vincent. 1977. On the Writing of Ethnography. *Dialectical Anthropology* 2 (1): 69–73.

Denton, Robert K. 1979. *The Semai: A Nonviolent People of Malaya.* New York: Holt, Rinehart, and Winston.

Douglass, Mike. 2003. The Singularities of International Migration of Women to Japan. In *Migration of Women to Japan, Past, Present, and Future*, ed. Mike Douglass and Glenda Susan Roberts, 91–121. Honolulu: University of Hawai'i Press.

Firth, Raymond. 1954. Social Organization and Social Change. *Journal of the Royal Anthropological Institute* 84:1–20.

———. 1967. Introd. to *A Diary in the Strict Sense of the Term*, by Bronislaw Malinowski. New York: Harcourt, Brace and World.

Gelles, Richard J., and Claire Pedrick-Cornell, eds. 1983. *International Perspectives on Family Violence.* Lexington, MA: Lexington Books.

Glionna, John. 2009. Part-Timers in Japan Confront Full-Time Woes. *Los Angeles Times*, January 29.

Gluckman, Max. 1963. *Order and Rebellion in Tribal Africa.* New York: Free Press of Glencoe.

Golde, Peggy. 1970. Introd. to *Women in the Field: Anthropological Experiences*, ed. P. Golde. Chicago: Aldine.

Harding, Sandra. 1987. Introd. to *Feminism and Methodology*, ed. Harding. Bloomington: Indiana University Press.

HELP Asian Women's Shelter. 2008. *Network News* (Tokyo), June, no. 53.

Incite! Women of Color Against Violence, ed. 2006. *The Color of Violence: The Incite! Anthology*. Cambridge, MA: South End Press.

Jongmans, Douwe Geert, and Peter Claus Wolfgang Gutkind, eds. 1967. *Anthropologists in the Field*. Assen, Neth.: Van Gorcum.

Knauft, Bruce M. 1987. Reconsidering Violence in Simple Human Societies. *Current Anthropology* 28 (4): 457–98.

———. 1991. Violence and Sociality in Human Evolution. *Current Anthropology* 32 (4): 391–428.

Leach, Edmund R. 1954. *Political Systems of Highland Burma*. London: Anthlone Press.

Lunsing, Wim. 1999. Life on Mars: Love and Sex in Fieldwork on Sexuality and Gender in Urban Japan. In *Sex, Sexuality, and the Anthropologist*, ed. F. Markowitz and M. Ashkenazi, 175–95. Urbana: University of Illinois Press.

Mackie, Vera. 2000. Feminist Critiques of Modern Japanese Politics. In *Global Feminisms since 1945*, ed. B. Smith, 180–201. New York: Routledge.

Marcus, George E., and Dick Cushman. 1982. Ethnographies as Texts. *Annual Review of Anthropology* 11 (1): 25–69.

Martin, Del. 1976. *Battered Wives*. San Francisco: Glide Publications.

McCann, Lisa, and Laurie Anne Pearlman. 1990. Vicarious Traumatization: A Framework for Understanding the Psychological Effects of Working with Victims. *Journal of Traumatic Stress* 3 (1): 131–49.

Merry, Sally Engle. 2008. Review: Commentary on Reviews of "Human Rights and Gender Violence." *American Anthropologist* 110 (4): 520–22.

Moeran, Brian. 1985. *Okubo Diary: Portrait of a Japanese Valley*. Stanford, CA: Stanford University Press.

Nader, Laura. 1970. From Anguish to Exultation. In *Women in the Field: Anthropological Experiences*, ed. P. Golde, 95–116. Chicago: Aldine.

Okely, Judith. 1992. Anthropology and Autobiography: Participatory Experience and Embodied Knowledge. In *Anthropology and Autobiography*, ed. J. Okely and H. Callaway, 1–27. New York: Routledge.

Oshima, Shizuko, and Carolyn Francis. 1989. *Japan through the Eyes of Women Migrant Workers*. Tokyo: Japan Woman's Christian Temperance Union.

Pagelow, Mildred Daley. 1981. *Woman-Battering: Victims and Their Experiences*. Thousand Oaks, CA: Sage.

Pelto, Pertti J., and Gretel H. Pelto. 1978. *Anthropological Research: The Structure of Inquiry*. Cambridge: Cambridge University Press.

Pettigrew, Joyce. 1981. Reminiscences of Fieldwork among the Sikhs. In *Doing Feminist Research*, ed. H. Roberts, 62–82. New York: Routledge.

Rabinow, Paul. 1977. *Reflections on Fieldwork in Morocco.* Berkeley: University of California Press.

Rosaldo, Renato. 1989. *Culture and Truth: The Remaking of Social Analysis.* Boston: Beacon Press.

Schechter, Susan. 1982. *Women and Male Violence: The Visions and Struggles of the Battered Women's Movement.* Boston: South End Press.

Sellek, Yoko. 1997. Nikkeijin: The Phenomenon of Return Migration. In *Japan's Minorities: The Illusion of Homogeneity*, ed. M. Weiner, 178–210. New York: Routledge.

Sokoloff, Natalie, and Cristina Pratt, eds. 2005. *Domestic Violence at the Margins: Readings on Race, Class, Gender, and Culture.* New Brunswick, NJ: Rutgers University Press.

Tedlock, Barbara. 1991. From Participant Observation to the Observation of Participation: The Emergence of Narrative Ethnography. *Journal of Anthropological Research* 47 (1): 69–94.

United Nations. 2000. Protocol to Prevent, Suppress and Punish Trafficking in Persons, Especially Women and Children, Supplementing the United Nations Convention against Transnational Organized Crime. *www.uncjin.org/Documents/Conventions/dcatoc/final_documents_2/convention_%20traff_eng.pdf.*

Walker, Lenore E. 1979. *The Battered Woman.* New York: Harper and Row.

Wintrob, Ronald M. 1969. An Inward Focus: A Consideration of Psychological Stress in Fieldwork. In *Stress and Response in Fieldwork*, ed. F. Henry and S. Saberwal, 63–76. New York: Holt, Rinehart, and Winston.

4

Crafting Community through Narratives, Images, and Shared Experience

Stephanie J. Brommer

In 1990, five first-generation Indian women and one Bangladeshi woman came together in the San Francisco Bay eastern shore region to help South Asian immigrant women deal with isolation and domestic abuse. By 1992, they formally named their organization Narika, which, in Hindi, means "of and for women," and offered a weekly support group with funding from a Bank of America grant. "But not that many women came," one of the founders, a prominent Berkeley attorney, said.[1] "It was very artificial, a Western notion that we would talk about our problems with other women. We did not know what we were doing when we started."

So the group of Northern California women swapped the support group for a monthly potluck where women could enjoy chai, homemade food, and friendly company and chat one-on-one—"the South Asian way of doing a support group," according to another co-founder who is still very active in the organization.

"It was clear from the beginning that we really made a big difference," the Berkeley attorney, a Christian Goan who immigrated from Delhi in 1970, said.

> We were helping women on a more informal basis and not getting hung up on statistics. We helped people transform their lives. We decided if we could help one woman change the cycle of abuse, think about it—how many can say they helped one woman not get beaten? We were not better, not experts, not sophisticated, and did not call them clients; we regarded them as members of our family, as peers. Every one of us through the force of circumstances could be placed in circumstances like this. Our at-

51

titude was that this does not mean you're a failure. We are like your sister or mother or cousin. We built a model on familial relationships in India. We thought we could provide the best of both worlds—cultural security and familiarity and not gossiping or taking sides.

This chapter examines how South Asian domestic abuse activists and frontline workers in Northern California integrate worldviews with the immigration experience to empower women to confront and overcome domestic abuse. Through mottos, themes, and models of caregiving, these frontline workers use discursive politics to signal an alternative vision of community that results in a weblike fictive kin relationship to promote women's empowerment and choice, while engaging in social change. Through their work and their discourse, these workers seek to break the silence and create a supportive community for women who are surviving domestic abuse.[2] Their emphasis on South Asian sisterhood and empowerment shapes their caregiving strategies and frames the way their work is viewed within the larger community. The South Asian immigrant community's status as a model minority, a label given to a group of people in a subordinate position in society that is associated with high educational achievement and financial success and strong family values, also contributes to the way in which they approach domestic abuse and the specter of abused women.[3]

By placing a high cultural value on family to appeal to South Asian abused women, frontline workers position themselves both as caregivers and as fictive kin. Their relationship thus functions as a kin network similar to the supportive kin network the immigrant woman left behind in South Asia. The frontline workers are reflecting familiar values, such as close family ties, and become culturally appropriate persons to talk with about family life. Drawing on this tradition of social life—the notion of women having kin, constructed as fictive kin, to turn to for support, as well as women helping women—is behind the names, symbols, slogans, and caregiving models of Maitri and Narika, two South Asian domestic abuse organizations in Northern California.

By speaking a language of empowerment, the Maitri and Narika frontline workers are feminist. As Katzenstein (1995, 35–36) points out, feminist interest groups are "word conscious" and seek to "change *understandings* of gender stereotyping." Katzenstein uses the term "discursive politics" to discuss meaning-making. "In discursive politics the careful thought given to word choices and language is sometimes instrumental but more often expressive. Its intent is to articulate clearly the differences in perspective and the revisioning of a feminist world view" (36). The discursive strategies articulated by these frontline workers include an empowerment discourse, differing experience discourse, and social change discourse.

The Organizations

When Maitri and Narika started in the early 1990s, they both faced community hostility, but by their tenth anniversaries in 2001 and 2002, respectively, the impact of their discursive politics had resulted in widespread community support. Emphasizing a discourse of differing experiences, South Asian caregivers of domestic abuse survivors recognize that a woman's action is situated within the discourses or frames of gender roles, cultural experiences, and community ideologies. Thus, a woman may hesitate to enter an emergency thirty-day shelter if she adheres to culturally prescribed dietary restrictions or is subject to familial and community pressures to keep her marriage intact, or lacks the necessary visa, job training, or language skills to be self-sufficient. A woman's behavior may be shaped by her position as a daughter-in-law or by the effect it might have on her family in the home country.

The frontline workers at these two Northern California organizations reflect and honor a wide South Asian feminist point of view that binds women from these diverse nations and regions regardless of geopolitical boundaries. To reach out to women from all South Asian countries, many South Asian domestic abuse organizations in the United States, including Maitri and Narika, socially construct themselves as "South Asian."[4] Women's subjugation by South Asian and Western patriarchal structures and institutions, including family, law, and politics, is the common thread linking women of South Asian background. For these organizations, domestic abuse itself, and combating domestic abuse, transcend nation-state boundaries. This identification is marked through the emphasis on South Asia and their goal to assist any woman of that regional background.

The number of Asian Indians in the San Francisco Bay Area, however, far exceeds the number of Pakistanis, Sri Lankans, and Bangladeshis. Of the region's total South Asian population, Asian Indians account for 94 percent, Pakistanis for 5 percent, and Sri Lankans and Bangladeshis for less than 1 percent each (Ahuka, Gupta, and Petsod 2004). According to the U.S. Census 2000, the population of Indians, Pakistanis, Bangladeshis, and Sri Lankans make up 2.8 percent of the San Francisco Bay Area's total population, which is the highest percentage of South Asian population in any area in the United States and equals 40 percent of California's South Asian population (U.S. Census Bureau 2002).[5] Overall in the United States, the Asian Indian population doubled in the decade after the 1990 census and is now the third largest Asian American population in the United States.[6] In 2000, the city of San Jose, the home of Maitri, had the largest Asian Indian population in California (26,606), representing 3 percent of the city's population and a 149 percent jump in Asian Indian population in ten years. In Santa Clara County (where San Jose is located), the Asian Indian population, totaling 66,741 people, grew 231 percent. Santa Clara County ranks third in the nation for Asian Indian population, and the neighboring Alameda County, which includes Berkeley, Narika's home, ranks fifth (Kang 2001).

Though the majority of the leaders, members, and clients of domestic abuse organizations are Indian, these organizations still claim the title "South Asian" because they aim to serve all people from the region, offering services in more than a dozen languages. Mohanty (1993, 352) explains the significance: "Obviously I was not South Asian in India—I was Indian. . . . Identifying as South Asian rather than Indian adds numbers and hence power within the U.S. State. Besides, regional differences among those from different South Asian countries are often less relevant than the commonalities based on our experiences and histories of immigration, treatment and location in the U.S."

"South Asian" in the appellation of an organization connotes inclusion and common concerns beyond national borders and throughout the diaspora (Passano 1995; Shah 1996). It is a political term because it threatens national and cultural boundaries and sets aside nationalistic differences. The countries of India, Pakistan, Sri Lanka, Nepal, and Bangladesh, and groups within them, are diverse in cultural beliefs, religious practices, and local histories, but many do share some historical commonalities and certain cultural practices, such as the caste system, a patrilineal form of patriarchy, joint family household, and patrilocal residence. Shah (1996, 53) points out that "while the term 'South Asian' can be problematic if it points to a group that is solely Indian and Hindu, it is useful for marking the region's shared histories and cultures." The term, she adds, is "particularly useful in a diasporic context—such as the United States—because it refers us to a collective homeland . . . [and] allows progressive workers for social change to bypass national allegiances and claim belonging elsewhere."

Like other domestic abuse organizations with a majority of their volunteers and clientele of Indian heritage, Maitri and Narika market themselves as "South Asian." But they are critically aware of the religious, cultural, and linguistic differences within the South Asian collectivity, as the Narika founder who is a Berkeley attorney makes clear: "We are not operating in the mainstream Indian community and are not comfortable with segregation in the linguistic and regional way. We're South Asian—from the beginning, we have had Bangladeshis and Pakistanis and we don't hang our cup in Indocentrism or Hindu or BJP [Hindu nationalist political party, Bharatiya Janata Party]. We are not caught up in any geopolitical game." A former Narika executive director reports that she sought to avoid communalism by making regionalism of foremost importance: "There are plenty of commonalities in the cultures of South Asia. That's not to imply it is a homogeneous culture. There are a lot of variations within South Asian cultures, but the pattern of violence and what we see here are similar." While class, caste, language, and religion differentiate both the volunteers and the clients of domestic abuse organizations, these differences do not subvert the solidarity of South Asian women in Northern California working together to address domestic violence in their immigrant communities. The common experience of growing up in patriarchal-based societies and families connects these women as they create their own community to reach out to women experiencing abuse.

South Asian caregivers tailor their programs and philosophies to the geographic and cultural displacement of their community. Maitri, for instance, prioritizes long-term transitional housing, and Narika supports collaborative ventures, including an overseas project aimed at alerting potential brides to the rights and services available in the United States. They post informational flyers in bathroom stalls in grocery stores and libraries so women can read them in private and take copies without being seen by the husband or in-law who accompanied them. Maitri and Narika volunteers also educate mainstream shelters, counselors, courts, and law enforcement officers about the dynamics of in-law collusion, family honor, immigration status, and the institution of arranged marriage that may impact a woman's life and obscure abuse.

Narika

The organization maintains a website that states: "Narika's mission is to promote the empowerment of women in our community to confront and overcome the cycles of domestic violence and exploitation. We work to build a movement to end violence against women and to support women's rights as human rights."[7] Its discourse empowers women by reinterpreting various practices and attitudes that lead to domestic abuse. Narika's frontline workers, the former executive director explained, integrate domestic abuse with other issues that affect the community and frame it as a public health issue, a woman's issue, and a man's issue. When dealing with domestic abuse, these frontline workers cannot ignore larger issues, such as immigration, and social factors—including forced marriage, female infanticide, and dowry demands—all of which are tied to the ways Indian women may be devalued. As a Narika employee, who is also a Berkeley graduate student, noted, "It's a social change movement dealing with political and economic issues." In fact, according to the former director, Narika volunteers will not refer women to housekeeper or nanny jobs, considering them avenues to exploitation and obstacles to empowerment. Katzenstein (1995, 36) conceives of discursive politics as "intended to challenge deeply held beliefs, but it directly challenges the way people write and think about these beliefs." These words describe the strategy of both Narika and Maitri.

Narika is located in Berkeley, a liberal, activist-oriented community with a sizable working-class South Asian population. Its staff consists of both first-generation women and younger, college-aged women, many of them second-generation immigrants recruited from the nearby University of California at Berkeley campus.

From the beginning, Narika represented regional and religious diversity. Its founders, all professional women, including an attorney, a journalist, a professor, and a filmmaker, are Sikh, Goan Christian, Bangladeshi Muslim, North Indian Hindu, and South Indian Hindu. They contributed their own money to pay for the telephone line and for cabs to whisk clients away from abusive homes. They spent several years, according to one founder, convincing the area's South Asian community that they were offering options and support rather than advocating divorce: "At the beginning, they would call us a bunch of lesbians and divorcees trying to break up the home. They would call us radical women feminists, and we got a lot of it because we are in Berkeley. What I saw was when people saw what was happening and women were leaving abusive situations and getting help, then attitudes started changing and we were tolerated and got some support from the community." Growing to twenty volunteers and representing at least a dozen languages, Narika opened an office in 1994 after years of meeting in volunteers' homes.

Narika, which sells a t-shirt bearing its logo surrounded by the words, "Changing the way we live—violence free," developed a symbol that displays two hands and two doves linked. This symbol connotes peace, nonviolence, friendship, and help and symbolizes Narika's collaborations with other organizations and services that address domestic abuse in Asian communities. These collaborations include Narika's Survivor Economic Empowerment and Development project, an initiative that uses a peer mentoring model and community resources to promote clients' professional growth and financial independence.

Maitri

A college professor, one of six women who helped create Maitri, conceived the name *Maitri* ("friendship between women" in Sanskrit) to connote the deep connection between women. "I thought of it right away," she said, "because our mission was to extend friendship toward these women, as a replacement for sisters, aunts, and the extended family they left behind. If they were in India, they would go to these resources. Here, they were alone; they came here after being married and did not have family in the community. They didn't know anyone." The name *Maitri* reflected the shared experiences of the women to whom the organizers sought to reach out, and it fit with their interaction models built on traditional South Asian familial relationships.

Among the founders is a woman who immigrated to the United States from Calcutta in 1984, two years after her arranged marriage to an engineer. She described her difficult adjustment: "When I came here, I had nobody, no relatives, no friends, no car. The people I met were his friends. I never drove in India, like so many women who come here. So I was not mobile. So I was stuck at home. I'm lucky I have a nice husband, a caring and responsible person. But if it was the other way, who would I turn to? They were his friends and they had known him for five years longer than me."

As her life took hold in California, she worked as a certified public accountant, brought up two daughters, made annual visits to family in India, and prepared to share her two-story suburban home with her husband's parents when they retire and move from India to California. By 1991, the woman, who comes from a family of activists—her mother and sister both run nonprofit women's organizations in India—was looking for a way to become involved with "something within my cultural group," she said. The opportunity arrived when the principal of her daughters' school asked her to help an Indian widow with a young son. Some of her friends, also originally from India and in professional occupations, had also been informally helping newly arrived Indian immigrant women. They felt the time had come to start a group to aid women with cultural adjustment issues because many immigrants do not have an extended family support system in the United States. She assumed that cultural adjustment would be the primary problem the immigrant woman would face. But, she revealed, "I was very naïve at that time. I'm embarrassed by it now. . . . I felt that Indian persons did not have domestic violence, that cultural adjustment would be more the focus than domestic violence. I was really unpleasantly surprised."

Maitri is based in San Jose, the heart of Silicon Valley and home to a significant number of engineers and professionals. At first, the community "responded rather negatively" to Maitri's mission, the college professor explained. "They didn't accept that there was a problem. They said we were being melodramatic, creating a sensation. There were a lot of negative feelings. When we'd go to public events and set up tables, people would say mean things to us, like, 'You just want to break up families' or, 'You're so Westernized, you've lost Indian values.'" Another woman, a longtime leader of Maitri, said, "We went to every community event that would allow us a table. We would stand there for four hours, six hours, eight hours, and not a single person would stop by. . . . Or people would come up and say, 'You're the home breakers,' 'You're the ones encouraging people to get divorced,' 'You're lesbians.' During the next five years, we were converting people 1 percent at a time."

Their aim was to create a space where women could find a sympathetic ear and cultural understanding, as well as referrals to legal, medical, and counseling services, job training, and other survival skills. "Our philosophy really is that abuse is absolutely unacceptable in any way, shape, or form, but ultimately it is her decision," a longtime Maitri leader said. She joined the organization in 1994 after separating from her abusive first husband, whom she had married in an arranged match when she was twenty.

By 2000, Maitri had evolved into what its advertisements in California's weekly Indian newspaper and monthly Indian magazine describe as a "free confidential referral service for South Asian Women experiencing domestic abuse, cultural displacement or unresolved conflict." Its volunteer base had tripled, to about twenty-five volunteers who had immigrated from the South Asian countries of India, Pakistan, Bangladesh, and Sri Lanka, enabling Maitri to offer services in at least fourteen South Asian languages.

Creating Community

The model of caregiving the frontline workers at these South Asian organizations in the San Francisco Bay Area use combines the concepts of fictive kin, community-building, and empowerment.[8] Drawing on ideas about South Asian sisterhood and empowerment, these workers create a language of empowerment intertwined with culture. They avoid positioning themselves as critics of the traditional culture that has, explicitly or indirectly, supported abusive relationships, promoting, instead, their services' consistency with familiar values, such as close family ties. Their goal is to assure abused women, whose natal family may not be supportive or available in the United States, that the space they are being offered is safe and that their disclosures are confidential. A South Indian native who was one of the founders of Narika said, "In the Indian family support network, a woman would have an aunt or mother or cousin on whose shoulder she could cry." Expanding on the issue of support, a longtime Maitri leader said:

> When a woman emigrates, she has left all of her support structure there
> [in South Asia]. There are a lot of festivals she can go to, and a woman
> gives birth in her mother's house. Here, there is no break for her; her only
> contact is by phone. The whole social structure that is meant to sustain
> you in the home country is shattered here. There is a lot of support
> structure, emotionally and physically [in South Asia]. When she's brought
> here, everyone's working and she is physically isolated. When she marries,
> she has to adjust to somebody else's life—if the family is very nice to you,
> it's a very happy situation. Can she really call her parents ten thousand
> miles away and say she's being abused here? They feel they do not want to
> burden their parents. She feels guilt, like a lot of Western women do, that
> it is her fault and she should do something different.

Narika's philosophy borrows the traditional Indian values of interdependence and sisterhood or support and the American problem-solving approach that emphasizes action based on options discussed with caregivers and the availability of social service resources that facilitate action. Its website states: "Narika's philosophy relies on incorporating our cultural affinities, our language capabilities and the most empowering practices from both South Asian and American cultures. Our volunteers and staff offer advice, helping hands, and a sisterly ear, providing the support and information women need to make their own decisions."

South Asian domestic abuse activists seek to redefine community for abused women by creating a social space that incorporates the positive and supportive aspects of familial relationships among women and allows choice. Their goal is to help the woman assume control of her own life and, supported by a network akin to an extended family, make a decision to stay or leave the abuser. An elderly Maitri volunteer who is a retired scientist said, "I provide them with all the options they have. I can't tell them what to do. I listen to them and say, 'What do you want, what do you think your options are?' If they want to go back, why. I've helped them go out and find cars and look at apartments. They know they can always keep in touch."

For these immigrant women whose support structures were left behind in their native countries, the counselor–client relationship becomes a kin network that operates as the woman's support network or extended family.[9] Volunteers at Maitri and Narika are often called by the Hindi terms *behen* (sister) or *didi* (elder sister) as a way of creating community, establishing trust, and developing bonds and support. Since elders are respected in the Indian community, some abused women seek the support and reassurance of older women. "The women call me 'Auntie,'" the Maitri volunteer who is a retired scientist said. "They never say 'Mrs.'; it's 'Auntie' or 'Sister.' It's a cultural thing."

The frontline workers adopt a *ma–behen* (mother–sister) model, where a volunteer becomes fictive kin to the client and hence an insider, as well as a caregiver. Thus, the workers become culturally appropriate persons to talk to about family life, and the client does not feel she is betraying her family by bringing the abuse to the public sphere. The caregiver as fictive kin shares her personal experiences with the client, meets for tea, and rejoices in the news of the client's baby taking his or her first steps or teenager graduating from high school. The boundaries between caregiver and client are more fluid regarding personal interaction, social contact, and gift giving and receiving than in mainstream activism (Kim 2002). An accountant who helped start Maitri noted:

> Sometimes [the clients] need to hold hands. One woman has called me off and on for three years. Now she has a good job with computer programs; we helped her with courses and her job search. She called me the day her divorce was final. They'll call with any little question. We approach as a friend because often they do not have their own friends. . . . I tell them that I am available and they can call me anytime. They will visit us, come to our homes.

South Asian familial relationships have both positive and negative attributes, she stated, adding:

> In India, all are involved in each other's lives, and to some extent this is really good—a[n abusive] man may be afraid of society; people are nosy; they talk to each other about each other's business. People are counseled within the family environment. But it can be bad—women are told that this is how it is and to just put up with it. Divorce is such a stigma in society.

Through its work and its discourse, Maitri fosters "self-reliance and self-confidence in its clients." Its stated mission reads: "Maitri believes that the best human relationships are characterized by mutual respect, open communication, and individual empowerment. To that end, Maitri's activities are designed to help South Asian women make an informed choice of the lives they lead."[10] Maitri's logo, developed in 1998, depicts a stick figure first curled in a ball, then starting to stand on bent legs, and finally standing upright. The word MAITRI appears below the three figures, and the organization's slogan, "Helping Women Help Themselves" below that. According to a Maitri project coordinator, "She is slowly rising to her feet. The 'Maitri' word is the platform to support her."

Maitri's slogan is supportive of the abused woman, enjoining her to find a solution that is comfortable for her, rather than putting pressure on her to take a certain action, such as staying in the relationship or leaving it. The slogan also announces to the South Asian community that since the woman is in charge of her life, Maitri is not responsible for devaluing families or advocating "breaking up families," an accusation that has been leveled at Maitri and other similar organizations by community members upholding the model minority stereotype. Since divorce is stigmatized among South Asians, keeping the marriage intact will often be a woman's first priority, according to caregivers. A longtime Maitri leader said, "A lot of South Asian women don't want to leave. They just want the violence to leave. By leaving, a lot are giving up their culture. They are told that if you are leaving, you are dead to us." She recalled the story of one woman who called the police, who then transported her and her two sons to a shelter. "The community was laughing at her because *she* was taken away," the Maitri leader said. "They said, 'See, that is what you get when you call the cops, *you* get arrested.' Are we going to be able to tell each person that no, she was not arrested but was taken away for her own safety?"

This discourse provides a language that shapes how the South Asian activists talk about domestic abuse. Hall (1997, 3–4) points out the importance of such language:

> We give objects, people and events meaning by the frameworks of interpretation which we bring to them. . . . The question of meaning arises in relation to *all* the different moments or practices in our "cultural circuit"—in the construction of identity and the marking of difference, in production and consumption, as well as in the regulation of social conduct. However, in all these instances, and at all these different institutional sites, one of the privileged "media" through which meaning is produced and circulated is *language*.

From the names of the organizations themselves to the frontline activists' use of the regional "South Asia" and emphasis on sisterhood, the activists' language constructs new meanings and shared understandings. Because they are actively creating community and bringing domestic abuse to the forefront, these groups are engaged in social change. According to Shah (1996, 55), "Domestic violence must be seen not as a personal (private) problem within the closed arena of the home, but as a political (public) problem influenced by cultural, social, and environmental factors."

Acknowledging the cultural patterns of, and responses to, abuse and giving voice to abuse previously silenced empowers the frontline workers as well. A Narika co-founder still very active in the organization stated, "We do a lot of outreach into our community and say we have got to take responsibility and not leave it a secret in the family because it is an open secret in the community; we need to rally our resources. . . . Everybody knows somebody who has been helped. The South Asian community is very small and I think it's like one big village out here. Our results have changed opinions about us."

Combating a Myth

Traditionally in the South Asian immigrant community, domestic abuse is silenced to keep the knowledge of abuse within the family and to allow the family to maintain its model minority status in the American society. The image of the abused woman is threatening to the South Asian community's cultural representation of itself. South Asian Americans generally consider themselves a model minority group because of their high educational achievement and financial success in the public sphere and strong family values in the private sphere (Abraham 2000; Bhattacharjee 1992). This myth symbolizes the essence of being South Asian. To preserve their model minority standing, many South Asian Americans may deny that domestic abuse exists, exhort family loyalty to conceal abuse from outsiders, or prevent the involvement of domestic abuse organizations in community events (Bhattacharjee 1992; Dasgupta 2000; Dasgupta and Warrier 1997; Lynch 1994; Shah 1996). Thus, immigrant leaders and community members in the past have ignored the issue, privileging instead the image of their community as built on family honor, women's deference to men, extended family, and cultural and community harmony. A longtime leader of Maitri noted, "We get the attitude that we are such a model minority, how can we have domestic violence? People bond to the model minority myth and ignore other issues."

South Asian women working with those experiencing domestic abuse must confront this model minority image or representation. This image is particularly strong in the San Francisco Bay Area of Northern California because of the high rate of economic success and educational achievement among the South Asian diaspora's members there. Through their brochures, their symbols, and their websites, Maitri and Narika have for more than a decade opened the community's eyes to the specter of domestic abuse. However, to counteract the notion that the organizations and support groups are corrupting South Asian women, the activists must tread very carefully when seeking support for their activities and services. They do so by labeling their services as responses to "cultural adjustment" problems, such as isolation from family members who remain in South Asia, or by emphasizing that they promote healthy relationships, not breaking up families.

These organizations also receive more support, donations, and media coverage by using phrases such as "We speak your language" that distance them from the mainstream American society while allying themselves with South Asians in general. For example, Maitri's slogan, "Helping Women Help Themselves," signals an alternative vision of community and is a nonthreatening way of saying they are combating the abuse of women and patriarchal authority, striving to make it no longer socially acceptable. Taking responsibility and rallying resources is key to these organizations' arguments.

Discourse and Silence

Both South Asian domestic abuse organizations in Northern California prominently feature slogans about ending silence in their informational brochures. Maitri's materials frequently say, "Stop the silence" and declare that the problem cannot be solved by neglect, denial, or wishful thinking. Narika points out in its publications that the presence of domestic violence, which is a serious and widespread crime against women, is continually disbelieved and ignored. Society's silence about the woman's suffering and the abuser's behavior, Narika says, permits the violence to continue, and the price of this silence is all too often paid by the victim, not the abuser. "We wish to break that silence," they declare.

By "breaking the silence," South Asian domestic abuse activists in Northern California are creating a community that stands by and takes care of its own. The narratives of community make a clear distinction between "we" and "they," marking the Indian diasporic community as different than mainstream, dominant American society. As discussed earlier, the differences between South Asians—religious, regional, caste—are eclipsed by their common immigrant experiences. So when Maitri and Narika seek to make the abused woman an accepted part of the community, they call on the commonalities of immigrants by emphasizing that the mainstream American community does not understand and is not serving the needs of South Asian abused women. A Narika women's advocate asked, "Our argument is that these are our women. The mainstream community is helping them, and we are putting the burden on someone else. The mainstream community is going to pick up the pieces, and how does that reflect on our community?" And one of the founders said, "We know what to ask. We know a certain kind of breakup is common in certain groups. We may ask, 'How much dowry?' 'Where is your jewelry?' 'Where is the stuff your parents gave you?' It may be the only thing she owns. We know what to ask." These frontline workers' dual roles, therefore, are to raise community awareness to confront abuse and to empower women. They redefine empowerment, focusing on building interdependence and a network of community support between women. They are positioning themselves to create kinshiplike relationships that will, in turn, help create and define community.

Discourse is informed by silence. As Brown (2005, 87) points out, "If discourses posit and organize silences, then silences themselves must be understood as discursively produced, as part of discourse, rather than as its opposite." Among the immigrant South Asian American community, the dominant model minority discourse prohibits speaking of abuse. "Silence and secrecy," Foucault (1978, 101) has written, "are a shelter for power, anchoring its prohibitions; but they also loosen its hold and provide for relatively obscure areas of tolerance." Silence, as a discourse prohibited from revelation, is broken by the frontline workers, thus becoming a subversive discourse. According to Foucault, "Silence itself—the things one declines to say, or is forbidden to name, the discretion that is required between different speakers—is less the absolute limit of discourse, the other side from which it is separated by a strict boundary, than an element that functions alongside the things said, with them and in relation to them within over-all strategies" (27). If silence is a part of discourse, then it can become a discourse. Thus, discursive politics becomes an important tool for these domestic abuse activists.

The words and meanings used by these frontline workers convey their understandings of, and their purposeful shaping of, domestic abuse in their community. They frame the issues, giving words and symbols to these issues, thus transforming the community perception and meanings accorded to domestic abuse and abused women. They discursively turn domestic abuse from a private, unspoken experience ignored by the community to an act reflecting unequal power relations, affecting the vitality of the community, and openly confronted by the community.

Conclusion

To combat the silence, Maitri and Narika found new ways to talk about abuse, framing it in terms of community and using a cultural model emphasizing fictive kin relationships. Shared experiences and a long-term support network have aided abused women and generated frontline workers who have in turn shaped the theory and practice of these organizations. One longtime Narika volunteer learned of Narika when her husband kidnapped her three-year-old son in 1991 after finding out she was seeking a divorce. She recalled the counselor who provided her home telephone number, urging her to call anytime, as well as volunteers' help and support in her court case, which also took her to Pakistan, where she recovered her son in 1992. Ever since, she has volunteered with Narika, and her experiences have given her a special perspective on helping other abused women. "We are forced to use the term *client*, but that's putting someone in a condescending position. I don't think of it as condescending help, but help that comes from love and equality," she said.

A Maitri frontline worker whose work with a homeless organization brought her into contact with several South Asian women abandoned by their spouses joined Maitri in 1995. "I take the time to do it because I believe in it," she said. Her sister-in-law is in an abusive marriage.

I'm not doing this for the fun of it. I work all day and then from 6:00 to 9:00 p.m. I am on the phone [with Maitri clients]. My husband has to take care of the little one, and sometimes it gets to him, but he understands because his sister is in an abusive situation [out of the country]. He went home for his brother's wedding—I couldn't go because I had just had my son—and there was an incident, so he would call me and have me talking on the phone to him about what to do. It always hits home when it's in the family. We keep a close eye on them, and we talk on the phone to her. It's hard because we have to maintain a cordial relationship with her husband.

Crafting support for abused women draws from this tradition of womanly support. Maitri and Narika are not filling a cultural gap but instead are revealing the need in caregiving models for a long-term support network and fictive kin relationships. While the Western model of intervention privileges social and legal services and a more clinical approach, organizations like Narika and Maitri train volunteer frontline workers to create an interdependency between themselves and the clients, rather than teaching them to be impartial observers as counselors are trained in the West. This model is contrary to the traditional Western concept of the detached counselor and client where counselors are prevented from becoming too emotionally attached and clients from becoming too dependent on one person.

A Maitri volunteer who works at both Maitri and the nearby Support Network for Battered Women, a mainstream domestic abuse agency, compared the two approaches.

Support Network is much bigger and better funded than we [at Maitri] are. There is more staff and a method to the madness. At Maitri, we are calling the lawyer and paying the bill and doing everything. Support Network is more hands-off. They make the assumption that the client only needs some help and then will take the ball and run. With the Support Network, they will give a woman the name of a lawyer and expect her to go. We [at Maitri] know she'll never make it. We do go and pick her up. [At Support Network] I will see someone one time to write a restraining order and that's all. The nature of our [Maitri's] clients is that many do not have any skills. They are new to the community. Our clients may not know how to drive or speak English. They aren't able to drive to pick up a restraining order. A bond between two people develops when they come from another country. They call us "sister" and not by our names. There's a little more emotional involvement and attachment, but we do keep our boundaries. My [Maitri] clients remain clients of mine for six months to four years.

These activists' approach to intervention and their discourse illustrates the political economy of domestic abuse as Adelman (2004) defines it. Emphasizing structural inequality, the normalization of gendered violence, the contested nature of culture, and local contextualized interpretations of violence and resistance strategies, these frontline workers shift conventional attitudes regarding domestic abuse toward contextualized cultural and historical approaches.

The political economy approach to domestic abuse also illustrates how caregiving and intervention in the United States emphasizes the individual, thus reflecting the individualistic worldview that permeates American society (Adelman 2004). The mainstream domestic violence movement developed around the abused woman's safety and permanent separation from the abuser, so its services center on shelters, restraining orders, and fostering self-sufficiency. These services are important in all domestic abuse organizations, whether mainstream or ethnically or culturally based, but the creation of a long-term supportive community is a vital caregiving approach that can be used by all frontline workers in the domestic abuse movement.

ACKNOWLEDGMENTS

I am grateful to and admiring of the frontline workers at Maitri and Narika who gave their precious time to discuss their work with me and perform such an important service to the community. I am grateful also to the University of California at Santa Barbara for providing financial support to this project, and I deeply appreciate my family and friends—particularly my parents, Penny and Jim Brommer, my brother, James P. Brommer, and my children, Cameron and Sarita Pauly—for their confidence in me and their encouragement while I researched and wrote this chapter. And thanks to my dissertation advisers, Mattison Mines, Mary Hancock, and Eve Darian-Smith, for their feedback and advice, as well as to the editors of this book for their dedication to this field of study.

NOTES

This chapter is based on my dissertation work with South Asian domestic abuse organizations in the San Francisco Bay Area of California. I conducted interviews with four dozen founders, volunteers, and donors and attended fund-raisers, meetings, community events, and training sessions over a period of eighteen months beginning in 1999. I interviewed people in their homes, their businesses, the organizations' offices, coffee shops, and restaurants. Several people were interviewed more than once. I held formal semi-structured interviews, as well as informal interviews when I met women at events. I also used secondary sources—including newspaper articles, Internet sites, court transcripts, and pamphlets—to find more contacts, as well as additional information on domestic abuse issues and cases among the South Asian diaspora.

1. Because of safety and confidentiality concerns, I do not use the names of my informants in this text.
2. Domestic abuse is a pattern of behavior, including physical, sexual, economic, verbal, and psychological attacks, where one partner in an intimate relationship seeks power and control over the other partner, causing that person loss of dignity, control, power, and safety. Rather than using the term *domestic violence*, which tends to connote the physical, I prefer to use the term *domestic abuse*, because it is more inclusive of psychological, economic, emotional, and other nonphysical forms. The term *domestic abuse* also connotes a social context. According to Sigler (1989, 75), "Domestic abuse has been defined as a social problem based in part on changing social values regarding the role of women and men in society and in domestic settings. Domestic violence is the dimension of domestic abuse that is visible, provable, and in extreme cases, shocking."
3. Though mainstream Americans often label South Asian Americans as a model minority, they still consider them the "other," distinguished by their skin color, food, clothing, accent, religion, and other features that place them as subordinate to the dominant mainstream. The model minority is defined as a role model for other minority groups.
4. South Asia encompasses the nations of India, Pakistan, Bangladesh, Sri Lanka, and Nepal. Some researchers and organizations also include Bhutan, Myanmar, and Afghanistan, and South Asians from elsewhere in the diaspora, such as Fiji, are often included in antidomestic abuse organizations' definitions of South Asians.
5. The U.S. Census 2000 was the official headcount of people living in the United States on April 1, 2000. While the census included U.S. citizens, permanent residents, visa holders, and undocumented immigrants, it was likely that many ethnic groups were underrepresented because of fear by undocumented immigrants, beliefs that temporary residents did not need to fill out census forms, and lack of education or awareness in non-English speaking communities about the importance of the census. The following Asian American ethnicities were queried in the census: Asian Indian, Chinese, Filipino, Japanese, Korean, Vietnamese, and Other Asian (with space to write in an ethnicity).
6. Comparisons with the 1990 census are available only for the Asian Indian cate-

gory, since the 1990 census did not have an "Other Asian" category where people could write in other ethnic groups, such as "Pakistani." Nationwide, the following Census 2000 statistics represent the number of people identifying with South Asian groups, either 100 percent or in combination with another ethnicity: 1,899,599 Asian Indians; 204,309 Pakistanis; 57,412 Bangladeshis; 24,587 Sri Lankans; 9,399 Nepalese; and 212 Bhutanese (Barnes and Bennett 2002, 9).

7. Narika's Mission, in "About Us," available from the Narika home page, *narika.org/index.php.*

8. Although *empowerment* is jargonistic, it is used by many South Asian women's organizations to describe their goals. Empowerment can mean women identifying for themselves what they need, such as safety, while remaining with the abuser; or women deciding to live autonomously by seeking housing, employment, or education (Fine 1989).

9. In many cases, a woman's natal family will provide support. But if an immigrant woman's natal family members reside in India, they may be unable to help her. Also, a woman may resist discussing the abuse with her natal family if she fears that her husband or in-laws will threaten or harm them.

10. Maitri's mission statement appears under "About Us," on the Maitri home page, *maitri.org/index.html.*

WORKS CITED

Abraham, Margaret. 2000. *Speaking the Unspeakable: Marital Violence among South Asian Immigrants in the United States.* New Brunswick, NJ: Rutgers University Press.

Adelman, Madelaine. 2004. The Battering State: Towards a Political Economy of Domestic Violence. *Journal of Poverty* 8 (3): 45–64.

Ahuka, Sarita, Pronita Gupta, and Daranee Petsod. 2004. *Arab, Middle Eastern, Muslim and South Asian Communities in the San Francisco Bay Area.* Grantmakers Concerned with Immigrants and Refugees. *sff.org/about/publications/AME_report.pdf.*

Barnes, Jessica S., and Claudette E. Bennett. 2002. *The Asian Population: 2000.* Census 2000 brief. U.S. Department of Commerce, U.S. Census Bureau, Washington, DC.

Bhattacharjee, Anannya. 1992. The Habit of Ex-Nomination: Nation, Woman, and the Indian Immigrant Bourgeoisie. *Public Culture* 5 (1): 19–44.

Brown, Wendy. 2005. *Edgework: Critical Essays on Knowledge and Politics.* Princeton, NJ: Princeton University Press.

Dasgupta, Shamita Das. 2000. Who Goes There, Friend or Foe? Finding Comrades in Domestic Violence Work. In *Breaking the Silence: Domestic Violence in the South Asian-American Community,* ed. S. Nankani, 161–71. Philadelphia: Zlibris Corporation.

Dasgupta, Shamita Das, and Sujata Warrier. 1997. *In Visible Terms: Domestic Violence in the Asian Indian Context; A Handbook for Intervention.* 2nd ed. Union, NJ: Manavi.

Fine, Michelle. 1989. The Politics of Research and Activism: Violence against Women. In Violence against Women, special issue, *Gender and Society* 3 (4): 549–58.

Foucault, Michel. 1978. *The History of Sexuality.* Vol. 1, *An Introduction.* Trans. Robert Hurley. New York: Vintage Books.

Hall, Stuart. 1997. Introd. to *Representation: Cultural Representations and Signifying Practices,* ed. Hall. Thousand Oaks, CA: Sage.

Kang, Cecilia. 2001. Valley Becomes Indo-American Hub for State. *San Jose Mercury News,* May 23.

Katzenstein, Mary Fainsod. 1995. Discursive Politics and Feminist Activism in the Catholic Church. In *Feminist Organizations: Harvest of the New Women's Movement,* ed. M. M. Ferree and P. Y. Martin, 35–52. Philadelphia: Temple University Press.

Kim, Mimi. 2002. Innovative Strategies: Themes and Questions. In *Domestic Violence in Asian and Pacific Islander Communities National Summit 2002: Proceedings,* ed. Asian and Pacific Islander Institute on Domestic Violence, 19–21. Arlington, VA: LGC, Inc., for the Office of Community Services, Administration for Children and Families, U.S. Department of Health and Human Services.

Lynch, Caitrin. 1994. Nation, Woman, and the Indian Immigrant Bourgeoisie: An Alternative Formulation. *Public Culture* 6 (2): 425–37.

Mohanty, Chandra Talpade. 1993. Defining Genealogies: Feminist Reflections on Being South Asian in North America. In *Our Feet Walk the Sky: Women of the South Asian Diaspora,* ed. W.o.S.A.D. Collective, 351–58. San Francisco: Aunt Lute Books.

Passano, Paige. 1995. Taking Care of One's Own: A Conversation with Shamita Das Dasgupta. *Manushi* 89:17–26.

Shah, Purvi. 1996. Redefining the Home: How Community Elites Silence Feminist Activism. In *Dragon Ladies: Asian American Feminists Breathe Fire,* ed. S. Shah, 46–56. Boston: South End Press.

Sigler, Robert T. 1989. *Domestic Violence in Context: An Assessment of Community Attitudes.* Lexington, MA: Lexington Books.

U.S. Census Bureau. 2002. *American FactFinder.* U.S. Census Bureau. Available at *factfinder.census.gov/home/saff/main.html?_lang=en.*

5

"We Couldn't Just Throw Her in the Street": Gendered Violence and Women's Shelters in Turkey

Kim Shively

In the past two decades, Turkey has made impressive efforts to deal with the problem of violence against women, by strengthening laws to criminalize batterers and developing public and private institutions to assist the victims of domestic violence. The new laws have largely been transplanted from international doctrines, and the institutions have been appropriated from and modeled on corresponding institutions in Europe and North America. This chapter investigates the process of what Sally Engle Merry (2006) has called the transplantation, appropriation, and translation of women's shelter models from Europe into the Turkish state social service system.

Based on research conducted into two women's shelters in the western Turkish province of Izmir, this chapter examines the de facto role that these shelters play in dealing with violence against women. Where in Europe and North America, women's shelters are set up specifically to provide refuge for victims of domestic violence (i.e., intimate partner violence), my research revealed that, even though the Izmir shelters were perpetually full, only a handful of the guests at the Izmir shelters were actually victims of domestic violence as defined in the United States and Europe. Indeed, the director of one of the shelters said that, quite frankly, among the women in the shelters only about 10 percent were there to escape domestic violence.

Initially, I was shocked by this revelation, since these shelters were often exhibited by politicians and activists as a viable (if not ideal) state response to domestic violence. The shelter director, Ummuhan, said that

71

she had also been surprised that there were so few women there because of domestic violence. She had expected to be dealing entirely with battered women and their children but was now confronted with a wide range of issues that affect mostly poor and marginalized women. In this initial conversation with Ummuhan, I had to ask: "Why are there so few battered women in these shelters? Who are the women in these shelters?" Ummuhan seemed to be so overwhelmed by the day-to-day logistics of running a very dynamic women's shelter that she had not really formulated a response to these questions, other than to say (to paraphrase), "What else can we do with the women who are here and need help, even though they are not battered? We can't just throw them in the street!"

As I made several visits to the shelters and spoke with the women and employees of these shelters, I came to realize that the process of institutional transplantation was not so clean and straightforward as the state might present or as some might presume. What I wish to show here is that a better way to think of these women's shelters is not as a response to domestic violence as "intimate partner violence." Rather, the domestic violence that women have to confront—and that the frontline workers have to deal with—can be characterized as structural violence that does not fit easily into the women's rights activists' discourse that dominates many human rights institutions with regard to domestic violence.

Research Setting and Methods

This investigation of the transplantation of the shelter system into the Turkish context is based on the status of two women's shelters (*kadın konukevleri*—literally, "women's guesthouses") in Izmir province in western Turkey.[1] I conducted research in the summers of 2004, 2006, and 2007 at these two shelters. One shelter, located in the northern Izmir municipality of Çiğli, was established in 2001, replacing a smaller shelter that had existed in Izmir since 1988. I visited this shelter in all three summers of my research, though in 2006 it was closed for a much-needed expansion. (I toured the expansion project in 2006.) During construction, the guests and staff of that shelter were transferred to the second provincial shelter—a newly opened establishment in Aliağa municipality about fifty kilometers north of the city of Izmir. By the summer of 2007, both shelters—plus a third smaller one that I did not have a chance to visit—were open and filled to capacity.

I conducted several long, open-ended interviews relating to women's issues and domestic violence with several frontline workers: a social worker (Türkan) and a psychologist (Birsen) in the Izmir office of the Social Services and Child Protection Agency (Sosyal Hizmetler ve Çocuk Esirgeme Kurumu [SHÇEK]). These were the personnel who referred women to the provincial shelters. I also interviewed the general director of Izmir SHÇEK, Zekarya Ertaş, and several private citizens involved in providing material support for the shelters in Izmir province, including members of the Çiğli Rotary Club and a representative of the International Women's Association of Izmir. I also visited the provincial shelters, interviewed the director, Ummuhan, as well as other frontline shelter workers, spoke with a number of the women who were temporary residents, and listened to some of their stories and hopes for the future.

Translating International Models into Turkish Reality

In the United States, domestic violence is seen as a form of gendered violence that requires special responses. This is a distinction that not every society necessarily makes or can afford to make. Domestic violence, for example, is defined rather narrowly in the United States and western Europe as physical, sexual, or psychological harm—or threats of harm—caused by a current or former partner or spouse (this is the current definition articulated by the Centers for Disease Control and Prevention [2006]; see also Saltzman et al. 2002). Indeed, there is a general trend to replace the term *domestic violence* with *intimate partner violence* as a way of more precisely defining the phenomenon. This tendency is also found in some international studies of domestic violence and in human rights documents (e.g., World Health Organization 2005).[2]

The focus on domestic violence as "intimate partner violence" in international human rights discourse creates problems when looking at domestic violence, gendered violence, and local institutional responses to various types of gendered violence in cross-cultural contexts. Domestic violence can take many forms, as I discuss later, and thus may require different types of institutional responses not commonly considered in Western settings. Even looking beyond domestic violence, international women's rights activists and transnational campaigns for women's rights have tended to focus on violence against women or "gender violence" in terms of individual injuries or individual acts of violence against individual women. But the most dire types of violence many women must confront are broader and more structural, such as armed conflict, economic disenfranchisement, environmental degradation, or loss of land. As Julie Hemment (2004, 829) has pointed out in her studies of women's aid organizations in Russia, "It is impossible to separate the problem of domestic or sexual violence from other issues women face."

In most European and North American countries, there are institutions established to cope with these structural forms of violence and marginalization, as well as with domestic violence. But like many other developing or unstable countries, Turkey has few social service institutions, and these are often overwhelmed by the social problems they are established to deal with. Thus, the direct transplantation of Western women's shelter models without much alteration into a social service system that is more limited in its scope of services has meant that the shelters—most often by accident—serve a much broader set of women's needs than do their Western models.

Transplanting Women's Rights

As Merry (2006) has pointed out, transplanting international human rights concepts and laws, such as notions of women's rights and gender justice, into local situations requires a process of appropriation and translation that may or may not be successful. For international standards for gender justice to be applied to the Turkish context, for example, mechanisms that promote gender equality—such as domestic violence laws, women's shelter systems, and other social service concepts—have had to be transplanted into a pre-existing set of social expectations, institutions, and laws that cannot always easily accommodate them.

Appropriation of international laws and institutions, Merry (2006, 135) points out, "means taking the programs, interventions, and ideas developed by activists in one setting and replicating them in another setting." Most often this process is transnational, since programs and laws are borrowed from other nations or from the international community and imported into the local context. In Turkey, the laws and institutions were appropriated—often wholesale—from European and international human rights discourses and transnational processes. The impetus for creating domestic violence laws and the model for programs and institutions aimed at combating gender violence derive from requirements made by the European Union accession process and the World Bank, as well as from requirements of the UN Convention on the Elimination of All Forms of Discrimination against Women (CEDAW), an international human rights document to which Turkey is a signatory. In 1990, in response to the CEDAW requirements, Turkey established the Directorate General on the Status and Problem of Women, which is directly affiliated with the Prime Ministry (Arat 1998; Levin 2007). The directorate mandated that every province have at least one women's guesthouse (*kadın konukevi*), to be run by the provincial SHÇEK.

Further legal transplantation took place in Turkey because of pressure from the European Union and a variety of Turkish women's nongovernmental organizations. The Turkish Civil Code was amended in 2001 and the penal code was updated in 2005 in part to improve women's position legally, including in situations of domestic violence (Ertürk 2008; WWHR 2002). The original Turkish Civil Code of 1926 contained clauses on marriage and family that contradicted the CEDAW requirements and were subsequently discarded in the 2001 amendments. For example, the original code placed familial authority and decision-making powers in the hands of the husband and delegated to the wife the roles of helpmate and household caretaker, while the 2001 code eliminated any idea of the head of the "conjugal union." In the 1926 code, husbands had also been deemed the ultimate authority over children and a husband's permission was required for a wife to work outside the home or to travel abroad with children, provisions that were rejected in 2001 (Levin 2007).

Similar progressive changes were made to the Turkish Penal Code in 2005. The previous penal code had defined rape as a crime against public decency rather than against the individual, thereby configuring women's bodies as repositories of public morality rather than construing women as rights-bearing individuals (Ecevit 2007; Uçan Süpürge 2005). The 2005 changes redefined rape as a crime against the individual and also introduced more than thirty amendments to advance the cause of gender equality and protect the bodily and sexual integrity of Turkish women (Levin 2007, 210). Among other provisions, the code has also criminalized marital rape, prohibited sexual harassment in the workplace, and introduced language by which honor killings (the murder of women believed to have sullied the honor of the family) are considered murder without mitigating circumstances (WWHR 2005b). Most important for this discussion, the 2005 penal code also defines domestic violence as a crime that can be punished by incarceration.

Other laws designed to curb domestic violence include the Law on the

Protection of the Family, no. 4320, approved in 1998 by the Turkish Parliament. This law permits a family member subject to domestic violence to file a court case for a protection order against the perpetrator of the violence (WWHR 2002). The protection order bars the perpetrator not only from using any further violence but also from approaching or harassing the victims. This law has provided some respite for women: CEDAW 2005 reports that between 1998 and 2003, 18,810 domestic violence cases were finalized in the courts under the provisions of the 1998 law. Part of this success may be attributed to the very active women's rights education efforts organized by women's nongovernment organizations (NGOs), such as Women for Women's Human Rights, Flying Broom (Uçan Süpürge), and the Purple Roof Women's Shelter Foundation (Mor Çatı Kadın Sığınağı Vakfı).

Lost in Translation

These legal transplantations have been welcomed by women's groups, frontline workers, and others in Turkish society. But those working most closely with women's issues and domestic violence, such as female activists and workers in the social service system, have noted that this process of appropriation has occurred sometimes without proper cultural translation. Translation, in Merry's terms (2006, 135), "is the process of adjusting the rhetoric and structure of [the] programs or interventions to local circumstances." Appropriation of programs tends to be most successful and popular if they are well translated.

In Turkey, a number of activists and frontline workers, including those I interviewed, have expressed concern that the European institutional models were dropped into a set of social structures, expectations, and political realities that could not easily accommodate these new mechanisms. For example, the establishment of the Directorate General on the Status and Problems of Women (as part of the CEDAW process) was not welcomed by nongovernmental Turkish women's organizations, because the organizations were suspicious of the directorate's intentions. The Turkish state is often heavy-handed when dealing with a whole variety of political, economic, and social issues, frequently imposing its own shortsighted solutions on civil society rather than allowing for more organic, bottom-up responses to emerge. The Turkish women's NGOs have thus been fearful that the directorate was set up to appropriate and control the independent women's organizations rather than deal with the "status and problems of women" as it was mandated to do. By now the directorate has gained some degree of acceptance by Turkish women's groups, but when I have discussed my research on the shelters with women involved in the NGOs, they have continued to express a great deal of suspicion (see Ecevit 2007).

Indeed, my original research plan was to investigate how politics at the national or provincial level affects the operations, especially funding, of women's shelters. Several female activists and academics had declared that conservative municipal governments often cut funds to women's services not only as a way to save money but also as a way to maintain a patriarchal social order in which women remain dependent on their families. When I first suggested this bias against the shelters to Türkan and Birsen, the Izmir SHÇEK social worker and psychologist, respectively, they looked genuinely puzzled. They were not aware of any government anywhere shutting down the state shelters for any reason. If anything they felt that the government at various levels was trying to find the resources and staff to create more shelters. As for the lack of funding, they argued that all social service divisions of SHÇEK, including those assisting orphans and the elderly, were chronically underfunded. The women's services, including the shelters, were not singled out in any way that they could see, a fact that was confirmed by the Izmir SHÇEK director.

These very different perceptions of the viability and vulnerability of women's shelters probably arise from there being different kinds of shelters: shelters run by the state and independent shelters established by Turkish women's groups and nonprofit organizations, such as the Purple Roof Women's Shelter Foundation. These independent shelters fulfill the state mandate for women's shelters—that there be at least one in every province—while the autonomy of the shelters allows them to target the issues and populations they choose. This autonomy makes them more effective than the state shelters at dealing specifically with intimate partner violence. But these independent shelters are unevenly spread through Turkey, and the funding for them is spotty at best. Interestingly, the work of these private women's organizations in constructing shelters for battered women provided much of the original impetus for the government, through the Directorate General for Social Work and Social Services, to develop women's guesthouses. In fact, municipalities have looked to women's organizations and NGOs for help to establish consultancy and educational services for battered women (Ecevit 2007, 199). I do not discuss these private shelters here but instead focus on those shelters put in place by the Turkish state and affiliated with SHÇEK.

Despite Türkan's and Birsen's objections, the administrative structures of government do leave the state women's shelters vulnerable to political manipulation. While in the past the Directorate General on the Status and Problem of Women has provided the initial capital for each shelter and funded on-going operations (food, salaries, utilities), a 2005 public administration reform process stipulates the transfer of all responsibility for opening and sustaining the women's shelters to local governments. Such a development is troubling, because, as pointed out in WWHR 2005a, "local governments . . . are subject to frequent changes in administrations every election period, and with highly volatile financial flows, are most likely to apply different priorities with respect to whether Women's Shelters . . . in their locality should be kept open; and if they are kept open, the operational guidelines under which they are to be monitored" (2). At least Izmir tends to be a socially liberal province, and the local government has maintained a relatively positive stance toward the women shelters, providing the funding for two shelters by 2006 and for a third by 2007. But such reliance on the largesse of local governments does nothing to guarantee institutional stability—not in Izmir, and certainly not in more socially conservative parts of Turkey. Indeed, the Purple Roof Foundation shelter of the Beyoğlu district of Istanbul lost its municipal funding at the end of 2008 because of a decision by the district's conservative government, despite that government's supposed commitment to a World Bank mandate that women's shelters be maintained in areas with a population over fifty thousand (see, e.g., Mor Çatı Kadın Sığınağı Vakfı 2008).

Turkey has difficulty upholding this World Bank requirement in many parts of the country, partly because of a continuing lack of resources. One of the most common criticisms directed at Turkey's institutional response to domestic violence is that there are simply not enough shelters available to battered women. In 2006, there were only twenty-four women's shelters in Turkey affiliated with the state, though the number of shelters is slowly increasing (Karabat 2008). Even as shelters have become more widely available since the 1990s, several international organizations, such as Amnesty International, have called for at least a four-fold increase in the number of women's shelters in Turkey.

The shortage of shelters also stems from an anemic investment in institutional resources. Turkey has only two schools of social work: one at Hacettepe University (Türkan and Ummuhan were both graduates of this program) in Ankara and a recently opened school at Başkent University. Thus, there is a constant shortage of social workers and no one expects an adequate increase in the next few years. The lack of personnel (social workers, managers, psychologists, etc.) has meant that while the legal way has been paved for opening shelters in all eighty-one Turkish provinces, many planned shelters will never open (see Shively 2006).

In the extant shelters, Turkish social services have attempted to translate the European shelters models they drew on to meet some specific needs of Turkish society. For example, Article 8 of the SHÇEK regulations (*Resmi Gazete 24396* 2001) states that the shelters may accept women who have left home for any sort of misunderstanding or who are escaping violence, women who are left destitute by divorce or widowhood, women who are escaping a forced marriage or who are being threatened for having a child out of wedlock, women who are overcoming addiction, and women who are newly released from prison. These regulations already demonstrate that the missions of the Turkish shelters are considerably broader than those shelters in the United States and Europe. The shelters take in women dealing with problems that in Europe and North America would be dealt with in a separate institution, such as a halfway house or rehabilitation facility.

Because of systemic issues relating to gendered violence, however, that are often outside the domestic violence discourse found in many Western countries, this official translation of the European institutional model to the Turkish context does not reflect the realities of shelter functions. Unlike in shelters in the United States, for example, the frontline workers in the Turkish shelters go well beyond their de juro functions and maintain a de facto policy of accepting almost any woman in need, despite the restrictions of Article 9 of the SHÇEK regulations, which forbids accepting prostitutes, women with addictions, women with mental illnesses, and women with substantial mental or physical handicaps. Thus, the official attempt at institutional translation was only partially successful in actual practice (as opposed to formal policies). As Ummuhan, the Izmir shelter director, complained to me:

The social services system was adopted directly from England but without adjusting for different customs. Turks are much more willing to help their neighbor and much more tied to the family than is the case in England, and setting up social services is harder under these circumstances. For example, the state wanted to set up the social services department and did so—but without personnel or training. It did no good. People aren't used to the idea of referring to an institution or to the government for dealing with problems relating to the family.

Rethinking "Domestic Violence"

Furthermore, as Ummuhan's comment suggests, common social attitudes toward violence within the family and the preferred remedies for that violence leave little room for institutional solutions. Domestic violence is common in Turkish society, as it is in most of the world. According to statistics reported by Amnesty International (2004), around two-thirds of Turkish women reported experiencing violence in the domestic context. But as Türkan explained to me, battered women often do not come to SHÇEK looking for help, since in Turkey there is such a widespread acceptance of domestic violence and internalized social norms that lead many women to believe that they deserve abuse or that domestic violence is simply the order of things (see also Gülçür 1999). This attitude may be gradually changing as public awareness of the problem has grown and violence is more publicly condemned in the Turkish media and political discourse. Certainly, Türkan, Birsen, and other members of the Izmir SHÇEK have invested considerable time, energy, and resources into conducting educational programs and advertising campaigns to mitigate the widespread acceptance of battering, including some training programs conducted in conjunction with a women's NGO for assisting police personnel in recognizing and responding to domestic violence.

Yet, even with this increased public awareness, many women either do not know of their options in applying to law enforcement or social service institutions for help or believe that the institutions would not help and could possibly make the situation worse. This opinion was certainly that of battered women I knew. This suspicion of the institutional arms of the state might also explain, in part, why so few victims of domestic violence seek out help from state institutions. The state has so long been seen as part of the problem for marginalized individuals—because of the state's inadequate economic development policies, antiminority rhetoric and actions, and abuse of human rights and the corruption that seems endemic to Turkish politics—that it may well be difficult for women to trust the state to be part of a solution to their individual suffering (see Adelman 2008). Thus, the very structure of the state shelter system and its political context already establishes barriers to the success of its mission.

Furthermore, because in Turkey, gendered violence within the family context is not necessarily confined to partner-on-partner violence, domestic violence cannot be conceptualized as only "intimate partner violence" as it is in Europe and North America. In patrilineal patrilocal households that are common in many parts of the world—including in parts of Turkey, India, Afghanistan, and China—the intrafamilial power dynamics and experiences of emotional intimacy may be more diffuse and arranged along diverse lines relative to nuclear families common in the West. As such, tensions and the potential triggers for violence against women in the family may diverge sharply from Western expectations (see Grewal 2008).

A patrilineal, patrilocal household generally encompasses an extended family where all women of the resident lineage will leave the household when they marry. Marriage for a woman means going to her husband's family. On the flip side, all resident married women are "outsiders," at least to the lineage segment that resides in the household. In Turkish, the word for "bride" and "daughter-in-law" is *gelin*, which means "the one who comes." Thus, all the married women in such a household are structural outsiders, a system that creates a series of tensions, especially between the in-laws and the daughter-in-law. The daughter-in-law is a foreign element that is nevertheless necessary for the perpetuation of the patrilineage, and she must be controlled. The husband certainly has a role in that control—and if violence does erupt, it is often within the marital pair. But the in-laws, especially the mother-in-law, are also part of the power dynamic. Indeed, a daughter-in-law is often under the direct control of her mother-in-law. Because many households are segregated by gender, a daughter-in-law often spends considerably more time with her mother-in-law than with her husband. This relationship is also a potential site for the eruption of domestic violence: the mother-in-law may beat or even sanction the murder of a disobedient daughter-in-law. Thus, domestic violence is perpetuated by a senior woman against a junior woman.

In many such situations, the husband's family is a wife's principal household—she cannot always return to her natal home, nor can she easily strike out on her own—so it is not a simple matter for a woman, especially a poor, rural young woman, to extricate herself from an abusive situation (cf. the case of China in Merry 2006, 149–50). This kind of domestic violence is not the "intimate partner violence" that occurs in a nuclear family that women's shelters in the United States and Europe are most commonly set up to deal with, and therefore the Turkish shelters must (and do) include provisions for women who are victims of violence from the extended family.[3]

Case Studies

Women seek out the shelters to deal with a whole series of life problems for which they have no other recourse. Some are escaping from bad marriages or family circumstances, others are threatened with honor killings. Some are simply destitute and cannot easily care for themselves. There are rules about who may or may not stay at the shelter, as I outlined earlier, but exceptions are often made. One woman I talked with, Meral, clearly had mental limitations, which according to the rules would disqualify her for the women's shelter.[4] But her family was not taking care of her and let her wander in the streets of her village. Local authorities had brought her to the shelter because they did not know what else to do with her. As Ummuhan explained in a refrain that I would hear many times, "They couldn't just leave her in the streets." Meral was bored at the shelter and deeply homesick for her village, but she could not take care of herself, and there was no other place for a young woman in her situation. (An elderly woman could be placed in a home for the aged.)

Türkan, the social worker for women's issues at the Izmir SHÇEK, said that Meral's case represents one of the agency's biggest problems: there are not enough treatment centers or halfway houses for people with various problems, and women like Meral are especially vulnerable because they, unlike men, cannot take advantage of informal forms of charity when in need. For example, while there are no homeless shelters, men may sleep in mosques or in the street, relying on the kindness of neighbors. But these options are not open to women. Mosques are, by and large, male spaces not open for casual female visitors. And a woman who sleeps in the street could lose her reputation and be suspected of sexual impropriety—a status that can be devastating and even life-threatening.

The women come to the shelters from all over Turkey, many from the east, which is considerably more impoverished and underdeveloped than western areas, such as Izmir and Istanbul. Indeed, many of the women from the east may be internal refugees—fleeing the frequent ethnic violence between Kurdish separatists and the Turkish military. When I began my research in 2006, a family had just arrived at the Izmir shelter. The family consisted of a woman and her two young daughters who came from Edirne in Thrace, though they were originally from the east. They had been abandoned with no nearby relatives and no means of support. The police did not know what to do with them but turn them over to the shelter system. "The police couldn't just throw them in the street," the shelter director Ummuhan again remarked to me. When Ummuhan asked the woman what her address in Edirne had been, the woman could give only the street name but did not know the house number. The daughter (nine years old) did not know her own birthday, and Ummuhan made it a game to keep asking the girl her birthday (which Ummuhan had learned from the girl's identity papers) until the girl could recite it herself. Clearly, this little family was at the mercy of the social service system and was fortunate to find refuge in a shelter.

The shelters have also taken in foreign women refugees and their children. Türkan reported that most such refugees are Turkish citizens born abroad or are non-Turks married to Turkish men. During my research stints in both 2006 and 2007, international refugees of a different sort found temporary refuge in the Izmir shelters. In 2007, a Somali woman and her newborn daughter, as well as some other Somali women, were housed at one of the shelters. In 2006, an Eritrean woman and her three sons had been dropped off by the police at the shelter for reasons that were not very clear. According to the oldest boy (he was twelve years old and spoke good Turkish and English, and therefore the mother mostly relied on him for translation), the family had been living in Istanbul under the auspices of the United Nations, but some sort of problem developed with their refugee status. Ummuhan had no information about them and did not know why they were there. And their situation never became clear. They had been scared about being brought to the shelter, and they disappeared one night. No one heard from them again.

The house takes in women with continuing alcohol or drug dependencies, even though such women are officially not supposed to be accepted into the shelters. These women simply have nowhere else to go, and hospitals deal only with acute cases, not chronic issues. Ummuhan maintained a lot of contact with hospitals to deal with any crises that might arise, but largely she had to cope on her own with women with severe problems. Basically, the shelter acts as a women's crisis center—any kind of crisis—not only as a shelter relating to domestic violence.

For women who do suffer from intimate partner violence, the shelters are not always a good option. This limitation is due to common social expectations rather than the merits of the shelters themselves. As mentioned earlier, many Turks have accepted the inevitability of domestic violence, and even when violence gets unbearable, most Turks would prefer to look to their neighbors or family for help. And because the shelters accept former prostitutes, they have become linked, at least to some extent, with prostitution. Therefore many women are reluctant to approach this institution for fear that they too will be associated with prostitution—again, a status that could be socially devastating and even life-threatening.

The shelters have little to offer many of the women who do end up in residence. While the guests may always participate in general activities in the shelter, such as cooking, cleaning, and child care, there are only a few organized activities, such as literacy or skill-learning courses, available to the women. For example, 80 percent of the women who come to SHÇEK for assistance are illiterate, and the shelters often try to provide some literacy training. The very first time I visited the Çiğli shelter in 2004, the director, whom I was interviewing, called in a young woman, Ferda, to demonstrate her newfound ability to write her name. She wrote her name with much pride and showed it to me, and I was duly impressed. Seeing my positive response, the director and a shelter volunteer both told me that Ferda is an exception, that very few women are successful at learning any literacy skills at the shelter for a variety of reasons. Several staff workers observed that most women seemed severely depressed and see no future for themselves, so it is difficult to motivate them to improve themselves or learn something new. Usually the shelter residents have no money, no skills, and little family support. Türkan noted that the women often do not know anything but housekeeping and never expected to be anything but housewives. The most common future they see for themselves after the shelter is getting married again. Because so many of the women are illiterate, they are unable to move from a life of dependency. Even if the shelters could offer consistent literacy classes, these classes would not be of much service, because the women usually stay for only a couple months and then move on. Likewise, children who are of school age and stay with their mothers at the shelters do not attend school, because they are not in the same place for long enough to be enrolled. Thus, a stay in the shelter can negatively impact the children's education.

Moreover, the shelters may have done less to improve the lives of women suffering from domestic violence than for other women. The normal practice of SHÇEK is to send the women back to the abusive situation they escaped from with no follow-up. This practice is followed not by choice but by necessity, since Türkan and Birsen were the only two SHÇEK personnel available to deal with women's issues and domestic violence in all of Izmir province (2006 population: 3.7 million). These two frontline workers were very dedicated to their work and were involved in many research and community-outreach activities. But it was clear that they could barely keep up with the new cases that came to them every day, let alone provide any follow-up to the cases they handled. So, when a battered woman comes to them, they can place her in a shelter and provide basic services, but once she leaves the shelter, they simply cannot keep track of her. Most of the women go right back to the situation they fled from—and there is no staff available to intervene on the women's behalf in the home setting to resolve the earlier tensions. Other women simply "disappear." With women at risk for honor killings, there is no way for social services to protect the women outside the shelters—that is left up to law enforcement.

It seems that so many end up where they started, perhaps even in a worse situation. Surely, battered women may pay a heavy price for having dared to leave in the first place. After all, a battered woman is at greatest risk of being killed by her abuser precisely at the time she tries to resist or leave her batterer (Kastenbaum 2008). These women often walk right back into the household they fled from, putting them at extra risk for reprisal, more severe abuse, or even death.

Furthermore, women who are escaping domestic violence may be stuck if they refuse to go home. I met Esen during an early visit to one of the Izmir shelters. Esen was a young woman who seemed very bright and had a high school education, but she had been crippled by polio since childhood and could not do any work requiring physical labor. She had fled from her family in the southeast Turkish city of Diyarbakır with her two-year-old son. She implied she fled from violence or threatened violence from her husband, but she did not want to discuss her life in Diyarbakır. After entering the shelter, she had given up her son to a foster family and would not be able to get him back until she was financially independent. She felt she was capable of doing work in an office, and because she is educated she thought she could contribute to any sort of job that did not require physical labor. But because of her handicap, she was having difficulty finding a business that was willing to take her on. She had been living in the shelter for a year when I interviewed her—despite the official three-month limit on stays. Esen was desperate to find work when I talked with her so she could get her son back. Her despair about her situation was palpable: she often seemed close to tears as she talked about her son, whom she visited only occasionally. She was losing hope about finding a job, and she could see no way forward. She left the shelter only after I completed my research, and so for reasons of privacy, Ummuhan could provide no details on her whereabouts or that of her son.

Beyond Intimate Partner Violence

There is no doubt that the women's shelters "do good" in general, filling very important gaps in the social services available in Turkey. Yet I genuinely wondered, Do these shelters do any good in dealing with the problem of domestic violence? Do they even make the situation for battered women worse? (Some of the frontline workers were asking themselves the same questions.) My original inclination was to be critical of the state's ability to point to the shelters as a demonstration that it is effectively addressing domestic abuse in accordance with CEDAW. And I do believe that it is misleading to characterize the shelters as institutions that deal primarily with intimate partner violence in the same way shelters in Europe or those set up by the Turkish women's NGOs, such as the Purple Roof Foundation, do.

Although the greatest problem with the women's shelters in Turkey is that there are not enough of them, the issue here is the institutional transplantation from transnational and international models to a particular local context. In Turkey, the legal transplantation was largely successful: the legal models were appropriated almost in their entirety and met the approval (more or less) of the parliament, the ruling classes, feminists, and other social progressives. Many of these Turkish citizens resisted the translation of these civil laws into traditional Turkish practices that gives priority to the husband in the family and establishes the wife as a dependent, that conceptualizes female bodies as repositories of family honor, and so on. Such a translation would have blunted the message of social change embedded in international discourse that reconfigures women as autonomous individuals with rights to bodily integrity and safety, independent of the family context—precisely the change that Turkish activists were seeking. As Merry (2006, 136) has argued, human rights activists often confront a dilemma when transplanting international expectations into a local framework: "If they frame human rights to be compatible with existing ways of thinking, they will not induce change. It is only their capacity to challenge existing power relations that offers radical possibilities."

For the institutional situation—those entities that actually apply the laws and deal with their consequences—the translation process was less straightforward. With the women's shelters, the government also attempted to translate their function to meet Turkish reality by establishing regulations stipulating who may and who may not be accepted into the women's guesthouses that are considerably broader than those traditionally established in Europe and North America. Women in transition—former prostitutes, former drug addicts, economically dispossessed women—are permissible guests in the Turkish shelters, whereas in Europe and North America such women could most often find state assistance in other institutions established for specific purposes (e.g., homeless shelters, drug treatment facilities, halfway houses). But the translation process was only partially successful, since the de facto operation of the shelters in Izmir and in Turkey in general goes well beyond—and sometimes directly contradicts—the official regulations to include women who simply need help for a whole array of problems. Recognizing that such women need assistance and that they cannot take advantage of informal forms of charity with the same ease that men can, the frontline workers, the police, and members of SHÇEK open their doors to anyone they can because, as they so often said, "What else can we do?" Not much, it turns out.

Because Turkey has so few institutional options for women with long-term difficulties, the shelters and SHÇEK personnel become the one institution that can help, and so it does. Although the situation is changing rapidly, Turkey has fewer social services available to the general populace than are found in Europe and North America. Furthermore, Turks are simply not used to looking to institutions of any sort to deal with issues relating to families or women's social welfare. Not only are Turkish women not accustomed to looking to institutions for aid, but they have little reason to trust that the state would protect them when the state is often also a threat (especially for ethnic minorities or impoverished women). Thus, when the European shelter model was appropriated into Turkey, it seems to have become the only de facto institution to aid any woman with any problem who was desperate enough to look to the social service agencies or who, like the refugees, happened to fall into the hands of law-enforcement officials.

Perhaps the best way to think of the state women's shelters in Turkey—or at least in Izmir—is to think of them as shelters from domestic violence, however it is defined, and as shelters that deal with gendered violence in all its forms.[5] The shelters do provide refuge to women who suffer from or are threatened by individual acts of gendered violence, such as rape, honor killings, or domestic violence (whether from the intimate partner or the extended family), though, as pointed out earlier, the institutional resources to assist such women are lacking over the long run.

At least, however, the shelters do provide some refuge to women who suffer from other, more structural forms of gendered violence. As Merry (2006, 39) has pointed out, the causes of gender violence may be social, economic, and political (see also Hemment 2004). Gendered violence may involve abandonment of support and ensuing poverty (economic dis-enfranchisement was probably one of the most common reasons women sought out the shelters in Izmir), displacement and armed conflict (many guests were "refugees" or immigrants from the impoverished and conflict-ridden eastern region of Turkey), and state policies (the international refugees). These shelters may therefore fall short of Western expectations or definitions of what defines a successful response to domestic violence. Instead, the Turkish shelters function by necessity, in response to the local situation, as institutions that serve the needs of victims of violence against women in the broadest sense of the term.

ACKNOWLEDGMENTS

I wish to thank Yeşim Arat and Ayşe Gül Altinay for allowing me to present portions of this chapter in a panel, "Gender-Based Violence: Prevention, Solidarity and Trans-formation," at the 2006 annual meetings of the Middle Eastern Studies Association in Boston. I also thank Karen Dugger for providing a forum for discussing issues of domestic violence in a cross-cultural context at the Institute for Teaching and Re-search on Women January 2008 conference in New Delhi. And I would like to ex-press my appreciation to the editors of this book, Hillary Haldane and Jennifer Wies, for their guidance and thoughtful input. I wish to convey a special thank-you to all those who made this research possible: Erol and Gaye Ertaş, Zekarya Ertaş, and the Çiğli Rotary Club. Finally, I would like to convey my deep appreciation to Türkan, Birsen, Ummuhan, and all the dedicated people of the Social Services and Child Pro-tection Agency of Izmir Province.

NOTES

1. The official name of the shelters is "women's guesthouse" (*kadın konukevi*), but I heard many other names used in reference to these houses: most often I heard the term *sığınma evi* (shelter) but also occasionally heard *barınma evi* (also trans-lates as "shelter").
2. For a discussion of definitions of domestic violence, see Merry 2009, esp. 27–29.
3. Interestingly, the women's shelter nearest to my university includes in its guide-lines the stipulation that women who are battered—or threatened with in-jury—by an intimate partner's family (in-laws) may also qualify to seek refuge in the shelter. But in talking with some professionals associated with the shelter, I found they were not aware of ever having women who were escaping "in-law" violence and were surprised that this provision was included in the shelter guidelines.

4. The names of all victims of domestic violence are pseudonyms to protect the women's identities.
5. A women's shelter I visited in New Delhi, India, seemed to operate on the same principles as those in Turkey. On a chalkboard in the director's office, the cause of each guest's presence in the shelter was listed. Only one guest was there for domestic violence; the rest suffered from more structural issues, such as abandonment, economic dispossession, and homelessness.

WORKS CITED

Adelman, Madelaine. 2008. The "Culture" of the Global Anti-Gender Violence Social Movement. *American Anthropologist* 110 (4): 511–14.

Amnesty International. 2004. *Turkey: Women Confronting Family Violence*. London: Amnesty International.

Arat, Yeşim. 1998. Feminist Institutions and Democratic Aspirations: The Case of the Purple Roof Women's Shelter Foundation. In *Deconstructing Images of the "Turkish Woman,"* ed. Z. F. Arat, 295–309. New York: St. Martin's Press.

Centers for Disease Control and Prevention. 2006. *Understanding Intimate Partner Violence*. Atlanta: Centers for Disease Control and Prevention.

Committee on the Elimination of Discrimination against Women (CEDAW). 2005. *Responses to the List of Issues and Questions for Consideration in the Combined Fourth and Fifth Periodic Reports: Turkey. www2.ohchr.org/english/bodies/cedaw/docs/CEDAW-PSWG-2005-I-CRP.2-Add.7-Turkey-E.pdf.*

Ecevit, Yıldız. 2007. Women's Rights, Women's Organizations, and the State. In *Human Rights in Turkey*, ed. Z. F. K. Arat. 187–201. Philadelphia: University of Pennsylvania Press.

Ertürk, Yakin. 2008. *Implementation of General Assembly Resolution 60/251 of 15 March 2006 Entitled "Human Rights Council": Mission to Turkey*. Report of the Special Rapporteur on Violence against Women, Its Causes and Consequences. United Nations, Human Rights Council, 4th sess.

Grewal, Inderpal. 2008. Postcoloniality, Globalization, and Feminist Critique. *American Anthropologist* 10 (4): 517–20.

Gülçür, Leyla. 1999. A Study of Domestic Violence and Family Life in Ankara, Turkey. Women for Women's Human Rights Reports No. 4. *www.wwhr.org/files/3_7.pdf.*

Hemment, Julie. 2004. Global Civil Society and the Local Costs of Belonging: Defining Violence against Women in Russia. *Signs* 29 (3): 815–40.

Karabat, A. 2008. Women to Sue Municipalities for Failing to Set Up Shelters. *Today's Zaman Online*, March 7, 2008. *www.todayszaman.com/tz-web/news-135798-women-to-sue-municipalities-for-failing-to-set-up-shelters.html.*

Kastenbaum, Robert J. 2008. *Death, Society, and Human Experience*. Boston: Allyn and Bacon.

Levin, Çelik Yasemin. 2007. The Effect of CEDAW on Women's Rights. In *Human Rights in Turkey*, ed. Z. F. K. Arat, 202–13. Philadelphia: University of Pennsylvania Press.

Merry, Sally Engle. 2006. *Human Rights and Gender Violence: Translating International Law into Local Justice.* Chicago: University of Chicago Press.

———. 2009. *Gender Violence: A Cultural Perspective.* Malden, MA: Wiley-Blackwell.

Mor Çatı Kadın Sığınağı Vakfı. 2008. "Sığınak İstiyoruz!" İmza Kampanyası ("We Want to Be Sheltered!" signature campaign). Available at *www.morcati.org.tr.*

Resmi Gazete. 2001. Özel Hukuk Tüzel Kişileri ile Kamu Kurum ve Kuruluşarinca Açilan Kadin Konukevleri Yönetmeliği (Regulations for the Establishment of Women's Guesthouses by Private or Public Entities). Resmi Gazete Sayısı 24396, May 8, 2001. *www.mevzuat.adalet.gov.tr/html/20702.html.*

Saltzman, Linda E., Janet L. Fanslow, Pamela M. McMahon, and Gene A. Shelley. 2002. *Intimate Partner Violence Surveillance: Uniform Definitions and Recommended Data Elements.* Atlanta: Centers for Disease Control and Prevention.

Shively, Kim. 2006. Women's Shelters and Responses to Domestic Violence in Izmir, Turkey. *Kadın/Woman 2000* 7 (1): 21–39.

Uçan Süpürge. 2005. *Türk Ceza Kanunu Kadinlara Neler Getiriyor?* (What Does the Turkish Penal Code Bring for Women?). *www.ucansupurge.org/arsiv/ www.ucansupurge.org/indexf6b4.html?option=com_content&task=view&id= 2140&Itemid=87.*

Women for Women's Human Rights (WWHR). 2002. *The New Legal Status of Women in Turkey. www.wwhr.org/images/newlegalstatus.pdf.*

———. 2004. *Shadow NGO Report on Turkey's Fourth and Fifth Combined Report to the Committee on the Elimination of Discrimination against Women. www.wwhr.org/images/shadowreport.pdf.*

———. 2005. *Turkish Civil and Penal Code Reforms from a Gender Perspective: The Success of Two Nationwide Campaigns.* Istanbul: WWHR–New Ways.

World Health Organization. 2005. *WHO Multi-country Study on Women's Health and Domestic Violence against Women.* Summary report. Geneva: World Health Organization.

6

Institutional Resources (Un)Available: The Effects of Police Attitudes and Actions on Battered Women in Peru

M. Cristina Alcalde

In 1985, Brazil became the first Latin American country to create women's police stations specifically to respond to women's complaints of violence. Research on women's experiences in Brazil's police stations suggests that some "police officers responsible for registering and investigating the incidents frequently treated the victims with hostility and indifference" and that "the line between acceptable and unacceptable treatment of women remains fuzzy in the minds of [female] police officers" (Nelson 1996, 135, 140; Santos 2005). Three years later, and largely as a result of pressure from women's organizations, Peru established women's police stations to focus on women's complaints of violence. By 2002, six women's police stations had opened in Lima, the capital, and seven more in other parts of the country. Women's police stations are staffed primarily by female officers. Regular police stations also include a family violence section. Based on a broader qualitative study of thirty-eight heterosexual indigenous and mestiza (mixed European and indigenous ancestry) women from poor and working-class backgrounds in abusive relationships in Lima, Peru, this chapter suggests that the situation some Brazilian women encountered is mirrored in Peru, where many women I interviewed faced indifference, hostility, and discrimination at police stations. After providing information on police officers in Peru, this chapter examines women's experiences in police stations in Lima and the effects of police attitudes and actions on women's ability to protect themselves and their children from abusive partners.

Among the women who spoke of interactions with police officers, fifteen described negative experiences they or women they had heard about had had at police stations and said that, as a result, they were less likely to go to the police; five mentioned placing complaints at police stations but offered few or no details about these experiences; and two reported that they were treated well at police stations and received the assistance they needed. Of these two women, one had a brother who worked as a police officer and who played an active role in helping his sister place a complaint. This chapter underscores the racism, class bias, and gender stereotypes women may encounter in police stations in Lima, cautioning us against the essentialism of equating female frontline workers, in this case female police officers, with feminism and gender sensitivity. I propose that women's interactions with the police play a significant role in prolonging the abuse of women in Lima.

The first part of the chapter presents a discussion of female police officers in Peru and their role as frontline workers, their backgrounds, their views, and forms of marginalization. In the second part, the focus shifts to the attitudes and behaviors women who sought assistance from the police encountered and the effects these attitudes and behaviors had on those women's lives. I present two examples of discrimination based on race and class and then focus on two gender-based ideas women encountered in police stations that negatively affected their ability to protect themselves from abusive partners. The first idea is that violence is a private, family matter and a woman's role is to keep the family together. The second idea is that women are responsible, and therefore to blame, for men's violence. In discussing women's experiences at police stations, I do not presume to provide a representative sample of all women's experiences at police stations. Instead, my primary goal is to contribute ethnographic depth to findings of police unresponsiveness and ineffectiveness in Latin America and, more specifically, in Peru (Flake 2005; Human Rights Watch 1999; Sagot 2005) by examining local cases and the effects of police treatment on a woman's ability to leave an abusive partner.

Background and Context

In Latin America, close to 50 percent of women experience psychological abuse and between 10 and 35 percent experience physical abuse throughout their lives (Morrison and Biehl 1999, 3). In two separate studies of domestic violence in Lima, 51 percent of women interviewed had experienced physical and sexual violence (Güezmes, Palomino, and Ramos 2002) and 88 percent of women interviewed knew someone who had experienced intimate violence during the previous twelve months (Espinoza Matos 2001). As in other parts of the world, in Peru the effects of men's violence include increased risk of poor health, such as injury, depression, and the development of a chronic disease (Coker et al. 2002).

In 1993, Peru passed a family violence law. As a result of modifications in 1997, 1998, 2000, and 2003, the law now includes physical, psychological, and sexual violence as forms of domestic violence, regardless of an individual's class, race, or gender.[1] The police are the state entity responsible for receiving domestic violence complaints, carrying out the preliminary investigation, and notifying the parties involved. Women can file complaints at specialized women's police stations, Women's Emergency Centers, or family violence sections in regular police stations.

Women's Police Stations and Female Police Officers

The world's first women's police station opened in India in 1973. Since then, specialized women's police stations have been established in South Asia, Africa, and throughout Latin America to address violence against women. Brazil opened the first Latin American women's police station in São Paulo in 1985. The day after the Brazilian station opened there five hundred women lined up to file complaints (Santos 2005, 155). In Peru, where the first women's police station opened in 1988, the primary mission of women's police stations is "to receive, prevent, combat, and investigate acts of family violence, to re-establish family harmony and unity, within a human rights framework."[2] In 1996, police in Lima received 6,181 domestic violence complaints. By 2001, the number had jumped to 32,821 (Fernández and Webb 2002, 260).

Despite the high demand for services provided by women's police stations around the world, female police officers in them face discrimination and marginalization. By 2003 in India, where women's police stations had been around for three decades, women made up just 2 percent of the entire police force and "general conditions for women on the force did not inspire confidence" (Hautzinger 2007, 212). In Brazil, women's police stations rank low within the police hierarchy and "policewomen clearly saw themselves as discriminated against, as women, in their police careers"

(224). In her work on women's police stations in Brazil, Santos (2005, 36) similarly notes that the creation of women's police stations "did not eliminate discrimination against policewomen and women's police stations."

In Peru, female police officers constitute 15 percent of the police force. Like their male counterparts, the majority of female officers come from working-class backgrounds. Police officers in Peru earn less than the average salary for civil servants and significantly less than employees in the private sector, making it common for officers to seek a second job to make ends meet (Instituto de Defensa Legal 2004). Police officers are also part of an entity whose duties have been increasing even as the number of officers available to perform those duties has decreased. In 1990, Peru had 129,000 police officers and a population of approximately 22 million. In 2004, the number of officers had decreased to 90,000, though the population had increased to 27 million (Instituto de Defensa Legal 2004). Of the dwindling police force, one officer who works in the domestic violence section of a police station commented, "[The number of] police officers will always be insufficient, [but] we have to have a strategy to reach the civilian communities and have them support us. The State will always have few resources, the solution lies in the leadership of the Comisariat [police]" (Movimiento Manuela Ramos 2007, 46). As exemplified by this officer, despite the obstacles confronted by the police, some officers highly value the responsibility of working with and building positive relationships with civilians.

Police officers as a group face several obstacles, but female police officers in particular confront sexism from within and outside the police. Although women were first admitted to the police force in 1956, it was only in 2009 that for the first time in the country's history three regular police stations (i.e., not women's police stations) were headed by female police officers. In March 2009, the police announced that Lima's notoriously hectic and dangerous traffic would be directed exclusively by female police officers. It was widely publicized that the rationale behind the decision was the belief that women officers are less corruptible and more disciplined than men (El Comercio 2009; *La República* 2009). And, although the bulk of the responsibility for overseeing traffic was placed in the hands of female police officers, the highest position within the traffic police was reserved for General Arturo Davila, a man.

Gender stereotypes of women heavily influenced both the decision to place traffic under the control of female police officers and the behaviors female police officers confronted on the street. In 2004, of the 244 police officers assaulted by angry motorists, more than 80 percent were women, which led the government to launch the "No more violence against female police officers" campaign (Grimaldo 2008). Today, female police officers continue to face resistance by male motorists who view female police officers more as women, who should not have power over men, than as police officers with the authority to stop, fine, and arrest.

Even though female police officers face marginalization and may be especially vulnerable to assaults in their role as officers, female police officers are not necessarily attentive to the victimization of women in domestic violence situations. In Brazil, Hautzinger (2007, 231) found that "many policewomen internalized and reproduced sexist or *machista* values."[3] Santos (2005, 48) underscores the heterogeneity of views and attitudes she found among officers in women's police stations in Brazil by outlining three basic positions officers held regarding feminism and violence against women. One group, referred to as "feminist policewomen," "made explicit alliances with feminists, fully embracing the feminist definition of violence against women as a crime." A second group, "masculinist female police," "opposed any contact with feminists" and "did not view violence against women as 'real' crimes." For the third group, "gendered police," "alliances with feminist organizations were indirect and ambiguous" and they "embraced aspects of the feminist approach to 'gender violence' but did not, or could not, make explicit alliances with feminists."

In Peru, female police officers also hold a variety of views regarding feminism and violence against women. Peruvian feminist organizations have consistently rejected conciliation as a solution in domestic violence cases in part by arguing that conciliation presumes two equal partners, while situations of domestic violence are characterized by unequal power relations between partners (Boesten 2006, 363). According to a recent study on the Peruvian judicial and police system in which both police officers in charge of receiving and processing domestic violence complaints and battered women were interviewed in three districts in Lima, police officers in two of the three districts favored extrajudicial conciliation between a woman and her partner in domestic violence cases. In the third district, however, one police officer clearly stated, "I do not agree with conciliation, because I don't think that after having been abused, she should have to allow a man who is hurting her [to be] in her bed. . . . I don't think so" (Movimiento Manuela Ramos 2007, 43). In the three districts, women complainants opposed conciliation (42).

Also in connection with domestic violence cases, another female officer explained that some women want to but do not follow through with complaints they initially filed. Their husbands, who are the ones who pay for everything—the house, electricity, and water—"threaten them with leaving and not paying anything," and because these women depend on the man, they regret the domestic violence complaint (Movimiento Manuela Ramos 2007, 46). This officer's statement underscores her understanding of that economic dependency is one of the factors that contribute to women's experiences of domestic violence. As the literature suggests, female police officers' attitudes and actions regarding domestic violence cases vary widely.

The Effects of Police Officers' Treatment of Battered Women on Women's Lives

Getting to the police station is itself a great challenge for many women. To reach a police station, a woman must temporarily escape her partner's surveillance, knowing she may be vulnerable to additional beatings if he discovers her plans to report the abuse. She may slowly and secretly set aside money to cover transportation costs to and from the police station, or, if she is unable to afford public transportation, she may walk long distances to the police station and risk being seen by her partner or someone who might inform her partner of her actions. What if, after taking all these risks, upon arrival at the police station, she is humiliated, told to go back home, and blamed for the violence?

Arrival at the police station is only the first step in an often long and complicated process. Women in Lima reported that the police would not pay attention to them unless they had severe and visible injuries and bruises, that police officers asked them for money for office supplies and snacks to process or speed up their claims, that police officers blamed them for the violence, and that police officers told them to go back home when what the women needed was protection from what awaited them there. In short, in women's experiences, a great difference existed between laws and practice, and between the rights they should have as citizens and the way police treated them as poor women and wives.

Once she files the claim at the police station, a woman must then decide whether she will return home, go to a shelter (if she is told of the existence of one and if there is space for her and her children), or stay with family or friends (if she has any in Lima). In the context of widespread poverty and rural-to-urban migration where few family members or friends are willing or able to offer a place to stay in Lima, it is not uncommon for women to return home after filing a claim and face further violence as they wait for the legal process to begin. After a woman places a claim, the police notify the batterer that a claim has been filed against him and that he must go to the police station to render his statement. The police also refer the woman to a forensic doctor who will evaluate the injuries she has suffered. A medical examination is often the most important piece of evidence against the batterer, yet not all women are given appointments for medical examinations on the same day or even week of the domestic violence complaint. An extended period between a woman's complaint and the date of her forensic examination may negatively affect the woman's case because of the likelihood that her bruises will have disappeared and injuries healed by the time of the examination. The claim will then go to the family prosecutor, who will evaluate the claim and may issue orders for petitioned protective measures. It was common for a woman to fear that the violence would escalate once her partner discovered that she had reported the abuse to the police.

In the United States, leaving a violent man is the most dangerous time for a woman (DeKeseredy and Joseph 2006). According to the accounts of women interviewed here, the same is true for women in Lima. Shortly after deciding to leave and filing a claim against their partner, many women feel disillusioned by the impossibility of achieving a satisfactory arrangement that ensures their safety in the short and the long term.[4] If they did not already know it, they soon learn of the prejudices and lack of funds available to help battered women and their children and that the process of filing a claim is a long one replete with bureaucratic hurdles.

Intersecting Identities of Race and Class

All of the women I interviewed agreed that they confronted more indifference and discrimination at regular police stations than at women's police stations and that women's police stations were "the best option," while also expressing dissatisfaction with police treatment in the latter. Several of the women believed they were treated with disrespect and turned away because they were poor and indigenous or mestiza in a society in which whiteness and wealth are highly valued. Perhaps even more important, how women were treated by the police had real, negative effects on their ability to protect themselves and their children from abusive partners.

The case of Ester, a poor mestiza mother of three in her forties, helps shift the focus from a unidimensional one on gender to a multidimensional one on intersecting identities that also inform women's experiences at police stations. Toward the end of a meeting with me, Ester asked whether I knew anyone at the main women's police station who could help her with the paperwork related to a domestic violence complaint she had filed but feared was not being processed. She had been to the police station several times since filing the complaint but was told each time to come back later. I had just spent several days speaking with a policewoman at the station named Office Ramirez, so I suggested to Ester that she ask for Officer Ramirez on her next visit since she appeared to be very helpful. Like several other officers at the main women's police station, Officer Ramirez participated in the occasional workshops for officers facilitated by Lima's feminist nonprofit organizations. Officer Ramirez fits into Santos's (2005) category of "feminist policewomen" because she allied herself with feminist organizations and defined violence against women as a crime.

A few weeks later, Ester told me that although at first the officers would not help her, once she asked for Officer Ramirez and told her I had sent her, things changed. Officer Ramirez told the other officers to help her because she was "a relative," and from that point on Ester was treated very well. Although Ester was treated well and ultimately received the information she needed, her experience points to the indifference women may face at police stations if they do not have the personal contacts (which most women do not have) that would elevate their social status in the eyes of some officers.

Amada, another woman who was turned away by the police, summarizes her reaction to two police officers—the (male) chief of the police station and a female police officer—who refused to honor her request to arrest her husband, who had violated a protective order and had beaten her. When she arrived at the police station, her face was bruised and swollen. After the officers refused to arrest her husband, Amada reproached them, stating:

> How is it that some women, because they have friends here or because
> they have boyfriends or I don't know what, acquaintances, as soon as they
> come in, as soon as they speak, all they have to do is open their mouths
> and a police car is there. And I, because I am a poor woman, or because
> I am not dressed up, or because the policemen haven't fallen in love with
> me, you don't pay any attention to me.

Amada's words eloquently demonstrate her awareness of her rights and underscore the discrimination she encountered within the institution responsible for protecting those rights. Both officers Amada spoke with blamed her for the violence, misinformed her about laws, dismissed her requests, and told her that the best thing for her to do was nothing, to avoid exacerbating her husband's violence. Fully aware of the importance the police placed on hierarchies and respect within the organization and of her low status as a poor, battered woman, Amada nonetheless rejected the police officers' interpretation of her situation. The police, however, refused to arrest her husband and ultimately she returned home.

In what follows, I discuss the two main gender-centered ideas women confronted at police stations: that violence is a private, family matter and women's role is to keep the family together, and that women are responsible, and therefore to blame, for men's violence.

It's a Private Family Matter and Women Should Keep the Family Together

In 2001, the "policeman of the year" shot and killed his wife (*La República* 2001). Although the honored policeman's wife had filed several domestic violence complaints against her husband, the police failed to consider these "private" actions in honoring him as "policeman of the year." This incident is disturbing because of what it indicates about what is considered private, and can therefore be easily ignored, in evaluating men charged with protecting civilians. Further suggesting that the belief that violence perpetrated by intimate partners is a private family matter is widespread are the findings of a longitudinal study in a poor district in Lima. In that study, the men who were interviewed expressed the belief that (women's) filing domestic violence complaints is not very useful and that a couple should resolve its problems without resorting to outside institutions, such as the police (Ríos and Tamayo 1990, 247).

Among the women I interviewed, Jimena, a twenty-six-year-old mestiza elementary school teacher and mother of two called the police on several occasions. As she explained, "I would even call the police station when I had problems. [The police would ask,] 'Señora, are you hurt? Can you walk? Then come and place a complaint [in person].' But how could I leave if my husband was there? He wouldn't let me leave. But the police said it was a private matter." As Jimena recounted the incident, the police directly told her that men's violence within the home is a private matter. As a school teacher, she viewed herself as a public figure whose responsibilities included being a positive role model for her students. She spoke with her students about domestic violence and had even counseled students on dealing with and reporting their experiences of domestic violence. Although Jimena taught her students that violence against women was a public issue, her experiences with the police reinforced the reality that violence against women was, in practice, widely viewed as a private matter.

Beyond the belief in men's violence against women as a private matter, beliefs about the primacy of the family and the need to keep the family together also affect women's ability to lead violence-free lives. In Peru, the belief that "the individual is worth little outside of kinship ties and is only fully realized when she is part of a relationship which produces a nuclear family" (Yanaylle 1996) is common. The cultural expectation that women will marry and have a family, the stigma of separation and divorce, and the fear of being a single parent prolong women's time with abusive partners. In this context, going to the police station constitutes "a major step resulting from a transcendental decision indicating an understanding of the public dimensions of their problem" (Sagot 2005, 1306). In police stations, however, women may feel disempowered because their own consciousness of violence as a public issue is challenged by those in positions of power and authority over them—a situation exemplified by Jimena's case.

Twenty-six year-old Ana's experiences illustrate both her wishes to escape from her husband's violence and the reality and effects of having the police reinforce her husband's power over her and her two young daughters (ages three and one). In the following excerpt, Ana describes her experience at the regular police station near her home, where she spoke with officers from the family violence section, soon after she had given birth to her second daughter. "I went to place lots of complaints. . . . I always reconciled [with my husband] at the police station. They would make me see, 'Señora, what are you doing separating?' . . . 'What are you doing?' they would say. 'Look at those babies. Think, you alone can't provide for them.' That. They always put my daughters in the middle of it. 'What are you doing?' they would say. 'Because of you, because of you your daughters are going to suffer.'" Ana was constantly under her husband's surveillance, forced to work with him in his welding workshop every day and locked in the house whenever he left home. She risked severe beatings each time she managed to escape with her daughters to the police station. She also visited the main women's police station downtown, but the response there mirrored the response she received at the regular police station in her neighborhood.

The main message Ana received from this institution was that she should go back home and worry about keeping her family together rather than attempt to create a new life for herself and her daughters. As Ana described the path leading to her arrival at the shelter at which we met, the central role of her interactions with police officers at both regular and women's police stations became clear. Ana did not know of the existence of shelters for battered women for at least one year after her initial visit to a police station because police officers failed to inform her about them.

Police treatment of Ana directly affected Ana's chances of leaving her abuser. Ana had one daughter and was pregnant with her second daughter the first time she visited the police station to report her husband's abuse. When I met her just two years later, she had two daughters and was pregnant with her third child. By the time we met, Ana and her daughters had entered a shelter, yet Ana's chances of permanently leaving her husband had significantly diminished. She feared no one would offer a pregnant, poor, abused woman with nowhere to live and two young daughters a job and that she would not be able to work very long hours because of her pregnancy and two young daughters. She also felt guilty about denying her daughters the possibility of living with both parents, especially each time one of her daughters asked where *papi* was.

Ana's experience is only one of several negative experiences at police stations that women reported during interviews. Another woman I interviewed reported that police officers told her to hurry up and return home with the children so that her husband would not find out she had gone to the station and become even angrier and more violent; a third woman was advised to be a better wife to avoid beatings; and a fourth woman was told to stop talking back to her husband to prevent future episodes of violence. In all of these cases, women failed to receive the protection they needed and had a right to receive.

Blaming Women for the Violence

Women who experience intimate partner violence may blame themselves for the violence, feeling they somehow provoked their husbands and thus feel ashamed to ask for help (Panchanadeswaran and Koverola 2005). Institutions can reinforce these feelings by questioning women's behavior at home and their efforts to seek help (Frohmann 1998), as well as by directly blaming women for men's violence.

Ana was directly blamed for the violence she experienced at a women's police station. When I asked Ana whether she had ever visited the main women's police station, she said, "The police officers in the women's police station . . . would tell me, 'You are to blame. It's your problem, don't come here [in search of help].'" Each time Ana left her house to report her husband's violence, she placed herself and her daughters in danger of her husband's finding out she was trying to leave him. Like the other women whose experiences I have described, Ana was dually victimized, first by her partner and then by the police.

Amada, a thirty-six-year-old mother of three, went to the station with a bruised and swollen face to ask for help after her husband beat her. Amada reported that she was told by the police chief to "be very calm and that I shouldn't look to fight with him. Not to do anything because it would just make it worse." The police chief's statement exacerbated Amada's powerlessness within an abusive relationship and pointed to Amada's behavior as the cause of her husband's violence.

Inés, forty-three years old and the mother of three, had experiences at the main women's police station that both embittered and empowered her. It took Inés several years to decide to go to the police station to report her husband's ongoing physical, psychological, and sexual abuse. In part, she was waiting for her children to get a little older so she would not deprive them of a father during what she considered to be their formative years. She was also hesitant to go to the police station because she had heard from acquaintances that "when people went there they treated them badly and so many of them did not want to return out of shame." She thought, she told me, "The police will say, 'Why do you let yourself be hit?' or maybe use vulgar language. So then, that was my fear." Inés eventually decided she needed to report the abuse to be able to leave her husband and have legal access to her belongings, regardless of how the police treated her. During an interview, Inés said that when she went to the station to file a claim, the psychologist there told her she should not cry about the violence because it was clear that she enjoyed being hit and was therefore to blame for the violence. Inés left the station feeling angry and disillusioned. As she recounted the incident to me several years later, she said she saw now that the experience made her so angry that it fueled her strength to keep fighting to free herself from the violence she lived. At the time, however, it did little to solve her problem. Similarly, Aurora, thirty-eight years old and the mother of two, also felt certain that going to the police station would only result in further victimization. Each time she had visited a police station, a police officer had suggested she had done something to provoke her husband. As a result of these experiences, Aurora feared police stations.

Women are commonly blamed for staying in abusive relationships. The reality, however, is that women have few options but to return to their homes after filing a complaint at a police station. For example, thirty-six-year-old Carmen Rosa went to the police station to file a complaint against her husband and as a way to begin the process of separating from him. The police officer who handled her complaint was scheduled to go on vacation for a month the following day and told her that because he had been assigned to her case she now had to wait one month, until he returned from vacation, to continue the filing process. After she complained about the waiting period, she received a referral to the forensic doctor. The appointment she was given, however, was for three weeks later. All her bruises would have disappeared by her appointment date. The delay in the appointment with the forensic doctor is significant in that it further disadvantaged Carmen Rosa and postponed the possibility of her permanently and legally leaving her husband. Carmen Rosa had no option but to return to her husband. Ultimately, she attempted to protect herself from further violence by appeasing her husband and reconciling. As in other cases, Carmen Rosa was dually victimized, first by her partner and then by the police.

Conclusions

In focusing on women's interactions with officers in police stations, my intention has not been to suggest that the police as an institution are solely to blame for the violence women experience or that all police officers treat women in ways that prevent them from finding alternatives to living with violent partners. Significantly, several women I interviewed noted that they encountered less discrimination in specialized women's police stations than in regular police stations. Nonetheless, police stations played a significant role in prolonging the amount of time the women I interviewed remained in abusive relationships.

An analysis of women's experiences in police stations is essential to our understanding of battered women's experiences in Lima because, after trying to get help from their families, many women turn to the police. In their interactions with police officers, women receive responses that trivialize the danger they experience. More specifically, women confront attitudes that disregard their welfare, encourage them to uphold the family despite the violence, and blame them for the violence men inflict on them.

Women's experiences in regular police stations and in women's police stations make clear that staffing police stations with women has its merits but cannot guarantee female victims the right to be heard or protected from their partner's violence (Hautzinger 2007; Nelson 1996). All women do not share the same opportunities or ideas, and gender solidarity cannot be assumed once we take into consideration issues of race, class, education, and economic standing (see Mohanty 1991). In Lima, as in other settings, individual police officers interpret existing laws through the filter of cultural values and norms, as well as individual prejudices, when interacting with individuals of the same, or different, race, class, or gender.

My findings that some police officers' biases negatively affect battered women's options for protecting themselves from abuse and leaving abusive partners mirror cross-cultural findings (for Brazil, see Nelson 1996; Santos 2005; for China, see Tam and Tang 2005; for Mexico, see Hijar 1992; for the United States, see Abraham 2000; Anderson et al. 2003; Wolf et al. 2003). This chapter provides ethnographic depth at the local level of Lima, Peru, for broader cross-cultural findings of police unresponsiveness and ineffectiveness. In the light of cross-cultural findings of inadequate police responses, in exploring why women stay or return to abusive partners, we should remember that, for some women, "in the absence of real protection, it is rational to want to put more faith in the promises and apologies of their batterers" (Anderson et al. 2003). But for women like Ana and Amada, even in the absence of these promises and apologies, there is little or no possibility other than to stay with or return to an abusive partner.

ACKNOWLEDGMENTS

A Fulbright Institute of International Education grant supported me during my initial fieldwork for this research. I am especially grateful to Jennifer Wies and Hillary Haldane for their vision for this book and for their continuous work to bring this book to life. I would also like to express my profound gratitude to the women in Lima who spoke with me about their experiences at police stations, and to the police officers who took the time to speak with me and explain how things work.

NOTES

1. The law applies to violence between spouses, *convivientes* (those living together but not legally married), former spouses, former *convivientes*, and those who have had children together, even if the man and woman never lived together.
2. The full text of the mission statement of the women's police stations is available at the police stations' official website, *www.comisariademujeres.org.pe*.
3. Writing on the revictimization of battered women in women's police stations in Brazil, Hautzinger (2007, 29) notes that "when police perceive that female complainants themselves originate from sectors of the population they identify

as marginal, they frequently direct considerable attention to pointing out to the women how the improper or immoral lives they lead set them up for the abuses they experience."

4. In Mexico, many women prefer not to report their partner's violence against them because of the legal problems and extended bureaucratic requirements women face when trying to file a claim (Hijar 1992). In Peru, many women face a similar situation.

WORKS CITED

Abraham, Margaret. 2000. *Speaking the Unspeakable: Marital Violence among South Asian Immigrants in the United States*. New Brunswick, NJ: Rutgers University Press.

Anderson, Michael, Paulette M. Gillig, Marilyn Sitaker, Kathy McCloskey, Kathleen Malloy, and Nancy Grigsby. 2003. "Why Doesn't She Just Leave?": A Descriptive Study of Victim Reported Impediments to Her Safety. *Journal of Family Violence* 18 (3): 151–55.

Boesten, Jelke. 2006. Pushing Back the Boundaries: Social Policy, Domestic Violence, and Women's Organizations in Peru. *Journal of Latin American Studies* 38 (2): 355–78.

Coker, Ann, Keith Davis, Ileana Arias, Sujata Desai, Maureen Sanderson, Heather Brandt, and Paige Smith. 2002. Physical and Mental Health Effects of Intimate Partner Violence for Men and Women. *American Journal of Preventive Medicine* 23 (4): 260–68.

DeKeseredy, Walter, and Carolyn Joseph. 2006. Separation and/or Divorce Sexual Assault in Rural Ohio: Preliminary Results of an Exploratory Study. *Violence against Women* 12 (3): 301–11.

El Comercio. 2009. Solo las Mujeres Policías Dirigirán Tránsito en Lima, February 28.

Espinoza Matos, Maria Jesus. 2001. *Violencia en la Familia en Lima y el Callao*. Lima: Ediciones del Congreso del Perú.

Fernández, Graciela, and Richard Webb. 2002. *Perú en Números 2002*. Lima: Instituto Cuánto.

Flake, Dallan F. 2005. Individual, Family, and Community Risk Markers for Domestic Violence in Peru. *Violence against Women* 11 (3): 353–73.

Frohmann, Lisa. 1998. Constituting Power in Sexual Assault Cases: Prosecutorial Strategies for Victim Management. *Social Problems* 45 (3): 393–408.

Grimaldo, Mirian Pilar. 2008. Valores en un Grupo de Policias de Transito de la Ciudad de Lima, Peru. *Revista Diversitas* 4 (2): 291–304.

Güezmes, Ana, Nancy Palomino, and Miguel Ramos. 2002. *Violencia Sexual y Fisica Contra las Mujeres en el Perú*. Lima: Flora Tristan.

Hautzinger, Sarah J. 2007. *Violence in the City of Women: Police and Batterers in Bahia, Brazil*. Berkeley: University of California Press.

Hijar, Martha. 1992. Violencia y Lesiones. *Salud Pública* 15:15–23.

Human Rights Watch. 1999. "Peru." In *Human Rights Watch World Report 2000*, 517. New York: Human Rights Watch.

Instituto de Defensa Legal. 2004. *Perfil del Policia Peruano*. Lima: Instituto de Defensa Legal.

La República. 2001. PNP Inicia Cacería en Piuria Para Atrapar al "Policia del Año." January 21.

———. 2009. Mil 600 Mujeres Policías Controlarán Tránsito en Lima. November 3.

Mohanty, Chandra Talpade. 1991. Under Western Eyes: Feminist Scholarship and Colonial Discourses. In *Third World Women and the Politics of Feminism*, ed. C. T. Mohanty, A. Russo, and L. Torres, 51–80. Bloomington: Indiana University Press.

Morrison, Andrew, and Maria Loreto Biehl. 1999. *Too Close to Home: Domestic Violence in the Americas*. Washington, DC: Inter-American Development Bank.

Movimiento Manuela Ramos. 2007. *Evaluación de la Ruta Critica del Sistema Political-Judicial en los Casos de Violencia Familiar en los Distritos de San Juan de Miraflores, Villa El Salvador, y Villa Maria del Triunfo*. Lima: Movimiento Manuela Ramos.

Nelson, Sara. 1996. Constructing and Negotiating Gender in Women's Police Stations in Brazil. *Latin American Perspectives* 23 (1): 131–48.

Panchanadeswaran, Subadra, and Catherine Koverola. 2005. The Voices of Battered Women in India. *Violence against Women* 11 (6): 736–58.

Ríos, José Maria García, and Giulia Tamayo. 1990. *Mujer y Varón: Vida Cotidiana, Violencia, y Justicia: Tres Miradas desde El Agustino, 1977–1984–1990*. Lima: Ediciones Raíces y Alas.

Sagot, Montserrat. 2005. The Critical Path of Women Affected by Family Violence in Latin America. *Violence against Women* 11 (10): 1292–1318.

Santos, Cecília MacDowell. 2005. *Women's Police Stations: Gender, Violence, and Justice in São Paulo, Brazil*. New York: Palgrave Macmillan.

Tam, Suet Yan, and Catherine So-Kum Tang. 2005. Comparing Wife Abuse Perceptions between Chinese Police Officers and Social Workers. *Journal of Family Violence* 20 (1): 23–38.

Wolf, Marsha, Uyen Ly, Margaret A. Hobart, and Mary A. Kernic. 2003. Barriers to Seeking Police Help for Intimate Partner Violence. *Journal of Family Violence* 18 (2): 121–29.

Yanaylle, Maria Elena. 1996. "Tiene Ventiocho Años y Aún es Virgen: Femineidad y Estereotipo de la Mujer sin Pareja." In *Detrás de la Puerta: Hombres y Mujeres en el Perú de Hoy*, ed. Ruiz-Bravo, Patricia, 73–90. Lima: Pontificia Universidad Católica del Perú.

7

Child Welfare and Domestic Violence Workers' Cultural Models of Domestic Violence: An Ethnographic Examination

Cyleste C. Collins

The Violence against Women Act (VAWA), first passed in the United States in 1994 and reauthorized in 2000 and 2005, and the policy changes that resulted have helped bring public and institutional attention to gender-based violence. An entire network of social services has been created to respond to the issues victims of gender-based violence face. Although most victims of gender-based violence never seek direct assistance relating to their victimization (Brookoff et al. 1997), the possibility that they will encounter frontline workers in the mainstream social service system at some point is high (Bell 2003). These workers, as victims' first points of contact with mainstream social services, have the potential for helping victims in several ways.

Frontline workers, defined here as human service professionals working in child welfare offices or domestic violence offices, can help shape victims' ideas about domestic violence, whether or not they self-identify as victims (Grauwiler 2008), as well as connecting victims to critical services (Purvin 2007).[1] These professionals also have the potential to retraumatize victims and their families further by responding to them by blaming or judging them for their predicaments (Danis and Lockhart 2003; Purvin 2007). A number of studies have found that it is common for frontline workers to hold biases and believe stereotypes about domestic violence (Bograd 1982; Danis and Lockhart 2003; Ross and Glisson 1991). Such biases and stereotypes might be made manifest by workers' failing to identify victims with whom they come into contact, actively discounting their experiences, outwardly blaming them, or simply not referring known victims to services that can help them (Eisikovits and Buchbinder 1996; Kok 2001).

Some research has suggested that tackling these issues requires identifying workers' ideas about the causes of and appropriate treatment for domestic violence (e.g., Davis 1984; Davis and Carlson 1981; Henderson 2001; Minsky-Kelly et al. 2005), but the question of workers' beliefs about domestic violence has become more complex since the passage of the VAWA as the awareness of domestic violence has become more commonplace. Screening programs and trainings in these organizations have increased because different human service areas, especially welfare offices and health care facilities, have been identified as important potential referral sources. Some programs train their frontline workers on the dynamics of domestic violence, the barriers that victims of domestic violence encounter, and available services and teach them how to identify victims and offer appropriate referrals when they come into mainstream social service agencies for help.

Despite the implementation of trainings about domestic violence to increase referral rates, studies are still finding that relatively few domestic violence victims make use of available services and programs (Brookoff et al. 1997). Whether victims do not receive referrals to available services through the mainstream social service systems with which they come into contact (Kok 2001, Levin 2001) or whether they choose not to use the available services, the discrepancy between estimates of the numbers of victims who enter the welfare system and those who take part in domestic violence services suggests that victims might not be aware of these services and programs.

Some welfare offices have addressed the low referral problem by training staff to screen for domestic violence by placing domestic violence advocates in welfare offices. Once victims are identified, they are referred to these advocates. The practice of incorporating domestic violence advocates in welfare offices is still relatively new, but the success of such programs so far has been limited. For example, research has found that only small numbers of victims tend to be referred to these advocates (Kok 2001), and that while some advocates are seen as being very helpful in navigating the system, others are unclear with victims about the variety of services, forms, and requirements needed to obtain services and do not refer clients to outside programs (Postmus 2004).

Several studies have found that even introducing domestic violence advocates into welfare agencies can be problematic. Saunders and colleagues (2005) found that victims can have such poor relationships with their welfare case managers that they are afraid to reveal their victimization or they may be pessimistic about being believed or helped if they do disclose their abusive situations. Other recent work has suggested that while collaborations between domestic violence and child welfare agencies are increasingly common, those relationships do not always translate to changes in practice (Banks et al. 2009).

It might be that increased attention to domestic violence issues through training has made workers more aware of common domestic violence stereotypes even while they continue to believe them. Training often focuses on myths surrounding domestic violence, and this focus might sensitize workers about the most appropriate ways to talk about domestic violence, even if their underlying beliefs do not actually change. Thus, although social service professionals such as welfare workers might not directly endorse domestic violence stereotypes (e.g., that the victim is at fault for her plight), domestic violence and welfare workers tend to misunderstand one another and appear at times to work at cross-purposes.

Domestic violence research and services have a long history of concern about collaboration and communication between different human service sectors. Much of this research has been large-scale and focused on identifying areas of difference using surveys (Davis 1984; Davis and Carlson 1981; Worden and Carlson 2005). The aforementioned increases in service provider knowledge about domestic violence, however, suggests that traditional survey methodologies might not be the most appropriate way to tap into providers' underlying domestic violence beliefs. Much previous research in this area has lacked a strong theoretical orientation and has relied on the results from surveys.

While surveys are often useful in understanding broad outlines of an issue, and can allow the researcher to generalize results when sampling large populations, they have several drawbacks. Chief among these drawbacks is the assumption that the researcher and informant share ideas about the domain of interest, in this instance, domestic violence. Typically, the researcher defines the terms of the domain and asks informants to respond to questions related to that topic. The counterpart to a strict quantitative approach is pure qualitative research that explores informants' experiences in a more open-ended format that allows informants' own ideas and perspectives to emerge. The following research combines qualitative and quantitative approaches and methods to investigate two distinct groups of workers' beliefs using data collection techniques and analysis that reveal perspectives of informants in their own words through ethnography with the goal of uncovering workers' underlying beliefs about domestic violence.

Theoretical Orientation: Cognitive Anthropology and the Cultural Consensus Model

This study adopts an emic point of view, in which the informant's own perspective and language are used, rather than that of the researcher. Such an approach makes few assumptions about how the informant thinks of or perceives the world. The theoretical orientation is rooted in cultural consensus theory (see Romney, Weller, and Batchelder 1986) and employs the concept of "cultural models," defined as socially distributed, shared schematic representations of reality that are used in thinking and behavior (Shore 1996). While culture here is defined as shared knowledge, sharing frequently varies both between and within informant groups; that is, intra-cultural diversity is common (Pelto and Pelto 1975). A cultural model, then, has both shared components and unique, idiosyncratic components. The premise is that if we can better understand the distribution of cultural models and how they influence behavior, we can potentially work to change that behavior.

The cultural consensus model developed by Romney, Weller, and Batchelder (1986) has been useful in previous studies that have examined the relationships between culture, health, and health behavior (Chavez et al. 1995; Chavez et al. 2001; Dressler, Dos Santos, and Balieiro 1996), culture and poverty (Dressler et al. 2004; Dressler et al. 2007), and culture in organizations (Caulkins and Hyatt 1999; Jaskyte and Dressler 2004). In this study, the cultural consensus model was used to assess frontline workers' cultural models of domestic violence.

From the Front Lines: Service Providers' Beliefs about the Causes of Domestic Violence

Recent research using the cultural consensus model supports the idea that different human service providers share beliefs on some aspects of the causes of domestic violence but disagree on others. A study of college students' beliefs about the causes of domestic violence found that social work students think about particular dimensions of the causes of domestic violence differently from other students (see Collins and Dressler 2008a). The follow-up to that study expanded the sample to include professional social workers and other human service professionals (see Collins 2005; Collins and Dressler 2008b). The research discussed in this chapter is part of that larger study, in which the extent to which different professionals share ideas about domestic violence was explored. The research was designed as a local-level ethnographic analysis and was conducted in four stages. Data were collected using free lists, pile sorts, and ratings—methods frequently used in cognitive anthropology in general, and cultural models research in particular (see Weller and Romney 1988). Here I describe the findings for two of the most important groups of service providers to victims of domestic violence: child welfare workers and domestic violence workers.

In the first stage of the research, informants were interviewed about what they believed causes domestic violence. Informants generated lists of causes. Domestic violence workers' lists tended to be shorter than those of other workers and included terms that were macrostructural, including "weak policy," "inadequate support systems," and "power and control." In contrast, child welfare workers' lists revealed that they thought about domestic violence in terms of micro issues, most frequently listing terms related to individual characteristics, such as addiction and mental health, especially drug and alcohol abuse and mental illness. On one hand, all child welfare workers listed drug use/abuse and alcohol abuse as causes of domestic violence, while no domestic violence workers did. On the other hand, every domestic violence worker informant listed power and control as causes of domestic violence, while no child welfare workers listed power, and only one listed control as a possible cause. These initial differences in domestic violence and child welfare workers' beliefs about domestic violence suggested not only that the two groups might think about domestic violence in fundamentally different ways but also that their interaction with victims could thus be affected. This idea continued to be explored through the subsequent stages of the research.

In the second stage of the research, informants were asked to organize their ideas more formally by completing pile sorts and, in semi-structured interviews, identifying overarching themes that they used in thinking about the causes of domestic violence generated in the first stage. The findings from this second stage of the research confirmed those from the first phase; here, domestic violence workers offered explanations that were fundamentally different than those of child welfare workers for how they grouped the causes of domestic violence. Specifically, child welfare workers tended to identify particular terms, including "low self-esteem," "depression," and "blaming oneself" as characteristics of victims, while domestic violence workers described those same terms as applying to victims, but as a result of experiencing domestic violence. Thus, domestic violence workers tended to be more specific, locating the terms in the context of the victim's domestic violence relationship as well as in a temporal context.

In another example, terms such as "job strains," "money problems," and "family pressures" were described as "tensions leading to victimization," "characteristics typical of victim experiences," or an "explanation for why victims stay." Domestic violence workers also tended to focus on macrostructural factors, such as acceptance of violence in the culture, gender inequality, inadequate support systems, and weak social policy as key causes of domestic violence, while child welfare workers tended to see these issues as irrelevant to domestic violence. While cultural consensus and other analyses (see Collins and Dressler 2008b for details) demonstrated that child welfare workers strongly agreed with one another with regard to how important different factors are in causing and contributing to domestic violence, post hoc analyses indicated that domestic violence workers' and child welfare workers' overall beliefs about importance were statistically significantly different, and in fact, did not overlap.

Investigating exactly what the two groups of workers disagreed on revealed that child welfare workers tended to rate alcohol abuse, anger, power, poverty, drug use/abuse, stress, and witnessing abuse as important contributors to domestic violence, while domestic violence workers tended to rate these terms as much less important (see Figure 7.1). Also, as demonstrated in an earlier stage of the research, the two groups of workers conceptualized the roles that these terms played in divergent ways, a difference the quantitative analyses were unable to detect. Thus, follow-up in-depth interviews sought to explore those differences in greater detail.

In the fourth stage of the research, frontline workers whose cultural consensus scores from the larger study indicated the greatest divergence of beliefs were selected and interviewed about how their ideas about domestic violence developed and how they use them in their everyday work. The interviews were conducted to examine, explore, and flesh out child welfare and domestic violence workers' differing beliefs about domestic violence, and how these beliefs are put into practice on a micro level with their clients.

Four domestic violence workers and two child welfare worker informants participated in the interview process. Domestic violence and child welfare workers were selected for inclusion for interviews based on their scores on a measure of agreement through cultural consensus analysis (Romney, Weller, and Batchelder 1986). The two child welfare workers with the highest cultural competence scores (and who therefore demonstrated strong agreement with the "typical" child welfare worker in the sample) were asked to participate in the interviews.

The domestic violence workers were also selected for inclusion in the study on the basis of their cultural competence scores from the third

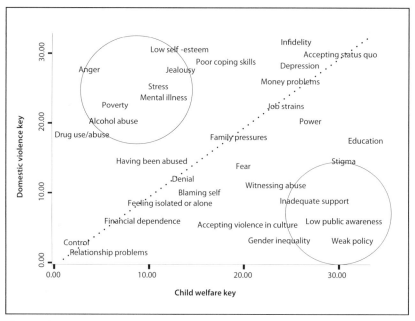

Figure 7.1. Domestic violence and child welfare workers' beliefs about the importance of different factors in contributing to domestic violence. The circles represent the divergence of agreement between the two groups. The circle in the lower right quadrant is a group of terms that domestic violence workers thought were very important but child welfare workers thought were very unimportant as causes of domestic violence. The upper left circle is the group of terms that child welfare workers rated as very important but domestic violence workers did not. Items closer to zero are considered more important, and items further from zero are less important.

stage of the research. Two domestic violence workers who had the highest level of agreement with child welfare workers and two who had the lowest levels of agreement were selected for interviews. The child welfare workers were recruited from the local branch of the state welfare agency. The domestic violence workers worked for a local nonprofit domestic violence agency or were employees of a local university's women's resource center.

The interviews were conducted to examine the extent to which informants' beliefs about domestic violence were evident in their descriptions of their interactions with domestic violence clients in their everyday work. The frontline workers were asked several questions, including how they developed their ideas about domestic violence in their work and how they deal with "typical" domestic violence cases, as well as how they see themselves as different than other human service professionals on domestic violence issues. The interviews were tape recorded, transcribed, and analyzed for thematic content.

Frontline Beliefs about Domestic Violence: Structural/Social Constraints in Contrast to Personal/Individual Choices

Consistent with findings from the previous stages of the research, domestic violence and child welfare workers responded differently when asked to talk in a relatively unstructured way about their beliefs about domestic violence. One child welfare worker expressed substantial cynicism about her experiences with victims of domestic violence. She said:

> I guess, you know, what, what I have just found here . . . is even if the woman leaves the male because he's abusing her, she's likely to find another male to abuse her. That's most likely who she's gonna end up with next time. . . . You know, and we joke here . . . is there a club they all go to? . . . I mean, how do these women find these men that were just like the husband they just left? What is it?

In acknowledging that victims sometimes return to abusive relationships, this worker recognized that domestic violence tends to be cyclical. At the same time, her comment, while said partly in jest, suggests that child welfare workers might not fully understand the dynamics of domestic violence and may even hold domestic violence victims at least partly responsible for their abusive relationships, especially if they end up with another abusive partner.

This same child welfare worker went further, stating that, at some point, child welfare workers have to draw the line in working with domestic violence victims and referring to the possible consequences of their clients' remaining in a domestic violence situation. She said, "And so I think, you know, yes, there have been workers here that have said, you have *got* to leave this man or we're going to have to take the children." The workers seem to suggest that domestic violence victims practically choose violent partners and that in so doing, willfully endanger their children. This response is consistent with the findings in previous stages of the research in which child welfare workers identified causes of domestic violence that lie within the victim or the abuser themselves, or within both, and may also, or instead, have pointed to character or personality flaws, as opposed to situational or structural constraints that might lead to domestic violence.

In contrast to child welfare workers' seeing victims of domestic violence as being flawed for "choosing" violent relationships, and feeling cynical about their experiences with domestic violence cases, domestic violence workers talked about how the circumstances of domestic violence victims' lives trap them in their relationships. This difference was revealed in one domestic violence worker's discussion of her experiences working with community groups to improve their understandings of victims in particular and domestic violence in general.

> And I have a lot of people, when I go and speak to churches . . . the older women, they'll say, well, I just don't understand why she just doesn't take her kids and leave. You know, I just do not understand that. And I explain to 'em . . . flat out, look, if you didn't have a job and you didn't have any money, and you had two kids, no friends, and no family, and you didn't know how you were gonna feed your kids tomorrow, I wouldn't go, either. You know? And so that's how I try to explain it to them.

Such an explanation demonstrates a deeper, more complex understanding of the issue than that of the child welfare worker. In particular, domestic violence workers mentioned having a heightened awareness of the issue, and that, especially as educators, they were keenly aware of how other people perceive domestic violence. This comment also speaks directly to the structural constraints that domestic violence workers identified throughout the study. While domestic violence workers steered away from discussing characteristics of victims that contribute to domestic violence, they commonly pointed out structural and social constraints as well as the circumstances of victims' lives that maintained the domestic violence relationship or kept victims from leaving. It also indicates domestic violence workers' desire to change people's image of the typical domestic violence victim, emphasizing that domestic violence is not due to personal or individual flaws but instead to structural constraints. As one domestic violence worker said, "That's *not* how it is, it affects all races, all socioeconomic, you know, groups. I mean, it affects everybody, and we see that, because we deal with it every day." Such a response suggests the domestic violence worker's desire to encourage others to identify with and empathize with the victim and her situation.

Putting Beliefs into Practice: Establishing Rapport in Contrast to Making Referrals

The workers were asked to describe the procedures they follow in dealing with domestic violence cases to better understand how their beliefs are manifest in their daily work. The domestic violence workers emphasized the importance of establishing rapport, specifically, showing victims that they care and dealing with them using sensitivity and compassion. They discussed the importance of timing, and that an assessment of victims' situation, especially their safety, is critical. The domestic violence workers said that assisting victims in creating a safety plan is a priority, and that educating them about domestic violence, while quickly identifying needs, potential options, and appropriate resources are all part of their protocol. The first meeting is considered essential for establishing rapport, gaining victims' trust, and making them comfortable enough to open up about their situations. They also try to send victims the message that they are not to blame for their situations. One worker in particular said that her first priority is making victims and their children feel comfortable in the shelter, assuring them they are safe, supporting them, and making sure they know their situation is not their fault. She said:

> You have to be very careful, as to, you know, when the lady walk[s] in the door, certainly she's afraid, . . . [she] don't know if she made the right decisions, . . . and she's looking to you for a lot of answers; . . . you gonna have to be very sensitive, . . . caring, compassion[ate], all of that . . . as to when you first make contact with them, especially [for] them coming into shelter; . . . time is important . . . when they come in . . . you have to move very quickly as far as if they need a PFA [order for protection from abuse], . . . or they just need safety, and you have to really assure them that they are safe, that he's not going to come here to take them or take the children. . . . and so, that's the main thing, and then, just to kinda educate them. So, your time with them and what you say to them is very important, the initial contact with them is very important.

Repeating the theme of the importance of the initial contact, another domestic violence worker said that the first thing she does is "tell them it's not their fault, let them talk to tell about [their] situation so I can identify what types of abuse it is and make a more informed decision on what to do, what services are available. Let them know they aren't alone." The domestic violence workers noted that this first contact is important because of victims' vulnerability following a domestic violence episode. This vulnerability involved their emotional states as well as their physical safety.

The domestic violence workers frequently referred to the cycle of violence, pointing out that following a domestic violence incident, there is typically a "honeymoon" period in which the abuser apologizes and the couple reconciles before the tension builds and the cycle of violence is repeated. Reaching, educating, and otherwise "arming" victims with resources, whether they return to their abusive relationship, enter shelter, or choose another course of action was considered important. One domestic violence worker put it this way: "I don't think that we need to make decisions for clients or pass judgment because of something, . . . [but we hope to] "help them be self-sufficient." This response suggests that one goal of domestic violence workers is to empower victims to take control of their lives and reduce dependence on their abusers.

While domestic violence workers talked about focusing on providing support and being caring and compassionate toward victims, they also emphasized that a key part of their job is providing education about domestic violence and resources—both to victims and to members of the wider community. One worker said that "educating about domestic violence, what it is, explaining the laws, giving information" is at least as important as any other function of her job. Domestic violence workers often referenced their own domestic violence–specific education and training and how it had shaped their views and affected their work. In particular, they discussed learning that the causes of domestic violence are rooted in power and control and embedded in social issues, such as gender inequality and patriarchy, and that social and structural factors, rather than individual ones, tend to keep victims and perpetrators locked in abuse cycles.

Child welfare workers described their approaches to victims somewhat differently. One worker hesitated in describing the "typical" procedures used, saying that there were no specific policies in place in her agency.

> I don't know that we have procedures that if we are aware of this, we do this, this, and this. We do try to be very, very sensitive; . . . we try to be very sensitive that when we're offering services, we're not also putting them in a situation where they may get abused that night, or indicating that something might be going on. . . . And we try to provide training to staff around here . . . [about] how to begin to recognize some of those signs, and how to respond without creating a worse environment.

This worker does mention the need for sensitivity and concern with victim safety, especially being aware of the potential for repeated abuse. This worker went on to say, "If they decide to go back, then it's their choice, but I think we have to give them different options."

One worker mentioned that her first priority is to counsel victims to leave the situation at least temporarily. In contrast to the domestic violence workers' approach of offering support, educating, establishing rapport, and developing a safety plan, child welfare workers placed the onus on the victims for taking responsibility for their situations. One worker described her approach this way:

> For most of the women I've encountered, I always encourage them [that] the first thing they need to do is get out. . . . Each situation is different, it may not always be where they need to divorce so much as it is they need to separate from each other and get some personal issues worked out on both sides . . . and then I always make sure that I have information of where they can go to get resources. [The local domestic violence agency] is the most obvious choice in this town, but I just tell them, get on the Internet, call people, do what you have to do.

This statement contrasts with that of the domestic violence workers who counseled women that they were not at fault. Although most child welfare workers were trained social workers, their approaches focused little on establishing an atmosphere of trust and compassion. Instead victims were told they must protect their children "or else." Child welfare workers, unsurprisingly, always brought the child's safety into the picture and often referred to the possibility of working with the perpetrator as well as the victim and her child or children. Another child welfare worker said:

> The social workers here, myself included, are very much aware of some resources in the community, both for the perpetrator and for the victim. Obviously, because we work with children and our focus and mandate is the protection of children, if it's a child that's involved or who could be the . . . recipient of the abuse, even accidental, if we feel like the children can't be protected, then we're going to proceed with our protocol, and the protocol of the court for removing those children. . . . Even when . . . we have an adult victim who chooses to stay with the perpetrator . . . we have children that want to return to the home, you know—we begin then, to really try to take a look at, through our treatment team meetings, and the service plan that we develop . . . really helping the family, uh, both the adult victim and adult perpetrator, of, what were the factors that lead up to this? What pushed you to the point that you reacted in this way? . . . [We begin] to really take a look at, was it stresses related to job, is it mental limitations that limit your ability to parent children at a difficult stage, you know, trying to really take a look, a broader look, at what leads up to the abuse . . . then try to match up what services need to address that. . . .

> We've really been able to open up and take an individualized look at each family and each situation, and, and if it's job readiness classes, or if it's anger management classes, or if it's an appointment at the employment office, you know, is it housing? Is it transportation, you know, are these some of the things that lead up to it, versus the idea that I've just got a mean, controlling person who chooses to maintain control by beatin' the fool out of somebody.

In keeping with earlier stages of the study, child welfare workers tended to focus on personal and individual factors leading to domestic violence. Child welfare workers did, however, consider a family's individual stressors that are related to social and structural causes, such as economic issues, but they specifically avoided the explanations of power and control and other larger, social and structural issues that domestic violence workers overwhelmingly thought were so important. These issues were simply not at the forefront of child welfare workers' awareness in domestic violence cases.

Divergent Perspectives: Domestic Violence and Child Welfare Workers

Although domestic violence and child welfare workers are employed in different agencies and have very different jobs, they all have contact with families involved in domestic violence situations. Because the sample of child welfare workers was drawn from a large, central child welfare agency, most had very similar job duties and worked together on specific cases. They were trained social workers, and as such, their focus was specific to protecting children and not necessarily supporting or comforting the child's parent or parents. As one child welfare worker put it, "I think when it comes to the children, we react a little bit faster than we do with the adults, because children, for the most part, are pretty helpless, and if their parents are not going to look out for them, then someone else has to. So, as far as the children go, . . . I feel like we're always on top of that." Another worker said:

> Since I work with children, it's of . . . the utmost importance that the children are in a safe, stable home. And in order to do that, they can't be that unless the parents are stable. . . . I would always . . . get the parents to do what they need to do to get things together, because I couldn't, I

wouldn't feel comfortable, or any of them that I know would feel comfortable, putting a child back in a home where the parents are fighting with each other and have undealt-with issues.

In keeping with their social work training, child welfare workers viewed the family as a system. Domestic violence workers, in contrast, dealt primarily with making the adult female victim and her children safe and did not mention working with male perpetrators at all. Thus, the child welfare workers mentioned seeing the entire family as their client, while domestic violence workers see the mother and her children as their primary client or clients.

When asked how child welfare workers are different or unique, one child welfare worker said, "[Domestic violence workers are] just looking at this one perspective of it, whereas with us, we're trained more so to look at the big picture." One child welfare worker said she believed that child welfare workers tended to take a more "holistic" approach than domestic violence workers, focusing on the whole family rather than one or two individuals within the family. Another child welfare worker explained that child welfare workers' approach is different than that of other social service professionals because child welfare workers tend to see the interconnectedness of people's troubles:

> It may just be, depending on what your profession is, you're just looking at this one perspective of it, whereas with us, we're trained more so to look at the big picture. . . . It's not that one piece stands alone, every piece somehow connects, . . . and I think that may be what one difference is. . . . I know particularly from the medical profession from what I've seen, is, they focused on this child needs this, this child needs that, and they're not seeing other things that came with it.

Domestic violence workers disagreed most with the child welfare workers' characterization of themselves as taking a more holistic view of domestic violence situations and the family system. One domestic violence worker, when asked about her thoughts on how child welfare workers handle domestic violence cases, said: "Well, it's their job to make sure those kids are safe. You know, and that's, that's the main thing, I mean, I'm sure . . . domestic violence is one of . . . the main reason[s] they take kids into foster care." Domestic violence workers acknowledged that it was perfectly understandable for child welfare workers to be most concerned about children because of their jobs. One domestic violence worker, in particular, when asked to comment about the difference between child welfare workers and domestic violence workers, said:

> With the child welfare worker, they're working with the children, and . . . removing children from the home and things like that. . . . As a domestic violence worker, you're seeing the whole picture. . . . You get the story from the victim. . . . Working with the children, I get to . . . hear the children's stories, and know . . . [how] they see, and how they feel about certain things. . . . I work with children to try to see how the domestic violence is actually affecting them, and whether it's causing them problems in school, or if they're acting out violently, or things like that.

Thus, when asked directly about differences between the two groups, domestic violence workers and child welfare workers responded that they are quite different. Their responses revealed, however, that the two groups actually have very similar styles, since both seek to support the family as a whole.

Finding Common Ground: Bridging Gaps and Breaking Down Barriers

Overall, the findings from the interviews indicated that child welfare workers' approaches to domestic violence cases were more focused on children and making referrals outside of their agency, while domestic violence workers saw a need for educating both victims and the community about the cyclical nature of domestic violence, identifying possible resources, focusing on their advocacy role, and perhaps most important, providing much-needed emotional support. With regard to overall causes, the interviews revealed that child welfare workers think about domestic violence in terms of family systems problems, while domestic violence workers, as women's advocates, tend to approach the issue with regard to gender inequality and society's role in perpetuating intimate partner violence. Domestic violence workers also focused on the adult victim, offering counseling and support, working with her on her legal needs and helping her craft a safety plan. Child welfare workers, in contrast, tended to focus on ensuring that the children in the family were protected, with substantially less emphasis on the adult victim. Child welfare workers discussed the need for identifying resources for individual case needs, as well as filing protective services reports, if necessary. Child welfare workers said that they tend to look directly at what lead up to the domestic violence situation, as long as those factors are in line with their own beliefs about domestic violence, and factors that cause people to want to stay together, all issues that speak directly to those examined in this study.

This study helped to construct a picture of the different ways frontline workers—specifically, child welfare and domestic violence workers—think about and approach domestic victims. As demonstrated in earlier stages of the study and supported by the interviews of the last stage, frontline workers show distinct differences in their beliefs, approach, and techniques for dealing with domestic violence cases, from their initial thoughts on the causes of domestic violence, to how they organize, categorize, and evaluate their ideas about the causes, and finally, to how they use these ideas in their everyday work. The beliefs that emerged from the quantitative and qualitative data provide support for the idea that different frontline workers think about domestic violence differently and tend to approach such cases in fundamentally different ways in their everyday work.

Compared with earlier studies, the multiple, iterative stages of the research better illuminated the similarities and differences between the two groups of frontline workers and provided a stronger basis from which to observe the differences between the two groups. While the two groups of workers did not necessarily have different cultural models, the elements of their models did vary, demonstrating intracultural diversity. Furthermore, the findings indicated that domestic violence workers' models were more elaborate, suggesting that the model might be contested—that is, that it contains elements of both agreement and disagreement (see Caulkins and Hyatt 1999). Comparisons between the two groups of workers throughout the study are summarized in Table 7.1.

This research supports previous studies that have found that victims fear that child welfare workers, because their primary focus is on the well-being of the child, might be vigilant to possible threats to child safety and therefore be more likely to recommend that the child be removed from the home in domestic violence cases (e.g., Postmus 2004; Purvin 2007). The workers in this study indicated that they concentrate on the needs of children and that a mother's staying in an abusive relationship is a matter of grave concern. Child welfare workers' discussions of individual character flaws and pathologies as principal causes of domestic violence and domestic violence workers' focus on structural causes in their interviews were also consistent with quantitative findings earlier in the study. The finding that welfare workers tended to be uncertain or uneducated about the aspects of domestic violence is also supported by previous phases of the

Table 7.1. Comparing Domestic Violence and Child
Welfare Workers throughout Stages of the Study

Stage/method objective	Domestic violence workers	Child welfare workers
1. Free listing; generating causes of domestic violence	Power and control as major causes	Alcohol abuse and drug use/abuse as major causes
2. Pile sorts; interviews; organizing causes	Structural causes; temporal arrangement of issues	Personal/individual pathology
3. Taking surveys; analyzing, sharing	Opposite agreement with child welfare; small group of university women's resource center with strong agreement	Strong, consistent agreement with one another on importance
4. Interviewing; employing ideas	Providing comfort, safe environment for disclosure; focus on compassion, safety plans, education	Counsel women about getting out, protecting children; focus on referrals
Overall	Focus on adult victim; in-depth understanding of dynamics of domestic violence; expanded, elaborated descriptions, with understanding of other people's views/biases	Focus on children; cynicism about dynamics of domestic violence; simplified categorizations, descriptions of domestic violence

research. Other research has come to the same conclusions. Collins and Dressler (2008b), for example, found that social work students tended to be skeptical about the efficacy of domestic violence interventions and to blame the violence on personal, internal issues in the person rather than in their environments. Some scholars have argued that it is imperative that child welfare workers understand the structural conditions that make victims vulnerable to domestic violence (e.g., Purvin 2007) as well as to the welfare system itself (Pélissier Kingfisher 1996).

The cycle of violence has an impact on frontline workers as they work to continually assess the victims' needs and most appropriate interventions, meeting each victim where she is in her process. Child welfare workers had a good deal of experience with domestic violence victims. Though they acknowledged that victims commonly leave and then return to their abusive partners multiple times before leaving permanently, this behavior was perceived as abnormal, and in some sense, victims were seen as willing partners in their abuse. The workers thus displayed little true understanding of the dynamics of violence relationships. These workers expressed their frustration when victims returned to abusive partners or were abused in different relationships, but domestic violence workers tended to view this same phenomenon in a larger context of the cycle of violence and the trajectory of the victims' experiences.

Furthermore, in working with domestic violence victims and their families, both sets of workers found themselves in a position to reproduce and maintain stereotypes, ideologies, and folk models about the causes of domestic violence, or to counter those mainstream beliefs with education and information about the issue. It is clear that despite undergoing training (conducted by domestic violence workers), not only do child welfare workers continue to hold stereotypical and misinformed ideologies about victims but also they are likely to communicate those messages to victims themselves in their frontline work. Domestic violence workers, in contrast, see it as explicitly their role to educate victims and others in a direct effort to counteract such ideas. These efforts are also clearly reflected in their frontline work, according to their own accounts.

The use of theory, methods, data collection techniques, and analytic approaches taken from the ethnographic analytic techniques of cognitive anthropology helps to give a voice to the experiences of frontline workers working on the local level. This study has uncovered, using their own words, the vocabulary these workers use to think about what causes domestic violence, how they organize these thoughts, the extent to which their ideas coincide with those of other workers, and perhaps most important, how these ideas play out in their everyday work with victims of domestic violence. The rigor of the anthropological data collection techniques employed here combined with a theoretical approach speaks directly to understanding how child welfare and domestic violence workers conceptualize the interplay between micro and macro issues. A trend in medical and social services is toward frontline workers' addressing people's needs according to evidence-based principles rather than the assumptions that researchers and practitioners make about people in practice. Because of this new focus, training continues to be important. Emic approaches such as those described in this research can inform such efforts and ultimately improve the plight of victims of domestic violence.

The findings from this ethnographic analysis suggest that despite increased training and knowledge, workers still experience frustrations and perhaps a basic disagreement on a fundamental level regarding the causes of domestic violence. For child welfare workers to continue to attribute domestic violence to individual flaws, such as alcohol abuse, low self-esteem, and mental illness is potentially dangerous to victims as domestic violence continues to be pathologized rather than characterized as an important structural issue rooted in social inequalities (Magen, Conroy, and Del Tufo 2000). Recent research on training child protective workers on domestic violence indicates that these workers often lack knowledge about domestic violence lethality and how to deal with frustrations in domestic violence cases (Button and Payne 2009).

Frontline workers in the two professions examined here must unite and strive to improve services for domestic violence victims, recognizing that an improved situation for a domestic violence victim who is a mother will necessarily improve the situation for the child as well. Offering support, advocacy, and meeting the client where she is are critical features of such an improved service model. Hope lies in promising collaborative models being piloted in cities across the country (see Friend, Shlonsky, and Lambert 2008; Moles 2008). Advances in training, implementing improved intensive (and extensive) screening procedures (Hazen et al. 2007; Magen, Conroy, and Del Tufo 2000; Moles 2008), and continuing education are excellent starts toward the goal of bridging the divide between two sets of frontline workers working in the same locality that can do much to improve the lots of traumatized families.

ACKNOWLEDGMENTS

This research was conducted with the funding from the University of Alabama Graduate Council Fellowship. The work would have been impossible without the cooperation of my informants, many of whom work to improve the lives of women and children in Alabama who are struggling financially, emotionally, and in other ways. Some informants gave me a great deal of their time, participating in all four phases of the research, and for that I am very grateful. Special thanks go to the Alabama Coalition Against Domestic Violence, the Alabama Department of Human Resources, and the DCH Health System for their support and allowing me to use their facilities. Many thanks go to William Dressler for his guidance, and Kathy

Oths, Jo Pryce, Debra Nelson-Gardell, Paul Stuart, and Daniel Goldmark for their helpful advice and comments at various stages of this research.

NOTE

1. The term *domestic violence* is used throughout this study because it is the terminology with which workers were most familiar. The agencies that served victims of gender-based violence used the term within the agency and in their communications with the community.

WORKS CITED

Banks, Duren, Andrea L. Hazen, Jeffrey H. Coben, Kathleen Wang, and Janet D. Griffith. 2009. Collaboration between Child Welfare Agencies and Domestic Violence Service Providers: Relationship with Child Welfare Policies and Practices for Addressing Domestic Violence. *Children and Youth Services Review* 31 (5): 497–505.

Bell, Holly F. 2003. Cycles within Cycles: Domestic Violence, Welfare, and Low-Wage Work. *Violence against Women* 9 (10): 1245–62.

Bograd, Michele. 1982. Battered Women, Cultural Myths, and Clinical Interventions: A Feminist Analysis. *Women and Therapy* 1 (3): 69–77.

Brookoff, Daniel, Kimberly K. O'Brien, Charles S. Cook, Terry D. Thompson, and Charles Williams. 1997. Characteristics of Participants in Domestic Violence: Assessment at the Scene of Domestic Assault. *Journal of the American Medical Association* 277 (17): 1369–73.

Button, Deanna, and Brian K. Payne. 2009. Training Child Protective Services Workers about Domestic Violence: Needs, Strategies, and Barriers. *Children and Youth Services Review* 31 (3): 364–70.

Caulkins, Douglas, and Susan B. Hyatt. 1999. Using Consensus Analysis to Measure Cultural Diversity in Organizations and Social Movements. *Field Methods* 11 (1): 5–26.

Chavez, Leo R., F. Allan Hubbell, Juliet M. McMullin, Rebecca G. Martinez, and Shiraz I. Mishra. 1995. Structure and Meaning in Models of Breast and Cervical Cancer Risk Factors: A Comparison of Perceptions among Latinas, Anglo Women, and Physicians. *Medical Anthropology Quarterly* 9 (1): 40–74.

Chavez, Leo, Juliet M. McMullin, Shiraz I. Mishra, and F. Allan Hubbell. 2001. Beliefs Matter: Cultural Beliefs and the Use of Cervical Cancer-Screening Tests. *American Anthropologist* 103 (4): 1114–29.

Collins, Cyleste C. 2005. Cultural Models of Domestic Violence: Perspectives of Human Service Professionals. PhD diss., University of Alabama.

Collins, Cyleste C., and William W. Dressler. 2008a. Cultural Consensus and Cultural Diversity: A Mixed Methods Investigation of Human Service Providers' Models of Domestic Violence. *Journal of Mixed Methods Research* 2 (4): 362–87.

———. 2008b. Cultural Models of Domestic Violence: Perspectives of Social Work and Anthropology Students. *Journal of Social Work Education* 44 (2): 53–74.

Danis, Fran, and Lettie L. Lockhart. 2003. Domestic Violence and Social Work Education: What Do We Know, What Do We Need to Know? *Journal of Social Work Education* 39 (2): 215–24.

Davis, Liane V. 1984. Beliefs of Service Providers about Abused Women and Abusing Men. *Social Work* 29 (3): 243–51.

Davis, Liane V., and B. E. Carlson. 1981. Attitudes of Service Providers toward Domestic Violence. *Social Work Research and Abstracts* 26 (4): 34–39.

Dressler, William W., Mauro C. Balieiro, Rosane P. Ribeiro, and José Ernesto Dos Santos. 2007. Cultural Consonance and Psychological Distress: Examining the Associations in Multiple Cultural Domains. *Culture, Medicine, and Psychiatry* 31 (2): 195–224.

Dressler, William W., José Ernesto Dos Santos, and Mauro C. Balieiro. 1996. Studying Diversity and Sharing in Culture: An Example of Lifestyle in Brazil. *Journal of Anthropological Research* 52 (3): 331–53.

Dressler, William W., Rosane P. Ribeiro, Mauro C. Balieiro, Kathryn S. Oths, and José Ernesto Dos Santos. 2004. Eating, Drinking, and Being Depressed: The Social, Cultural, and Psychological Context of Alcohol Consumption and Nutrition in a Brazilian Community. *Social Science and Medicine* 59 (4): 709–20.

Eisikovits, Zvi C., and Eli Buchbinder. 1996. Pathways to Disenchantment: Battered Women's Views of Their Social Workers. *Journal of Interpersonal Violence* 11 (3): 425–40.

Friend, Colleen, Aron Shlonsky, and Liz Lambert. 2008. From Evolving Discourses to New Practice Approaches in Domestic Violence and Child Protective Services. *Children and Youth Services Review* 30 (6): 689–98.

Grauwiler, Peggy. 2008. Voices of Women: Perspectives on Decision-Making and the Management of Partner Violence. *Children and Youth Services Review* 30 (3): 311–22.

Hazen, Andrea L., Cynthia D. Connelly, Jeffrey L. Edleson, Kelly J. Kelleher, John A. Landverk, Jeffrey H. Coven, Richard P. Barth, Jennifer McGeehan, Jennifer A. Rolls, and Melanie A. Nuszkowski. 2007. Assessment of Intimate Partner Violence by Child Welfare Services. *Children and Youth Services Review* 29 (4): 490–500.

Henderson, Angela. 2001. Factors Influencing Nurses' Responses to Abused Women: What They Say They Do and Why They Say They Do It. *Journal of Interpersonal Violence* 16 (12): 1284–1306.

Jaskyte, Kristina, and William W. Dressler. 2004. Studying Culture as an Integral Aggregate Variable: Organizational Culture and Innovation in a Group of Nonprofit Organizations. *Field Methods* 16 (3): 265–84.

Kok, Anne C. 2001. Economic Advocacy for Survivors of Domestic Violence. *Affilia* 16 (2): 180–97.

Levin, Rebekah. 2001. Less Than Ideal: The Reality of Implementing a Welfare-to-Work Program for Domestic Violence Victims and Survivors in Collaboration with the TANF Department. *Violence against Women* 7 (2): 211–21.

Magen, Randy H., Kathryn Conroy, and Alisa Del Tufo. 2000. Domestic Violence in Child Welfare Preventative Services: Results from an Intake Screening. *Children and Youth Services Review* 22 (3, 4): 251–74.

Minsky-Kelly, Debbie, L. Kevin Hamberger, Deborah A. Pape, and Marie Wolff. 2005. We've Had Training, Now What? Qualitative Analysis of Barriers to Domestic Violence Screening and Referral in a Health Care Setting. *Journal of Interpersonal Violence* 20 (10): 1288–1309.

Moles, Kerry. 2008. Bridging the Divide between Child Welfare and Domestic Violence Services: Deconstructing the Change Process. *Children and Youth Services Review* 30 (6): 674–88.

Pélissier Kingfisher, C. 1996. *Women in the American Welfare Trap*. Philadelphia: University of Pennsylvania Press.

Pelto, Pertti J., and Gretel H. Pelto. 1975. Intra-Cultural Diversity: Some Theoretical Issues. *American Ethnologist* 2 (1): 1–18.

Postmus, Judy L. 2004. Battered and on Welfare: The Experiences of Women with the Family Violence Option. *Journal of Sociology and Social Welfare* 31 (2): 113–23.

Purvin, Diane M. 2007. At the Crossroads and in the Crosshairs: Social Welfare Policy and Low-Income Women's Vulnerability to Domestic Violence. *Social Problems* 54 (2): 188–210.

Romney, A. Kimball, Susan C. Weller, and William H. Batchelder. 1986. Culture as Consensus: A Theory of Culture and Informant Accuracy. *American Anthropologist* 88 (2): 313–38.

Ross, Martha, and Charles Glisson. 1991. Bias in Social Work Intervention with Battered Women. *Journal of Social Service Research* 14 (3, 4): 79–105.

Saunders, Daniel G., Mark C. Holter, Lisa C. Pahl, Richard M. Tolman, and Colleen E. Kenna. 2005. TANF Workers' Responses to Battered Women and the Impact of Brief Worker Training: What Survivors Report. *Violence against Women* 11 (2): 227–54.

Shore, Bradd. 1996. *Culture in Mind: Cognition, Culture, and the Problem of Meaning*. New York: Oxford University Press.

Weller, Susan C., and A. Kimball Romney. 1988. *Systematic Data Collection*. Thousand Oaks, CA: Sage.

Worden, Allisa Pollitz, and Bonnie E. Carlson. 2005. Attitudes and Beliefs about Domestic Violence: Results of a Public Opinion Survey. *Journal of Interpersonal Violence* 20 (10): 1219–43.

8

Gender-Based Violence: Perspectives from the Male European Front Line

Uwe Jacobs

This chapter is primarily a first-person account of direct service work and an attempt to reflect on motivations and issues encountered. It is secondarily the perspective of one who has created and directed a program for survivors of gender-based violence (GBV) who have fled to seek political asylum protection in the United States. This chapter is issued from a relatively protected and privileged front line and removed from the primary trauma of GBV.

During the past five years, my colleagues and I at Survivors International, in San Francisco, California, have assisted several hundred asylum seekers who suffered rape, trafficking, domestic violence, female genital cutting, and persecution on account of their gender, sexual orientation, or transgender identity. GBV, from our point of view, includes all these forms of violence inflicted on women and sexual minorities in the context of political, social, cultural, and economic structures that perpetuate oppression, exploitation, and violence through either direct harm or the refusal to protect against violence. We are health professionals and social service providers—frontline workers—who assist refugee survivors of GBV by providing medical and psychological treatment, case management, advocacy, and access to self-help activities and resources. We work with immigration attorneys who represent these survivors in their quest to obtain political asylum, and we provide medical-legal and psycho-legal documentation and perform expert witness testimony in immigration courts. Through our research, comparative studies, and firsthand experiences, we have demonstrated that the effects of GBV are equivalent to those of political torture perpetrated by state actors.

129

Our perspective on GBV is one of conceptualizing the rights of women and sexual minorities as inalienable human rights, where freedom from violence and persecution has to be demanded and achieved as a restorative act and within the context of international human rights law. Survivors of GBV, from this perspective, are entitled to refugee status under U.S. asylum law and deserve access to medical and psycho-social assistance as they rebuild their lives in their new country of refuge. This conceptualization is not to be separated from the context of our work, which takes place in a country of refuge and exclusively with survivors, rather than in communities where the violence took place. While this context is in some important respects still adversarial, nevertheless it holds a certain position of privilege because no compromises need to be made with local community actors in the survivors' communities of origin. Survivors have no further need to get along with husbands, other family members they depend on, or officials who have refused to protect them. In cases where abusive husbands have come after survivors in the United States, they are able to obtain protection for themselves and their children from local law enforcement.

The roughly twenty health professionals at Survivors International, consisting predominantly of clinical psychologists and clinical social workers, may here be defined as frontline workers in the sense that we come face-to-face with survivors of GBV in order to engage with them in a process of examining their histories of violence and its consequences in both clinical and forensic settings. In many cases, in-depth confrontations with the details of survivors' trauma histories result directly from the pressures of the legal claim to asylum. Survivors cannot ask for protection without a full disclosure of their victimization, which tends to be retraumatizing and shameful. One of the principal challenges for frontline workers in this situation is to engage survivors in a paradigm of forced exposure and investigation, which is illustrated and analyzed in a later section.

The Political Context

For most of my time spent in the field of human rights, I have focused on the issue of torture as perpetrated by agents of the state. In my over ten years of work with survivors of torture, during which time I became a specialist in evaluating political asylum seekers, I was increasingly faced with individuals who had fled their home countries after having been abused by their husbands and other family members, as well as by others in their communities. Like political refugees, the women and gay men have no freedom, protection, or recourse where they came from, and their lives were shattered by cruelty and violence. As some of us in the torture rehabilitation field began to serve more of these survivors, it soon became apparent to us that the level of violence they had endured was often on par with what many survivors of state-sponsored torture had experienced. We had to ask ourselves whether we would do the right thing and respond. We decided to add GBV to the mission of our organization and to seek specific funding for undertaking more work in this arena. The broadening of our mission was made in the hope that a single-issue organization that had worked exclusively on torture for fifteen years would be able to communicate that GBV is a form of torture, even though it may not meet a legal definition that requires perpetrators to be state actors.

Refugee and asylum law in the United States and the world over was not written with the rights of women and sexual minorities in mind. The international laws that define the status of refugees and govern their protection came out of the experiences of the Holocaust and other genocidal campaigns, as well as the use of torture by dictatorial regimes. In this context, GBV appeared to be a domestic affair until women and sexual minorities began to flee their countries of origin to save their lives and build lives in freedom elsewhere. The effort to bring asylum protection to survivors of GBV has required much ground-breaking advocacy and fundamental rethinking of what may constitute a form of persecution (Musalo and Knight 2000). In the United States, asylum seekers must demonstrate a "well-founded fear of persecution" on account of race, religion, nationality, political opinion or "membership in a particular social group." The legal battles on behalf of GBV survivors have revolved around the argument that they are members of particular social groups enduring systematic persecution.

The effort to support GBV survivors is thus embedded in the powerful politics of immigration rights. These politics are driven by enormous economic and ethnocultural forces. Women who flee from GBV and who have frequently suffered from violence in a context of abject poverty are faced with the added burden of proving, even if implicitly, that they did not enter the United States "only" to escape from poverty, since poverty is not grounds for asylum protection. The double jeopardy of gender-based injustice and economic injustice is thus compounded misery at home and an added burden of proof later, when petitioning for protection abroad. If a well-to-do woman flees violence and asks for asylum protection elsewhere, she is not likely to be suspected of trumping up a "common" story of domestic violence to obscure that she "really" came to get a job and send money back home. She is more likely to have been educated and have some idea of what her rights are, more likely to have access to competent legal representation, more capable of explaining the depth and details of her situation, and—for all these reasons—in a better position for her quest for protection.

For GBV survivors seeking asylum, however, the price of asking for protection is submission to painful legal, physical, and mental scrutiny. What is known in psychology as *forced exposure* is usually the least helpful thing for a victim of trauma. The confrontation with painful and shameful memories in an adversarial legal context is retraumatizing because exposure does not occur in a context of interpersonal safety or in doses that are therapeutic. The helping mental health professional does not escape from this equation of trading exposure for the goal of immigration relief but has the consequences of worsening symptoms as a result of legal proceedings on his or her hands to deal with. More important, in the process of documenting the consequences of violence, we also have to ask for the story, whether we would otherwise, in a purely therapeutic context, ask for it or not.

Coming Face-to-Face with Violence: Personal Reactions

In examining the personal experiences of the frontline mental health professional in relation to GBV survivors, I begin with an ad hoc e-mail I sent out to colleagues one evening about two years ago, here reproduced without editing.

> Dear All—
> I apologize in advance for being melodramatic but I feel the urge to communicate about my day at the office after a 2-week absence because now it feels less routine than it will again tomorrow. As I am writing on a psychological evaluation report for a domestic violence victim from Mexico this evening, which was due today but which the attorney had neglected to tell me, as it is often the case, I am thinking back to the other woman from Mexico I saw this morning, who also got savagely brutalized by her ex-husband. It took considerable time to arrive at the decision that it was safe to let her go and not hospitalize her in relation to her desire to kill herself. She has made two prior attempts and she has three children to care for. I listened for a long time to her stories about being behind on the rent,

making promises she can't keep to her kids about buying them clothes, getting cheated and abused at work, which is the street sale of flowers, about walking the streets at night looking for work, not being able to sleep and eat etc. It was interesting to see her arrive looking very much together and presenting like the school teacher she used to be. She displayed a sense of humor and intelligence and I thought that she was probably coping quite well until I asked her about her symptoms. When she had to admit that she had every single one of them to the max, she began to sob uncontrollably and then launched into the account of her incredible reality, which included the wish to end it all. Finally, I told her that I had seen many before her on a first visit at the end of their ropes and that it usually gets better as we tackle one problem at a time etc. She took this in and left, saying that this gave her some hope and that she would be back. In this task, I wasn't alone, however. Anna is setting her up with all kinds of social service help and she will go and get free food, clothes, medical visits etc.

Then I ran into the attorney from next door who looked ashen. I asked him what was the matter and he told me he had just met with a woman who survived domestic violence and he was doing her asylum case, and how difficult these stories were. He said he decided to get into therapy for the secondary trauma. These stories are not unusual for us at all but I see them today in the context of working on a grant that would allow us to continue to serve these women and to spread the message. I am running into all kinds of resistance from my friends in the torture rehabilitation movement who are afraid that if we do this work for survivors of gendered persecution in an organized manner, the torture definition will be watered down, or that the suits in Washington who fund most of our sister agencies (but not us) won't like it because they are against giving asylum on the basis of gender claims, or that it will become further evident that some of our sister agencies are already surreptitiously serving these survivors with torture rehabilitation money because they, too, realize that some of these survivors are much more affected by the violence they have suffered than some folks who got clubbed at a demonstration and held in jail overnight somewhere (for example).

The experience that moved the lawyer I mention to seek therapy is typical. Who can emotionally contain the accounts of beatings, insults, rape in front of the children, getting kicked in a pregnant abdomen to the point of a miscarriage, being thrown down the stairs, being dragged around the house by the hair like a rag doll and beaten to a pulp, all rolled into the case of just one wife and experienced every day for years on end?

Can we imagine running away to avoid some form of female genital cutting, seeking protection from the police, only to be raped by the police and returned to the people who are preparing to do the cutting? Any response ranging from rage to helplessness to despair appears merely human.

What privileges us in our role is that we can channel these difficult emotions into responses that are highly technical and professionally organized. If all goes well in our endeavor, and it frequently does, we are able to witness inspiring levels of resiliency and the most heartening transformations in the lives of survivors. Ultimately, I was able to provide expert witness testimony in immigration court on behalf of one of the women I describe in the e-mail message. She was granted immigration relief by a compassionate judge and her former husband's attempts to create difficulties for her with the custody of her children were successfully thwarted. She has made tremendous efforts to heal and to help her children recover from the trauma they suffered. She brings one of her daughters, now an adult, to our weekly support group. There she acts as a big sister for newcomers who are beginning the same, difficult process.

The Politics of Gender, Ethnicity, and Class

In having consulted with women who work face-to-face with GBV survivors, I have reflected on the power differentials that are at work in these relationships. They include dynamics of class, gender, and ethnicity, with the disempowerment of the survivor at the center.

A common scenario is this: a Latina went through hell in her home country, having endured a lifetime of poverty, lack of education, and years of severe abuse, including death threats. She makes the gut-wrenching decision to leave her children with her sister and to try to enter the United States. With what little money she has scraped together, she pays the coyote (smuggler). The coyote gets her across the border but also rapes her. Once she has arrived, she stays with relatives without immigration documents. She tells no one about the depth of her past misery, keeps her head down, and tries not to be anyone's burden. She has never heard of political asylum protection and simply assumes the identity of another undocumented immigrant living in fear of discovery and deportation.

That the survivor's fear of deportation is also one of getting abused or killed is rarely processed in any conscious manner. Once she discovers that she has a right to asylum, she has missed the one-year filing deadline. To overcome that deadline requirement, she must produce psychological documentation that certifies "mental illness" to establish the "extraordinary circumstance" that allows for the requirement to be waived. She now has to submit to the same questions from her lawyer, the asylum officer, the immigration judge, and the prosecutor for the government about the details of her life and the abuse she was subjected to. Additionally, she has to cooperate with a mental health expert.

Although this mental health expert is only trying to help, there is no way to do that without putting her through yet another investigative procedure: interviews, questionnaires, psychological tests, and so on. The more thorough the examination, the more weight it stands to be given by the adjudicator. Simple therapeutic or emotional support will not do. Survivor and health professional are locked into an investigative process that has both supportive and retraumatizing aspects. The frontline worker and the client can shift to the genuine emotional concerns of the survivor only after the force field of the legal case has been navigated.

Compared with the survivor's situation, the one of the mental health worker seems easy. I understand this as both a male clinician and a consultant for my female colleagues. They have described to me feeling torn in all kinds of directions. Using the example of the Latina client, my colleagues find themselves wondering whether the client is "gaming the system" to get legal papers. And if she were, then what? All of us struggle with becoming the arbiter, in a sense, of how much misery and emotional suffering is required for a case of persecution or an "extraordinary circumstance," as if the trauma symptoms present were not perfectly "ordinary" in these cases.

At times, I bear witness to my female colleagues' experiences at the front lines. I have listened to them describe both expected and unexpected personal reactions, for instance, a colleague's feeling critical of clients for running away and leaving children behind, then feeling critical of herself for her own attitude. She may disclose to me that, at times, the severity of what she has heard overwhelms her, makes her cry, and gives her nightmares.

My role then is serving as a link in a chain of empathy and support: the survivor tells the story and cries; the clinician listens, helps and cries sometimes, and then she tells the story, too; the consultant listens, lends emotional and technical support, and cries less. In the end, through this chain of solidarity, the work gets accomplished, the survivor gets her papers and improves in her suffering, and the clinicians at the front line see the kind of change that looked unattainable some time earlier. This chain, of which we are all a part, helps us considerably in working through traumatic material and in containing cynicism and burnout.

A European Male Perspective

Some of the most painful encounters with GBV survivors I have had were with those who reacted to my male presence with either guardedness or outright terror. I have avoided these encounters where possible or kept them brief, conducted them in the presence of other, female staff, and allowed them to last only long enough for necessary clarifications before giving assurance that the survivor will be interviewed by women from this point forward. Nevertheless, the survivor shows outward signs of fear, sits as far away as she possibly can, seemingly ready to run, and in no way relieved by assurances of safety. This kind of interaction can leave a clinician feeling despondent because the impulse to offer help and create a supportive environment, with which we identify as healers, is negated. One ends up feeling like a perpetrator, or at least someone who lacks understanding and sensitivity. Interpersonal violence, unlike impersonal forms of traumatic experiences, destroys trust in fundamental ways.

One of the symptoms of secondary trauma I have observed in myself is a kind of deep disgust I have felt with my fellow men. It reminds me of an interview I once listened to in which a domestic violence expert was asked, "Why do men abuse women?" and her answer was, "Because they can." This response reflects a kind of cynicism and misanthropy I have felt in dealing with human rights violations generally, here directed specifically at men. It has moved me at times to assert that men are generally unfit to advance our civilization and that the only hope we have is to put power into the hands of women. Such sentiment might be seen as natural, because of what we have seen men do throughout history, but I feel that, in the end, it is a sign of trauma and has to be analyzed as such and put into proper perspective. More precisely, this is to say that the impulse to give up on men is not limited to women and, since it is a psychological defense against emotional distress and cognitive dissonance, is not likely to be helpful.

A related painful lesson has been the degree to which women are caught up in the cycle of male domination and violence. One woman who had tried to escape from female genital cutting and forced marriage told the story of her grandmother's way of telling her that her rebellion would not be tolerated: she asked her granddaughter's young son to urinate on his mother's head to show her who was boss. A good friend and female clinician worked on this case, and she stated to me that she found this to be one of the hardest traumatic narratives to digest. It makes me wonder, too, whether the woman would have told me this story or not because of my gender.

The first torture survivor I had ever worked with was an African woman who had suffered, among other things, acts of sexual violence by male prison guards, which she found extremely difficult to remember and discuss. She had been referred to me by a female supervisor of mine. In doing more than a year of psychotherapy with her, I came to realize that her capacity to relate to me was more determined by the idealized relationship she had with her father, who had, according to her, always been good to her. By contrast, she continued to suffer from a very difficult relationship with her mother and she had, in life in general, more trouble relating to women than to men. I was in some ways astonished to find that this pattern of relating, established early in life, had not been fundamentally altered by her subsequent victimization.

Since then, I have come to see much more of the same. Many survivors of torture and abuse retain a way of discerning who is trying to help them, regardless of their gender, ethnicity, class, or other group characteristics. The way in which we deal with "the other" is complicated and highly variable. There is no doubt that having an individual who shares key characteristics with us, whom we perceive as "our own" by our side can be invaluable and comforting. Women will need women and gay men will need gay men somewhere along the path of recovery. Plenty of abused women absolutely require female therapists, and who would wish to deny them the need or the request? Similar considerations apply to culture, ethnicity, and language. Still, in my experience, women have benefited from nonabusive, healing relationships with male professionals and have reported that some of their healing came specifically as a result of relating to a man in this way.

These truths co-exist side by side with the overwhelming facts of men's domination and abuse of women and these are difficult to digest. Keen awareness of this emotionally confusing reality may help us to not get mired in self-hate and paralysis or blind romanticism. Apart from self-defense, the male observations offered here spring from the hope of building a common humanity, one of pluralism rather than sectarianism. Such a conception has plenty of space for groups who take care of their own because they are their own; it is merely not limited to this approach.

Self-conscious privilege need not deter us from being clear and direct about the underpinnings of what we offer. The values I bring to the work here described are grounded in the Enlightenment, and in this instance without apology. From this point of view, no differences can be split when it comes to the principles of liberty and equality and the necessity of rational discourse when these issues are being settled.

Conclusion

In view of the painful material covered in these pages, it is gratifying to end on a note of hope. The first African American President of the United States and his administration moved to issue new guidelines for women seeking asylum protection on the basis of domestic violence, explicitly recognizing that such women may constitute social groups eligible for protection under asylum law. There are many who will need this protection and who depend on increased recognition of their situation by lawyers, health professionals, and the public at large. Sadly, there will also be those who suffered GBV but are, for any number of technical reasons, not eligible for asylum protection. At the very least, however, increased awareness of GBV can lead to efforts at general support and healing.

The work toward universal protection of human rights is ultimately one of an emerging consciousness in an emerging global community. The rights to freedom of women and sexual minorities today remain less clear in the global citizen's mind than the rights of political prisoners or the rights of children. The efforts of frontline advocates and healers combating GBV have a critical function in forging a network of international solidarity that will gradually change this imbalance. The domination and abuse of women and girls and sexual minorities will be seen as inextricably linked to tyranny in general and will serve as tyranny's markers, along with censorship of the press, prisoners of conscience and torture. As existing gender and religious power structures hold on, this vision is still summarily rejected in many parts of the world. However, individual rights to freedom are indivisible and so is the idea that no one group has the right to dominate another. There are no exceptions, for if there were, they would negate the entire principle.

For this simple reason, further progress in building communities that reject and seek to abolish GBV is inevitable. In the future, the efforts of the frontline workers described in this book will likely be prized by societies that have come to consider the relative absence of GBV as one more indicator of what it means to be compassionate. Until then, the efforts to combat and eradicate GBV must take care to be inclusive and diverse, as diverse as the workers and projects described in this book and beyond.

WORK CITED

Musalo, Karen, and Stephen Knight. 2000. Gender-Based Asylum: An Analysis of Recent Trends. *Interpreter Releases* 77 (42): 1533–43.

Cultural Politics of a Global/Local Health Program for Battered Women in Vietnam

Lynn Kwiatkowski

As many anthropologists and other scholars have shown, wife battering is a practice that is shaped by complex cultural and social contexts involving historical and modern cultural ideologies, and economic, political, and other social processes (Adelman 2003, 2004; Alonso 2002; Burbank 1994; Erez, Adelman, and Gregory 2009; Gutmann 1996; Hautzinger 2007; McClusky 2001; McWilliams 1998; Merry 2006, 2009; Mrsevic 2000; Plesset 2006). In Vietnam, discourses of wife battering and domestic violence have become more public and diverse in recent years. Wife battering can no longer be understood only through local cultural logics particular to contemporary Vietnamese communities. Instead, transnational discourses of wife battering have penetrated several areas of Vietnam society and have intersected with local ideologies and practices.

In recent years, personnel from international organizations, local and national government institutions, and local nongovernment organizations (NGOs) have been working collaboratively in Vietnam to address the needs of battered women. Recognizing that battered women's health and well-being need to be addressed within a larger social context, a new international health program in Hanoi, the Violence against Women Health Program, combines hospital and clinic care with community-based prevention programs.[1] Through a local-level, ethnographic analysis, this chapter analyzes the perspectives of the participants in this international health program, including international organization personnel, local NGO workers, health professionals, and community leaders, to understand the diverse ways that global and local cultural ideologies intersect as the program's participants attempt to accommodate these sometimes competing ideologies. The approach to analyzing the perspectives of individuals working with battered women that I take in this chapter is situated in the realm of anthropological studies of gender violence that have recently addressed the transnational circulation of discourses of gender violence.

In Vietnam, the way in which people conceptualize what they consider to be appropriate responses to wife battering is shifting (Romedenne and Loi 2006). This shift is occurring particularly as Vietnamese scholars, government-sponsored mass organization leaders, and local Vietnamese NGO workers move between national boundaries and accumulate and offer knowledge and resources that address wife battering, and generate transnational networks of support. Sally Engle Merry (2006) has discussed this transnational circulation of people and ideas through the international human rights movement against violence to women. She asserts that this international social movement "provides a valuable site for understanding how new categories of meaning emerge and are applied to social practices around the world" (1). In Vietnam, new cultural conceptions of gender and violence have been emerging with the transnational circulation of discourses of gender violence (Merry 2006, 2009).

The recent expansion in Vietnam, since the mid-1980s, of international health and development organizations and NGOs has also been an important catalyst of change in moral conceptions of and responses to wife battering. Addressing these transnational processes in a local-level ethnographic study that assesses the perspectives of gender-based-violence frontline workers is crucial to understanding wife battering in contemporary Vietnam. In this instance, the frontline workers include local NGO-based professional counselors, health personnel, and community leaders who directly assist battered women through the international health program. This approach can also help us to understand the interplay between international, national, and local community realms, as individuals and groups aiding battered women and preventing wife battering negotiate contested meanings of this form of gender-based violence in societies. It can also help us to better conceptualize wife battering as an ongoing and shifting cultural and social process that implicates actors from the global to the local level.

An anthropological approach to the study of wife battering that considers transnational processes highlights the ways that historically specific global practices involving wife battering are played out in local communities. In Vietnam, community, state, and international actors intersect with each other within programs that are often initiated or supported by international sponsors and are intended to reshape the experience of wife battering. In assessing changes stemming from global discourses and practices that address wife battering, we must pay close attention to how powerful local understandings of family and marriage, and political conceptions of society, nation, and development held by individuals working directly with battered women intersect with global processes.

It is also important to recognize that within one society there may be multiple and sometimes conflicting approaches to wife battering implemented by frontline workers. The emergence of multiple approaches to wife battering may occur particularly in a period characterized by openness to experimentation, which we can find among government institutions in contemporary Vietnam, as well as among local NGOs that have been emerging as part of the growing civil society in Vietnam. By addressing this diversity, we can draw from an anthropological approach to gender violence that asserts that culture is not a fixed entity that stands in the way of change (Merry 2006) but that instead, the process of change can be observed to involve cultural negotiation and contestation among a variety of actors.

An examination of the discourses and practices of individuals and groups involved in assisting battered women within the Violence against Women Health Program operating in Vietnam allows for an analysis of the intersection of global and local forces through a local-level ethnographic analysis. For instance, state discourses and practices have played a powerful role in recent decades in constructing conceptions of womanhood, marriage, family, and wife battering in Vietnam (Pettus 2003). Yet, in recent years, international health and development processes operating in Vietnam have also emerged to play an important role in influencing and regulating individual and collective experiences of these same conceptions.

Methodology

The analysis in this chapter is based on research I conducted during two research periods in 2004 and 2007. During this time, I assessed international organization, government, and local NGO programs that were addressing wife battering. I focused on an international health program that initially was located in two communes of Hanoi and a nearby biomedical hospital. Later, the program expanded to another hospital and additional communes. I conducted qualitative, ethnographic research in a women's counseling center of the hospital and in two of the communes in which the program was operating. I conducted twenty-eight in-depth interviews with battered women and approximately fifty in-depth interviews with Vietnamese individuals and international health and development personnel who were actively responding to wife battering.[2]

In this chapter, I examine wife battering in Vietnam as a particular form of gender-based violence. While at times I use the term *domestic violence*, I have chosen to emphasize the term *wife battering* in this chapter to specify that the form of domestic violence I am addressing is husbands' abuse of and violence against their wives. The use of this term also points to the gendered nature of the violence I am analyzing. In Hanoi, while a number of terms are used to discuss this form of violence, a Vietnamese term commonly used among frontline workers, and Vietnamese people more generally, to discuss a husband's abuse of his wife is *đánh vợ* (or *đánh đập vợ*). This term refers to the beating or hitting of a wife. Many frontline workers of the international health program revealed that before participating in the program's training they had only a limited view of what violence against a wife or violence in the family (*bạo hành trong gia đình*, or *bạo lực trong gia đình*) directed at a wife entailed. In addition to a husband's beating or hitting of his wife, they now understand violence against a wife to include sexual, emotional, and economic abuse, and a husband's committing adultery. This perspective is held by the frontline workers I discuss in this chapter.

Vietnam and Change

Political-economic processes in Vietnam have had a significant influence on domestic violence, and wife battering specifically, as well as battered women's health (Kwiatkowski 2008). Madelaine Adelman (2004) has identified a political economy of domestic violence that positions domestic violence within a cultural-historical context to understand the intersection between domestic violence and the organization of the polity, the arrangement of the economy, and the dominant familial ideology expressed through a state's policies. In Vietnam, the state has been recently undergoing a shift from a centrally planned and state subsidized economy to a market economy that operates through state regulations (Tran and Le 1997). Policies associated with this shift, referred to as *đổi mới*, or Renovation, were formalized by the Vietnamese state in 1986. This transition has involved greater integration of Vietnam into the global market economy and has also led to increased involvement of international organizations in Vietnamese social life.

Approaches to wife battering have also been changing in Vietnamese society in the context of this political-economic shift. While violence perpetrated by one family member against another has been outlawed at least since the emergence of the communist government in Vietnam, the Vietnam National Assembly approved the first anti–domestic violence law, called the Law on Domestic Violence Prevention and Control, in November 2007 (National Assembly 2007). Dialogues among international organizations and local individuals and groups, including NGOs, mass organizations, and government leaders, resulted in the development of the new law. Participants in these dialogues included Deputies to the Vietnam National Assembly, international organization personnel, Vietnamese scholars, local NGO personnel, health professionals, other Vietnamese professionals, and individuals from other Asian countries who had experience with domestic violence laws and programs.

Also, personnel working through state agencies and state-supported organizations had long been the only members of institutions available to provide assistance to battered women and their families. By the late 1990s, international and local health and development organizations began to establish programs in greater numbers in the country. By the early twenty-first century, many international organizations and local NGOs had implemented programs that address wife battering, as well as other forms of gender-based violence.

Wife Battering and International Health and Development Programs

The promotion of Vietnamese women's health through the Violence against Women Health Program was initiated in a Hanoi district in 2002. I visited the program in 2004 and 2007. It has been supported by two international organizations and the government's Hanoi Health Service and has involved counseling and other forms of assistance from a local NGO. Funding from the Vietnam Women's Union has also been drawn on by volunteers to aid in supporting community-level clubs organized in communes participating in the international health program.[3] The program provided education for government biomedical health personnel employed by a general hospital of the Hanoi District, enabling them to offer a wide spectrum of services to battered women. Some of the trainings were conducted by foreigners, including an Australian social worker and an American counselor. The program taught the health personnel to identify battering, to provide basic counseling for battered women, and to refer the women to other health personnel who were trained to counsel battered women more extensively. This training aimed to reorient the Vietnamese biomedical personnel's common practice of providing only physical treatment for battered women and introduced a contemporary Western health and social approach to aiding battered women. The program also involved education for individuals who would train other health personnel; and the creation of a curriculum for this education, monitoring indicators, and medical record forms for treatment of battered women and other patients who experienced gender-based violence.

The program also established a women's counseling center on the hospital grounds. The program trained and then employed counselors in the women's counseling center, to whom health personnel referred battered and other women who were in need of counseling. Although rare, spouses and men who batter could also be counseled at the center.

In addition to the hospital-based resources, the international health program trained health personnel at nearby commune health clinics to counsel and care for battered women who live in the communes and coordinate their services with other local government officials. In the same communes, the program also established women's and men's clubs that addressed and tried to prevent wife battering. This program included ensuring that battered women in the communes received appropriate health care and social services.

Within two of these communes where I conducted research, members of the local Women's Union had been addressing wife battering before the establishment of the international health program. In recent years, the work of the local Women's Union members in this area has included providing information to women about their legal rights, assisting battered women, reporting some cases of battering to police officers, and participating in government reconciliation committees. In wife battering cases, government reconciliation committees have been oriented toward ending gender violence perpetrated by a husband and reconciling the spouses (Vu, Vu, and Nguyen 1999).

This international health program was a pilot project that, in 2006, was extended to other Vietnamese communities, with, as I noted earlier, a new counseling center having been established in another Hanoi hospital and community-level programs linked to this counseling center established in additional communes. Funding for this project, which included two phases and evaluations of the project, ended in 2009. Personnel from hospitals outside of Hanoi also have requested information from this program, to establish their own health program to address wife battering in their province.

Choice

In discussing gender violence, Merry (2009) argues that we must understand interpersonal violence, such as wife abuse, in the context of larger systems of power and inequality, and other forms of institutional or social violence. Further, international discourses of gender violence, such as United Nations discourses, as well as some local government and NGO gender discourses, frame gender violence as a human rights violation. For instance, in Vietnam, a representative of the international organization that funded the health program for battered women said to me that while the project was institutionally under the reproductive health rubric, she viewed domestic violence more as a human rights issue. Merry (2006, 220) also wrote that "human rights are part of a distinctive modernist vision of the good and just society that emphasizes autonomy, choice, equality, secularism, and protection of the body." Susan Bordo (1997) argues that a contemporary popular postmodern discourse about the body in the United States emphasizes and celebrates individual choice and self-determination in a wide range of contexts and criticizes this view for effacing the material and social realities that shape and constrain the choices we are able to make.

Additionally, in discussing development processes in Nepal, Stacy Leigh Pigg (1997, 281) argues that development programs do not "act on a stable field of indigenous understandings and practices." Thus, in Vietnam, cultural ideologies and practices associated with gender, marriage, and violence are not fixed or homogeneous. Therefore, new conceptions of wife battering being introduced into Vietnam society through international organizations are contributing to ongoing constructions of these cultural ideologies. For instance, Vietnamese women's ability to make independent choices, as well as the kinds of choices women are able to make, has expanded over the past century. Still, cultural norms and political and economic realities have constrained many women's ability to make choices. Following Bordo, Vietnamese women's choices, therefore, are not completely free and self-determined.

This point is relevant since *choice* is a key term found in the international organization personnel's discourses about wife battering. The concept of choice has introduced a new way of conceptualizing how to approach battered women and the violence the women are facing. One example of this emphasis on choice is found in a 2001 document entitled *International NGO Perspectives on Reproductive Health in Vietnam: An Invitation to Dialogue*. This document is pertinent to this discussion since one of the contributing international organizations to this document was the international organization that funded the health program in Hanoi discussed here. The document, which includes domestic violence under the rubric of reproductive health, reads, "International standards and goals set out at the ICPD [International Conference for Population and Control (held in Cairo in 1994)] emphasized the need for reproductive health policies and programs which highlighted choice, information and empowerment as key ways to ensure lasting improvements in reproductive health" (INGOs 2001, 8).

These ideals continued to be promoted through internationally sponsored reproductive health and gender-based violence programs in Vietnam during the early twenty-first century. Vietnamese counselors at the women's counseling center have stressed the importance of providing women with the ability to make their own choices about how to approach the violence they are experiencing, rather than pressuring women to return to their husbands as part of a process of reconciliation. One of the counselors of the women's counseling center said:

> Even though some doctors and nurses referred battered women to People's Committees, the Women's Union, or the police before this program was instituted, it did not result in any improvement for the women. These government organizations are the last to help the battered women. . . . In the People's Committee, there were so many departments . . . [but they] had no commitment, between the different authorities, to the management or treatment of the battered women. . . . The People's Committee and Women's Union took care of battered women, but it was a cycle. When battered women were beaten they told the Women's Union, but then they went home again, and they went to the reconciliation committee to keep the peace, but things did not improve for the women.

In contrast to the government emphasis on reconciliation of husband and wife, "the substantive development of this [international health] program," one of the counselors at the women's counseling center stressed, "is that after the women enhance their knowledge, they can choose how to solve their problem by themselves, not by others." A pamphlet, entitled *Guide for Health Personnel Working with Victims of Gender Violence*, which was distributed to health personnel participating in the training program, provided the following instruction: "[Health workers] should not tell the patient what they must do, but instead help her to learn the different options, so that she can make her own decision about the matter."

The counselors regularly provided information to battered women who visited their office about divorce law and laws that prohibit violence within the family.[4] The counseling center also offers free legal information and assistance to battered women that could facilitate the process of divorcing their husbands, if the women chose to do so. While the counselors also try to reconcile couples, they emphasized that they prioritized focusing their efforts on battered women's stated choices. Allowing women to choose a means of addressing their husband's abuse was viewed as a key shift in approach from previous ones. This process has involved a decision to pursue divorce for some women visiting the counseling center. For instance, one counselor said to me, "We have helped women to obtain a divorce, as in the case this morning, but we try to reconcile first. Mostly here, we provide counseling about emotional issues and laws, and after we provide the counseling, women themselves can choose to divorce or not. Their choice of help is their own decision. We have seen many get divorced." In one case, a woman visited the counseling center a few times while I was present, seeking assistance in filing for a divorce. The counselors helped her to obtain a divorce application, and she came to the center for assistance in filling out the application. The counselors told me the woman also asked to learn how to speak in the court in a manner that would help her to acquire a divorce. Counselors went to court proceedings with battered women if they did not feel comfortable going alone. Sometimes the counselors were even asked to testify on the women's behalf. In most cases, the testimony of the counselors, who are also physicians, focused on women's medical injuries. One of the counselors said at another time, "For battered women who have some knowledge [about legal procedures], it is not difficult for them to go to court. But for farmers who have little knowledge, it is difficult because they do not know where to go, what their rights are, and, with pressure from their family and emotional feelings for their husband and children, it is very difficult."

In 2007, a counselor said that approximately 5 to 7 percent of battered women who visited their counseling center acquired a divorce. Divorce has been increasing in the nation at large. A survey, conducted by the Vietnam government Committee for Population, Family, and Children, was reported in 2007 to have found that the number of divorces in Vietnam increased from twenty-two thousand in 1994 to between fifty-three thousand and fifty-five thousand in 2005. The survey also found that domestic violence accounted for 60 percent of the divorces (*Vietnam News* 2007).

While divorce rates have been increasing in Vietnam, especially in urban areas, not all battered women may have the resources or social networks that would enable them to make this choice, even if they desired to divorce. Some battered women I spoke with did not feel that they had the economic resources or social support to live independently, or that they would be awarded custody of their children if they divorced. Some women held a cultural view that their children would be harmed emotionally by the divorce of their parents. Women I interviewed were influenced by personnel of government groups or institutions, or family members to remain with their husbands. For instance, a counselor at the counseling center said that many victims who visit the clinic would like to divorce, but because of problems related to their economic situation, children, and housing which are not easily solved, they must maintain their marriage. He also said that after receiving assistance from members of the community, including personnel of government institutions, family, or friends, many battered women often give up their pursuit of a divorce.

Complexities of Local Responses to International Health Approaches

As I noted earlier, anthropological approaches to examining the discourses and practices of international health and development program participants address the complexities and contestations surrounding local interpretations and appropriations of these discourses and practices. While the program was conceived of and implemented as a holistic program that brought health into the realm of the larger society, personnel and volunteers working within the hospital and community club sectors of the program did not always implement the program with the same orientation. Subsequently, the international organization personnel's discourse that emphasized allowing battered women independent choice in how to approach the battering was not employed by volunteer leaders at the community level through the community clubs that the international health program helped to establish.

In each commune, program participants attempted to form at least one women's Club for Family Happiness, and a Club for Male Farmers, which would address the problem of gender violence. The male farmers club was generated as a part of the larger local Farmers Union mass organization. These clubs worked in conjunction with the hospital-based counseling center and local government officials. One of the communes had two clubs for women: the Club for Volunteers for Family Happiness, which included a network of volunteers who were working with the international health program to address and prevent wife battering; and the Club for Family Happiness, which had as its members battered and nonbattered women, including the members of the Club for Volunteers for Family Happiness. The groups advocated for greater surveillance of men's behavior in their homes and in their interactions with their wives, by both women and men in the commune; prevention activities; counseling of battering men; and provision of support, counseling, and other forms of assistance to battered women. The leaders of the women's clubs are also commonly Women's Union leaders, who integrate information about wife battering into other commune club meetings.

While the counseling center emphasized a battered woman's choice in deciding how to address the battering she is experiencing, the clubs emphasized reconciliation of a battered woman with her husband, and encouraged the women to remain within their families. Some battered women turned to the police and the legal system or were led to these government institutions by club leaders or leaders of the local Women's Union. Since leaders of the women's clubs tended to be Women's Union leaders, some were also members of reconciliation committees. The club leaders said that if a case of wife battering was very serious, they would support divorce. But reconciliation was the most common avenue pursued by club leaders. A professional of one of the international organizations sponsoring the program also recognized this tendency by the club leaders when she said, "It seems that they [the clubs] are still like the reconciliation committee." One leader of a women's club said to me:

> Yes, the most important thing in the program is to keep the family together. But in cases in which it is useless to keep [the family together], then we will help them to get divorced, to be liberated. [Keeping the family together is important] because in Vietnamese culture, the family

is the most important element in all people's lives, that is why we want to keep families together. If they can solve the problem in the family it is best, not only for the Women's Union but for all of the unions, in order to help families to have a happy family and keep the family together; so children will not be in a situation of living without a mother or father; to decrease the rate of divorce; and so that children can be brought up well. And reducing the divorce rate will help to decrease the rate of social evils.

Another women's club leader, who was also a local Women's Union leader, relayed to me her concerns about battered women's well-being following a divorce. These concerns influenced other women's club and Women's Union leaders to emphasize reconciliation of spouses in cases involving wife battering.

The Women's Union always reconciles [spouses] in order to maintain families' happiness. There are a few cases of divorce. . . . Women usually have the most disadvantages when they divorce. So we never want to solve [wife battering] through divorce. Especially in the view of Vietnamese people, divorced women usually have a bad reputation. They are regarded as having had many faults, so their husbands just left them. However, we had to solve some cases through divorce. But there are very few cases like this.

While the clubs met with the counselors of the women's counseling center and medical personnel often, I interviewed several battered women referred to me by the leaders of the women's club and Women's Union who did not know about the women's counseling center. One of the professionals of an international organization supporting the health program told me that the club leaders do not regularly refer battered women to the women's counseling center, because they said that they handle the cases themselves. The community has not greatly shifted its conception of the importance of the stability of the family. Women's Union and other government leaders and community members continue to implement programs around the ideas of the reconciliation of spouses and the happy family, an idea also promoted by the government. Some battered women were still being told by some club leaders that it was their fate to suffer in their families. The international organization professional said about the club leaders: "I am concerned about their capacity, since they may not have learned the [international health program] ideas. They may just work like the reconciliation committee worked, because they have their support."

Within the same communes, unlike the women's club leaders, some health clinic personnel do refer battered women to the women's counseling center. As one commune physician noted, in discussing the care she gives to battered women she treats, "I talk to them and give advice. In cases of patients who trust us, we advise them to go to the health care center and give them the address if they still have problems . . . [the address of] the [women's] counseling center."

In contrast to the women's club's and Women's Union leaders' emphasis on family unity, a counselor of the women's counseling center argued, "in Vietnam, the family is an extended family, and maybe this is good, but also there is pressure [from the family] that outweighs women's rights." The common extended-family form in Vietnam may, in part, influence local club members to focus on maintaining family unity, while simultaneously working to end wife battering.

Community members targeted by international development programs are not homogeneous in their views or interests. On one hand, women's clubs and Women's Union leaders do not emphasize battered women's making individual choices. On the other, commune-level health clinic personnel refer women to a counseling center that prioritizes a woman's choice. We can see divergent local discourses and approaches to wife battering among frontline workers within the same international health program.

International program personnel and volunteers sometimes only partially accept ideas introduced by the programs and, thereby, potentially give the battered women they serve mixed and contradictory messages. The personnel and volunteers of this international health program also faced contradictory messages, since the new international program approach that emphasized women's choice did not replace the government approach. With women's club leaders participating in both approaches simultaneously, as club leaders and Women's Union leaders, they seemed to draw on the approach that they had more experience with and that they perceived to provide a better solution, in order to maintain battered women's economic stability and moral social standing. Still, the women's club leaders drew on elements of the international health program that they perceived to provide beneficial outcomes for battered women, such as focusing on preventing wife battering, ending battering that women in their communes were facing, and providing social support, health care, and other forms of assistance to battered women. As Pigg (1997, 281) writes, members of communities targeted by development "are already assuming and seeking certain kinds of relationships to development." This international health program demonstrates the multiple ways in which transnational ideas and approaches introduced into a new culture can be apprehended by local program participants.

Choice and Social Constraints

The concept of *choice* was integrated into the everyday implementation of the international health program for battered women in varying ways and degrees among a variety of actors in the program. Furthermore, personnel of the international organizations involved did not seem to conceptualize battered women's process of making choices as being located within a broader context of social and material constraints, such as class inequalities, or power exerted through government institutions or through cultural ideologies of gender and family. The focus of the international health program was specifically on gender violence. In a few cases, the counseling center did aid women economically through the help of the Women's Union small loan program and local government officials' provision of funds. These approaches, though, appeared to be limited, since most of the women I spoke with who visited the counseling center did not report having received economic assistance.

Even a Vietnamese counselor of the women's counseling center said that a serious problem women face is difficulty in financially supporting their families if they divorced their husband. Vietnamese women's choices are also often made relative to or in conjunction with their families, as Tine Gammeltoft (2007) argues in regard to many pregnant Vietnamese women's decision-making following their receiving a prenatal diagnosis. Battered women I interviewed often spoke of their natal families and whether they could depend on them for economic and moral support or whether they and their children would pose a burden on their parents and siblings.

The international health program club leaders at the community level considered the negative economic and social ramifications of divorce for battered women and drew on their experience as local Women's Union leaders and members of reconciliation committees to assist battered women to reconcile with their husbands. Unless the economic and social constraints that battered women face are considered and addressed practically within international health programs, or other programs for battered women, local program participants may be hesitant to advocate the concept of choice as they assist battered women.

NGO Personnel, Government Law, and Women's Rights

The contested ideas of preserving battered women's rights and keeping families intact through reconciliation processes were found in local Vietnamese NGO organization perspectives as well. One local Vietnamese leader of an NGO that was involved in training participants of the international health program had been influenced by international conceptions of human rights. She asserted:

> The Women's Union is very good in implementing activities, but sometimes they lack skills. They are very concerned about keeping the family together, not about individuals' safety or human rights. They are not concerned with human rights or women's rights. . . . The government officials talk a lot about the reconciliation approach, but this approach focuses on maintaining the marriage, and they think about the whole family. They are not concerned with the rights of the woman, and the people who use this approach have no skills in counseling. They just focus on analyzing who is right and who is wrong; their counseling is not based on the rights of those involved. They are not concerned about what they want. The people who apply this approach have a limited knowledge about gender and just advise women to accept the situation according to traditional values; . . . this approach can be successful for a short time, but women have to suffer for a long, long time. They just focus on the security of the society, such as no fighting in the community, and they don't see things underneath that the woman has to suffer.

Another counselor within this local NGO said the following about government-sponsored reconciliation committee members: "If they obey the ideology of tradition, they think it is necessary to reconcile [the couple], and then that is what they will do. But if they know about women's rights, then things will be different. The main aim of all reconciliation groups will be to do what the women want." The local NGO leader and counselor have adopted modern conceptions of human rights, individual bodily safety, and choice in regard to gender-based violence. This NGO provided another local space for conceiving of battered women's options in terms of human rights and choice in the international health program, ideas that did not necessarily correspond with local community views of battered women's position in the family and society.

The Vietnam government provides yet another local space within which some global discourses have been integrated with local cultural ideologies and social structures. The new Law on Domestic Violence Prevention and Control, approved in 2007, is viewed by some as linking Vietnam to the larger global community. For instance, one counselor of the women's counseling center said, "This law is a great step to respect and improve human rights, especially for women. It proves that Vietnam now has been integrating into the world."

Through the new domestic violence law, the Vietnam government has addressed some of the issues I have raised. Still, while international organization and local NGO personnel influenced the development of this law, the international organizations' emphasis on prioritizing battered women's choices is not found in the law. Instead, this new law "encourages international cooperation in domestic violence and control on the basis of equality," while it simultaneously continues to promote reconciliation of conflicts and disputes through families, clans, institutions, and grassroots reconciling teams (National Assembly 2007, 3, 5). The law also provides for community criticism targeted at perpetrators of domestic violence who are sixteen years old or over, and who have continued to perpetrate domestic violence following attempts at reconciliation by reconciliation teams.

While at least one shelter has been established by international organizations through the Women's Union, the new domestic violence law also encourages the organization of "reliable addresses in the community" (National Assembly 2007, 11). These can be described as shelters or safe houses located within communities where battered women are living, and to which the women can go in times of crisis for temporary residence. Reliable addresses were initiated in Vietnam by NGOs. There are different models for these houses. The house can be that of a family in a community, which is designated and supported by government leaders and the police to protect battered women who seek their assistance. In some of these houses, battered women do not usually sleep overnight, since their doing so may be viewed as inappropriate if a married man lives in the house. But in other models women can sleep in these houses. Some of these programs are funded by international development organizations.

Houses designated as reliable addresses within the communities of the battered women are viewed by many in Vietnam as more culturally appropriate than shelters for battered women, since there is a lower degree of separation of the women from their community and family. One NGO leader pointed out that a woman is expected to live with her family, and therefore it would be very difficult for a battered woman to reintegrate into her community and with her family after living in a shelter, because the woman would be living apart from both and the address of the shelter would not be widely publicized. The NGO leader also asserted that if a battered woman lived in a shelter and then returned home, she would face more danger, because her husband would be angrier than he had been before she left their home and therefore more violent.

One program has organized intervention teams, made up of local community officials, leaders, and members who are trained to counsel battered women and men who batter and who work in conjunction with the houses designated as reliable addresses. The intervention teams actively intervene in wife-battering cases during a crisis. They call on the husband to join the intervention team and his wife to solve the problem immediately, rather than wait until a later time. Yet, there is some concern about the safety of the battered women and the family living in houses designated as reliable addresses, since the batterer continues to live nearby, within the same community.

In regard to economic problems battered women face, a section of the new law on domestic violence states that one of the responsibilities of the Vietnam Women's Union is that of "Organizing vocational training, credit and saving activities to support victims" (National Assembly 2007, 12). This mandate for the Women's Union may aid in increasing the limited funds already being provided to battered women by the local Women's Union organizations and thereby aid in reducing the economic constraints battered women encounter.

The government ideology of maintaining family integrity and the government approaches that involve family and community members' addressing the problem of domestic violence, counter the more individualistic approaches espoused by international programs. While the international health program encourages community participation in preventing and eliminating domestic violence, it also advocates a more individualistic approach to decision making and conflict resolution by battered women. It was sometimes difficult for international organization personnel to integrate these divergent views. For instance, a representative of the international organization that provided funding for the international health program held ambivalent views of the proposed new law on domestic violence. When I spoke with her in 2007, she said:

> I am frustrated that the reconciliation process is still in the law, because they are placing an illusory happy family above individual rights. But I do not want to exclude family needs. On the other hand, I've come to realize

that we need to be careful as outsiders about not recognizing the value placed on family and community in Vietnam by dichotomizing the individual and the family. And by taking these issues head on, we undermine ourselves and Vietnamese local groups who may be trying to seek a delicate balance, and also may themselves see things differently than us. We need to understand the value of the family and the collectivity, and try to think of ways to talk about it that bring out the point of reconciliation occurring at the cost of anybody's rights.

In this discussion, we see an international organization actor grappling with integrating her perspectives of wife battering into the cultural and social context within which she is operating, as she introduces concepts associating gender violence with individual human rights into Vietnam society and implements programs that are based on these new ideologies. This discussion depicts the kinds of culturally and politically based struggles, negotiations, and compromises that occur as international organization personnel introduce transnational ideologies into new social spaces. These kinds of cultural, political, and even economic negotiations also can be found to occur among local frontline workers, as they interpret and implement internationally inspired programs for battered women within the cultural and social contexts in which they work and live.

Power and Ambiguity

Some anthropologists have argued that participation in international development programs can disempower individuals as their lives become reorganized and managed by the development apparatus (Escobar 1995; St. Hilaire 1993). In the international health program addressing wife battering in Vietnam, the implications of participation as personnel and as volunteer community leaders in the program were ambiguous, with some aspects of the program empowering these participants, and others leading to feelings of frustration or dismay.

For instance, association with the international health program provided individuals who worked at the commune level with a new form of authority in relation to men who battered their wives. For some female volunteers in the clubs, overcoming their husband's resistance to the program accorded them the ability to exert agency in preventing wife battering. However, the infusion of Vietnamese cultural ideologies of family into program practices, practical considerations, and problems of dependency on national or international support simultaneously disempowered some of the same participants.

During my research, I attended two meetings of the women's clubs: a Club for Volunteers for Family Happiness meeting, and a Club for Family Happiness meeting.[5] At the monthly meetings of the Club for Volunteers for Family Happiness, women come together to share their experiences of educating men and women about wife battering, and of intervening in battering cases. At the Club for Family Happiness, volunteers discussed similar issues, but in addition some battered women attending the meeting shared their own experiences of battering. Goals of the meetings generally included learning from one another, assisting one another in problem solving, providing support for battered women, and generating solidarity among volunteers as they address wife battering.

Although women in Vietnamese communities may already be highly aware of cases of wife battering within their neighborhoods, the organization and integration of the women into these state-sanctioned clubs provided them with a legitimacy that allowed them to overtly intervene in cases of wife battering. Members of the Vietnam Women's Union had the authority to intervene in cases of wife battering for decades before the introduction of this international health program, particularly when they served on reconciliation committees. Yet, through the mechanism of the new women's clubs, the women's intervention had a different character. Through the development of the new women's clubs, the number of women who were sanctioned to intervene in cases of wife battering was greatly increased. Between fifty and sixty women attended one meeting that I observed, and approximately thirty women, and two men, attended another meeting I observed. One intervention strategy of the women's clubs is very similar to that of the Women's Union, in that the women assist battered women who seek out the help of the club volunteers. However, a different strategy involves club volunteers' seeking out cases of wife battering in their community. During a women's Club for Volunteers for Family Happiness meeting held in the month of July, the president of the club said, "Women, in August, try to find more and more violence, and try to ask other women to arrange their time to attend this meeting monthly and weekly in the small groups. Try to counsel the husbands who are so violent and see whether they beat their wife or not." Through this statement, women are encouraged to seek out cases of violence before battered women request their assistance. During one of the women's club meetings, the president reported that women in the club had counseled fifty-one couples during that month. One member of the club said during the meeting, "Now there are more volunteers who can counsel many people and reconcile the problems in their family."

This international health program has allowed community women working as volunteers to assert some authority in relation to batterers, with their authority legitimated by the state and the internationally sponsored program. This authority may only entail speaking to male batterers to alert them of the women's awareness and surveillance of their abuse of their wife. Yet, with the introduction of the international health program, female volunteers, as well as male volunteers of the men's clubs, can assert power to change men's violent actions toward their wives in an arena from which they had previously felt restricted. Before their involvement in the international health program, many of the volunteers had perceived wife battering to be a private problem of families. Speaking about the intersecting work of the leaders of the international health program's women's clubs and the Women's Union, a woman who is both a women's club and a Women's Union leader said, "After having this [international health] project, we informed and mobilized women, so that now they understand that being beaten is not their problem alone. Instead, it is necessary to denounce the husband's behavior and for the whole society to intervene. It is not a private affair."

A few women said during the club meeting that their own husbands, or the husbands of other women, had initially prohibited their participation in the clubs. One woman said, "Some women are prohibited by their husbands from coming to the club meetings. They are banned by their husbands, but after some time they realize that they [their wives] should come to the club." Women in these cases overcame their husbands' restrictions in order to pursue their own interests and needs, as women and as members of their community. This process can also be viewed as empowering women as they seek to work with battered women and male batterers.

Additionally, medical surveillance by health clinic personnel working directly with battered women has increased in the communities targeted by this international health program. A doctor of a commune health clinic said that since she had received training to recognize signs of wife battering and to respond to them, she and her fellow doctors and nurses have been looking for and finding signs of violence on the bodies of women in their commune. She said, "We also have a counseling center here for battered women. People come here for an annual exam. If the doctors and nurses find signs of violence, they transfer the women to the hospital, where the doctors know better and more treatments to cure them, and they have more advice to give to the women to stop the violence." This doctor was referring to the hospital that houses the women's counseling center I am addressing.

A counselor of the women's counseling center said that the center's staff held meetings with government officials and mass organization leaders of the communes for each battered woman whom they treated in order to seek further social approaches to assisting the women. This process, in turn, increased local government officials and leaders' awareness of men who batter their wives in their community, thus increasing the state's surveillance of these men. This program could potentially weaken the power of men in the community to abuse their wives.

With their new authority to seek out wife battering, rather than passively wait for battered women to approach them, both female and male volunteers and health personnel working directly with battered women and men who batter have become more active in meeting battered women's needs. Their power to effect change in the male batterers' behavior may be undermined to some degree, however, by the volunteers' emphasis on family unity over women's choice.

A frustration expressed by the international health program club leaders was the cutting, and later renewal, of program funds to help support the activities of the commune clubs. More significant, however, was providing club meeting participants with funds that could compensate for their loss of work during the meeting period. One female club leader said that their commune's women's Club for Family Happiness no longer functioned, "Because after two years, the project ended, and the club was no longer active; . . . if we want to form a club like that, we need funding. . . . In fact, if we want to be active, we have to have funding to invite experts and to give [funds] to members who come to the meetings, since this affects the time that they have to work." The latter was viewed as especially important for poor participants. The club leaders felt that the funding provided an incentive for women and men to attend the club meetings. The international health program funding had been terminated following what was later determined to be the first phase of the program. After this initial phase, a professional at the international organization that funded the program said that the organization personnel decided that "the time was right and advantageous to expand the program to two more communes and another hospital." Still, during the second phase of the program, club leaders said they needed further funding. When I asked one club leader, who is also a Women's Union leader, whether there were changes that could be implemented to improve the health care provided for battered women, she said,

"It is necessary to have funding in order to assist them, and then they will be more enthusiastic [to attend the club meetings]."

Another difficulty the frontline workers cope with is a heavy workload. This same club leader also said, "There are both advantages and disadvantages [to the program]. The advantages are that all agencies participate in the program and support each other, and we have the sponsorship of [the international organization]. The difficulties are that we have much work, which overlaps, and sometimes we feel overwhelmed."

While the international health program is oriented toward aiding battered women, and promoting women's ability to cope with their problems, the difficulties that the female club leaders faced as they implemented the program created a sense of dismay and frustration as they worked with limited resources and time.

Conclusion

Global and local ideologies have intersected in multiple ways in Vietnam, as diverse participants of an internationally influenced health program working with battered women have attempted to meet and accommodate these sometimes competing ideologies. While international organizations are powerful forces introducing new meanings of gender inequality, gender violence, marriage, and family into Vietnamese society, Vietnamese individuals working with battered women appropriated new concepts and invested them with their own meanings to generate diverse and at times competing approaches to wife battering. The international health program has aided the battered women it served in many ways and has opened up a new approach to addressing wife battering in both the biomedical and community realms. Yet, while the international health program for individuals affected by gender violence advocated providing women with the right to choose their own course of action, the program did not include initiatives to address structural and cultural constraints, such as class inequalities, or power exerted through government institutions or cultural ideologies of gender and family, on women's ability to make choices in a comprehensive manner. International development programs may also have ambiguous impacts on local participants who serve as frontline workers to assist battered women, such as according them new forms of power while simultaneously limiting their ability to successfully implement the program's goals.

Although a focus of studies of international health and development programs has been on local participants and workers' responses to the programs, international organization professionals may also reinterpret their own approaches in ways that come to meet the contemporary needs of battered women. It is important to also recognize that a single internationally sponsored program addressing wife battering, or gender violence more broadly, may have different influences on battered women because of multiple interpretations that different social actors may have of program ideologies and approaches, and to possible changes in the views of these actors over time.

ACKNOWLEDGMENTS

I am highly grateful to Dr. Le Thi Quy, director of the Research Center for Gender and Development, at the Hanoi University for Social Science and Humanities, and Dr. Nguyen Thi Hoai Duc, director of the Institute for Reproductive and Family Health, of Hanoi, who provided me an affiliation with their institutions and offered their generous guidance and support during my research in Hanoi. I thank my research assistants, Le An Ni and Trinh Phuong My, for their tremendous assistance to me. I extend my deep appreciation to the many members of the Vietnamese communities in which I conducted research who shared their knowledge and valuable insights with me. I am also grateful for the very perceptive and helpful comments of the editors of this volume. The Centers for Disease Control and Prevention (Grant Number R49/CCR811509), the Colorado Injury Control Research Center of Colorado State University, and the Office of the Vice President for Research and Information Technology, Colorado State University, provided generous funding for my research in Vietnam. This chapter's contents are solely the responsibility of the author and do not necessarily represent the official views of these institutions.

NOTES

1. This program name and the names of organizations and individuals in this chapter are pseudonyms, which I use to maintain the confidentiality of the individuals I interviewed.
2. I conducted additional research in Hanoi and a town in the former Ha Tay province in 1997 and 2000, focusing on culturally informed perceptions of wife battering and masculinity. (In 2008, Ha Tay province merged with the city of Hanoi.) This earlier research has also informed my analysis in this chapter.
3. The Vietnam Women's Union is a government-related mass organization that has a network that operates throughout the country. It is "a women's social-political

and developmental organization" that advocates for women's rights and gender equality (Vietnam Women's Union 2002, 2).
4. Currently, this information includes the recently approved Law on Domestic Violence Prevention and Control, but this law had not yet been adopted at the time of my research.
5. I was unable to attend a meeting of a men's club, because they met less frequently than the women's clubs, and no meetings of the men's clubs took place while I was conducting my research.

WORKS CITED

Adelman, Madelaine. 2003. The Military, Militarism, and the Militarization of Domestic Violence. *Violence against Women* 9 (9): 1118–52.

———. 2004. The Battering State: Towards a Political Economy of Domestic Violence. *Journal of Poverty* 8 (3): 45–64.

Alonso, Ana Maria. 2002. "What the Strong Owe to the Weak": Rationality, Domestic Violence, and Governmentality in Nineteenth-Century Mexico. In *Gender's Place: Feminist Anthropologies of Latin America*, ed. R. Montoya, L. J. Frazier, and J. Hurtig, 115–34. New York: Palgrave Macmillan.

Bordo, Susan. 1997. Material Girl: The Effacements of Postmodern Culture. In *The Gender/Sexuality Reader: Culture, History, Political Economy*, ed. R. N. Lancaster and M. di Leonardo, 335–58. New York: Routledge.

Burbank, Victoria Katherine. 1994. *Fighting Women: Anger and Aggression in Aboriginal Australia*. Berkeley: University of California Press.

Erez, Edna, Madelaine Adelman, and Carol Gregory. 2009. Intersections of Immigration and Domestic Violence: Voices of Battered Immigrant Women. *Feminist Criminology* 4 (1): 32–56.

Escobar, Arturo. 1995. *Encountering Development: The Making and Unmaking of the Third World*. Princeton, NJ: Princeton University Press.

Gammeltoft, Tine. 2007. Prenatal Diagnosis in Postwar Vietnam: Power, Subjectivity, and Citizenship. *American Anthropologist* 109 (1): 153–63.

Gutmann, Matthew C. 1996. *The Meanings of Macho: Being a Man in Mexico City*. Berkeley: University of California Press.

Hautzinger, Sarah J. 2007. *Violence in the City of Women: Police and Batterers in Bahia, Brazil*. Berkeley: University of California Press.

International Non-Governmental Organizations (INGOs), Vietnam. 2001. International NGO Perspectives on Reproductive Health in Vietnam: An Invitation to Dialogue. Hanoi.

Kwiatkowski, Lynn. 2008. Political Economy and the Health and Vulnerability of Battered Women in Northern Vietnam. In The Economics of Health and Wellness: Anthropological Perspectives, ed. Donald C. Wood, special issue, *Research in Economic Anthropology* 26: 199–226.

McClusky, Laura J. 2001. *"Here, Our Culture Is Hard": Stories of Domestic Violence from a Mayan Community in Belize.* Austin: University of Texas Press.

McWilliams, Monica. 1998. Violence against Women in Societies under Stress. In *Rethinking Violence against Women,* ed. R. E. Dobash and R. P. Dobash, 111–40. Thousand Oaks, CA: Sage.

Merry, Sally Engle. 2006. *Human Rights and Gender Violence: Translating International Law into Local Justice.* Chicago: University of Chicago Press.

———. 2009. *Gender Violence: A Cultural Perspective.* Malden, MA: Wiley-Blackwell.

Mrsevic, Zorica. 2000. Belgrade's SOS Hotline for Women and Children Victims of Violence: A Report. In *Reproducing Gender: Politics, Publics, and Everyday Life after Socialism,* ed. S. Gal and G. Kligman, 370–92. Princeton, NJ: Princeton University Press.

National Assembly, Socialist Republic of Vietnam. 2007. Law on Domestic Violence Prevention and Control, Law No.: 02/2007/QH12. Hanoi.

Pettus, Ashley. 2003. *Between Sacrifice and Desire: National Identity and the Governing of Femininity in Vietnam.* New York: Routledge.

Pigg, Stacy Leigh. 1997. "Found in Most Transitional Societies": Traditional Medical Practitioners between Culture and Development. In *International Development and the Social Sciences: Essays on the History and Politics of Knowledge,* ed. F. Cooper and R. Packard, 259–90. Berkeley: University of California Press.

Plesset, Sonja. 2006. *Sheltering Women: Negotiating Gender and Violence in Northern Italy.* Stanford: Stanford University Press.

Romedenne, Magali, and Vu Manh Loi. 2006. *Domestic Violence: The Vietnamese Shift.* Hanoi: United Nations Population Fund and Swiss Agency for Development Co-operation.

St. Hilaire, Colette. 1993. Canadian Aid, Women and Development: Re-baptizing the Filipina. *Ecologist* 23 (2): 57–60.

Tran Thi Van Anh, and Le Ngoc Hung. 1997. *Women and đổi mới in Vietnam.* Hanoi: Woman Publishing House.

Viet Nam News. 2007. Divorce on the Rise; Spousal Abuse Blamed. June 29, p. 5.

Vietnam Women's Union. 2002. *Vietnam Women's Union.* Hanoi: Vietnam Women's Union.

Vu Manh Loi, Vu Tuan Huy, and Nguyen Huu Minh. 1999. *Gender-Based Violence: The Case of Viet Nam.* Hanoi: World Bank in Viet Nam.

10

Global Civil Society and the Local Costs of Belonging: Defining Violence against Women in Russia

Julie Hemment

In May 1998, activists from crisis centers all over Russia gathered in Moscow for a conference to discuss the formalization of their thus far loose network into a national association. The conference was a veritable gala. I was stunned to see almost all of my Moscow-based women's movement acquaintances, as well as representatives of the main international foundations and agencies (the Ford Foundation, the Open Society Institute, the American Bar Association, the British Embassy, Amnesty International). Everybody who was anybody in the field of women's community activism and development was there.

At the conference, the theme of universalism sounded loud. The first speakers—mostly representatives of international agencies—emphasized cross-cultural commonality. One of the first to the podium was a British woman, a representative of an expatriate club and a longtime benefactor of antiviolence campaigns. As she put it, "Violence against women is not a Russian problem but an international problem, affecting women of all religious and national backgrounds. We are all vulnerable to violence from men; most of us in this room will have experienced violence at some stage in their lives." She offered words of encouragement to the new network— "My point is that we were where you are now." Her remarks were intended to bring the women in the room together. They were met, however, with weary frustration by some attendees. Nadya, an activist of a Moscow-based group with whom I was well acquainted, muttered, "I always switch off when foreigners speak"; another woman groaned, "Men are people too."[1] Dissent such as this erupted at the margins (during the coffee breaks, in the corridors, in whispered asides). This remark and these objections, however, remained unheard.

This chapter focuses on interactions between Russian women's groups and transnational feminist campaigns during the 1990s. This vignette highlights some of the key tensions of transnational women's activism that this chapter explores: the divisiveness of Western aid, the ambiguous role of nongovernmental organizations (NGOs), and the local costs of belonging in transnational or global campaigns. During the 1990s, the campaign against violence against women was one of the most prominent campaigns of the Russian women's movement. Almost all the main women's organizations participated in it, in some form or another. (Indeed, I was attending the Moscow conference as both researcher and advocate, representing the women's group I worked with to set up a crisis center.) The ubiquity of the issue in Russia testified, however, less to local perceptions of needs than to the success of transnational campaigns and the work of international donor agencies. Beyond limited, elite circles, the work of crisis centers was not understood.

This point raises thorny questions about women's activism and social movements in contemporary conditions of globalization. The effectiveness of the global women's movement surely rests on its ability to heed local concerns. I argue, however, that the campaigns and the logic of grants and funding that drive them impede this process. The framing of violence against women screens out local constructions of events and deflects attention from other issues of social justice, notably the material forces that oppress women. This is a troubling outcome for a movement that intends to challenge the global inequities that contribute to women's marginalization. It suggests that we need to be more attentive to the context within which feminist initiatives are nested. Examining my own participation in the campaigns as a Western scholar and activist, I argue that we need to interrogate our use of Western feminist models and concepts in order to be responsive to local knowledge and to achieve truly democratic transnational engagements.

Russia offers an interesting vantage point from which to interrogate these processes. Russian women's rights activists are relative newcomers to the international stage; bar a few early connections during the Soviet period, they first entered into dialogue with Western feminists following the collapse of the Soviet Union in 1991.[2] As walls and boundaries were dismantled and democratization got under way, feminist scholars and activists rushed to join in solidarity with Russian women; a mass of horizontal relationships formed under the rubric of sister city schemes, academic exchanges, and later, NGO activity. This context helps to explain the tone of the British speaker's remarks. The excitement that was generated by the democratic "revolutions" in the Eastern bloc gave rise to a dizzying sense of possibility and a climate of liberal triumphalism that legitimated this stance and these kinds of interventions.[3] Contrary to what she supposes, however, we were not where they are now. Russian women's activism is shaped by a distinct history and a distinct set of gender alignments. What is more, activism around women's issues emerged not only in the context of the euphoria of democratic change but in the context of intense economic dislocation, too.[4] Women's groups formed in response to the devastation wrought by "shock therapy," the market-oriented economic reforms implemented in the early 1990s by democratic Russian politicians under the tutelage of U.S. and western European economists. These structural adjustment policies led to the dismantling of the social security system and sharp cutbacks in the health care system, affecting women disproportionately. These changes inform their perceptions of needs and definitions of problems.

The best way to evaluate the effectiveness of transnational campaigns is to examine their local manifestations; this "place-based ethnography" does just that (Escobar 2000). Drawing on nineteen months of ethnographic fieldwork conducted between 1997 and 2001, I examine the new crisis centers from the two vantage points my research afforded me—high-profile foundation-sponsored events and interactions with provincial women's groups. Presenting insights gained in the context of an action research project that I undertook with one group, this chapter highlights local contestation about the campaigns, exploring the competing conceptions of the "crisis" facing Russian women that the campaigns displaced. In highlighting these alternative constructions, it examines the extent to which activists were able to translate the issue of gendered violence and to root it in their concerns.

Whence the Transnational Campaigns?

Before considering these local understandings and concerns, I examine the campaigns themselves. The presumed transparency of the issue in international development circles is interesting in itself. Since the 1990s, the campaign against violence against women has had broad resonance across locations. It is assumed to address a universal problem, the content of which is taken for granted, as my opening vignette suggests.

By the late 1990s, violence against women had grown from a feminist issue that concerned women's groups to an international development issue. It had won broad acceptance at the United Nations and is still prioritized by international foundations that work with women's community groups. The campaigns are determinedly transnational. The formulation (or framing, to use the language of recent social movements theory) of violence against women is deliberately inclusive, pitched in terms that encompass diverse social practices—from spousal abuse to female genital mutilation. How was this change achieved?

Gendered violence has long been a concern of local women's movements. In the United States and western Europe, the battered women's movement was a prominent component of second wave organizing. The first women's crisis centers were survivor-led grassroots organizations. The provision of shelters—secret safe houses where female victims of domestic abuse could take temporary refuge—was central to these early campaigns. Elsewhere, women's groups organized around local manifestations of violence—in India around campaigns against dowry deaths, in Latin America against the state-sanctioned violence perpetrated by authoritarian regimes.

Until the late 1980s, gendered violence was a feminist issue and was not regarded with much seriousness at the international level. In the late 1980s and early 1990s, because of the efforts of activists of the international women's movement, the framing of violence against women went global.[5] Margaret Keck and Kathryn Sikkink (1998), in their influential account of the development of transnational advocacy networks (networks of activists that coalesce and operate across national frontiers), explain how the issue achieved such currency. Violence against women emerged in the 1980s as a framing that had the power to unite women from the global North and global South. Until that point, attempts to unify in global campaigns had been largely unsuccessful. Women's rights activists of North and South had been deeply divided and unable to achieve a common agenda. While Northern (or "first world") feminists had been preoccupied with issues of gender discrimination and equality, Southern (or "third world") women were more concerned with issues of social justice and development, which affected both men and women, though in different ways. Violence against women was a framing that could encompass a broad range of practices and hence bring about dialogue between women from different locations.

Its success at the international level was due largely to the innovation of linking women's rights to human rights, bringing together two powerful constituencies for the first time—human rights activists and feminists. Feminist activists first pushed the issue to international prominence at the 1993 Vienna UN human rights conference. Their strategizing coincided with international concern about the systemic use of rape in war in Bosnia, and it was effective. In 1994, the UN High Commission on Human Rights appointed the first special rapporteur on violence against women, and rape in warfare was recognized as a crime against humanity by the Hague Tribunal.

The UN Fourth World Conference on the Status of Women in Beijing, 1995, was a pivotal moment for the success of the framing. Combating violence against women emerged as a central policy agenda of the international women's movement and of international development. The campaigns have galvanized support across diverse constituencies, among politicians and donors. In the late 1980s major U.S. foundations decided to make violence against women a funding priority, channeling funds to NGOs that address the issue.[6] As one American male coordinator of a crisis center training I attended explained to his Russian trainees, "[In the United States] we've found that domestic violence is an easy theme to go to the public with. People give readily. We're at the point where it's politically correct to support this type of organization."

Clearly there is much to celebrate here. Indeed, many feminist scholars regard the prominence of the campaigns as an unqualified success. The campaigns have been analyzed in terms of the increased influence and effectiveness of transnational social movements or transnational advocacy networks.[7] Such accounts are in keeping with celebratory accounts of NGOs and civil society; here, transnational social movements represent the positive, liberatory side of globalization. However, there are alternative, less sanguine ways to view this.

While it is true that transnational campaigns such as these unite women's groups across different locations, they do so at a cost. Aihwa Ong (1996) provides a critical reading of the "strategic sisterhood" that is the basis of this and other North–South alliances in the post-Beijing conference era. She presents it as an alliance driven by the desire of Northern women that ignores geopolitical inequalities and that is insensitive to non–first world cultural values. She argues that transnational campaigns are based on a distinctly individualist formulation of "rights" that is Western specific.[8] The skepticism among activists that I detected in my research points toward similar frustrations in the postsocialist context.

Building on this and other critiques, I wish to introduce a note of caution in my account of the campaigns. First, I suggest that the very success of the framing can also be regarded as its weakness. Although the framing certainly yields cross-cultural clarity, it does so at a cost. At the transnational level, it works insofar as it is a catchall. However, this catchall quality screens out crucial nuances in the ways people define violence against women in different local contexts. In this chapter, I go on to argue that in postsocialist "democratizing" contexts, as in "developing" ones, the framing deflects attention from issues of redistributive justice.

Second, it is important to consider the political-economic context of the campaigns. The issue achieved prominence at a time of crucial shifts in global development agendas. The rise of NGOs and the success of the campaigns took place at a time when a neoliberal vision of development had achieved hegemony. This vision has introduced "a new kind of relationship between the state and civil society and advanced a distinctive definition of the political domain and its participants—based on a minimalist conception of both the state and democracy" (Alvarez, Dagnino, and Escobar 1998, 1). Concerns about these processes have been raised by both scholars and activists, in Southern or "developing" contexts as well as the postsocialist one (see, e.g., Alvarez 1998; Feldman 1997; Kamat 2002; Lang 1997; Paley 2001). Support for NGOs is provided within this new rubric and comes with strings attached; NGOs that accept donor support are required to take on the responsibilities of the retreating state, picking up the slack for the radical free market.[9] What is more, the sudden influx of grants and funding brings about dramatic changes in organizing. Ironically, "NGO-ization" has demobilized social movements. It has contributed to the formation of new hierarchies and allowed former elites to flourish. In many cases it also signals the triumph of Washington- or Geneva-based agendas over local concerns.[10]

The gendered violence campaigns do not operate outside this political-economic context. Indeed, the forces that enable them, the logic that drives them, and their effects demonstrate their complicity. Concern about violence against women originated in the second wave political slogan "The personal is political," which challenged the inviolability of the home and politicized it. The radical critique of patriarchy and gender-based economic inequality, however, that was fundamental to the battered women's movement in the United States and western Europe has fallen out of the transnational campaigns. In a grotesque inversion, the campaigns reprivatize the problem of domestic violence by focusing on interpersonal relations between spouses to the exclusion of structural factors outside, specifically the economic upheavals that most women believe pose the greatest threat to themselves and their families.[11] In a disturbing way, the work of the campaigns thus overlaps with the privatizing intent of neo-liberalism. Indeed, this overlap helps to explain the success of the issue among donors in the West. It is easier to garner support and international outrage around issues concerning sex and that position women as victims than around issues of social justice (Snitow 1999).

Accounting for the Rise of Crisis Centers in Russia: Foundations, Funding, and Feminists

For complex reasons, violence against women is not an issue that local groups were likely to have raised by themselves. The issue was discursively created by the meeting of Western feminists and Russian women activists in the early 1990s. These feminist-oriented Russian women set up the first crisis centers, in Moscow and St. Petersburg and then in provincial cities. In the decade of their existence—a decade of rapid and tumultuous transformations in Russia—the crisis center network has undergone significant change. Donor support has been a key factor in its development, and feminist-oriented Russian activists have played a crucial role as brokers of ideas.

Since their arrival in Russia in the early 1990s, donor agencies have channeled a proportionally small but ideologically significant portion of civil society aid to women's groups. They met with a diverse range of women's organizations. While some set up during the mid-1980s, when Mikhail S. Gorbachev's liberalizing reforms permitted the formation of independent groups for the first time, most were founded in the early to mid-1990s in response to the dislocations of the market I have described. And while some had their roots in official Soviet-era women's organizations (*zhensovety*), others regarded themselves as determinedly independent from the former regime. A small but prominent minority identified as feminist. These groups of highly educated women were mostly clustered in institutes and universities. Familiar with Western academic literature, they brought insights from Western feminism to bear on Soviet gender relations and on the effects of political and economic reform. They were also committed to practice and spearhead attempts to bring about unity among women's groups, organizing two Independent Women's Movement forums in 1991 and 1992. This latter group found itself particularly well positioned to take advantage of the new opportunities of democratization aid. Members' knowledge of foreign languages, experience of travel, and familiarity with liberal democratic and Western feminist concepts made for easy dialogue with the representatives of donor agencies. The crisis centers they founded, often in collaboration with Western feminist activists, were greeted enthusiastically by international donor agencies and were among the first women's projects to receive support.

Although these initiatives won a great deal of international attention, they were less successful at home. The Independent Russian Women's Movement was marginal in Russia and did not have broad support. On the contrary, most men and women regarded women's groups with suspicion and hostility, particularly those that identified as "feminist."[12] For complex reasons, there is no commonly shared perception of gender discrimination in Russia or other former socialist states. As many scholars have noted, the commonly held notion is that the socialist state "spoiled" both men and women, emasculating men and making women too aggressive and assertive, denying them natural expression of difference and self-realization *(samorealizatsiia)*.[13] Men and women perceived themselves to be equally victimized by the state. As Watson (1997, 25) puts it, "Under state socialism, society was excluded as a whole, and citizens, far from feeling excluded relative to each other, were held together in a form of political unity."

I found that among feminist-oriented women's projects, crisis centers were regarded with particular incomprehension and skepticism. Indeed, even some women activists involved in the campaigns admitted that they did not think gendered violence was the most pressing issue facing Russian women and expressed concern that so many resources were put into it.

There was plenty of conflict in the private realm in the USSR. However, women with violent spouses were unlikely to recognize their experience in terms of gendered violence. Crisis centers are premised on a set of property relations that are bourgeois and on an alignment of public and private that is liberal democratic. They presume that women are economically dependent on men and stuck in the private sphere. This presumption was not true for Soviet women, who were brought into the workforce and guaranteed formal equality by the socialist "paternalist" or "parent" state (Verdery 1996, 63). Soviet-era property arrangements also complicate the picture. The nationalization of all property meant that there was no ideology of private ownership to give Soviet citizens the illusion of domestic inviolability. Many Soviet citizens lived in the notorious communal apartments, sharing kitchen and bathroom facilities with their neighbors. What is more, few married couples lived autonomously as nuclear families. Chronic housing shortages meant that many people lived with extended family, grandparents, in-laws, and siblings. For all these reasons, domestic conflict most commonly expressed itself in the form of tension over rights to living space, interpersonal strife, or alcoholism. Although patterns are certainly changing with the introduction of a free market, lack of housing remains the most chronic problem. Indeed, the persistence of this problem helps to explain why women's shelters have not taken off in Russia.[14]

A further obstacle to crisis centers has been that during state socialism the private sphere was constituted as a kind of "refuge" for both men and women. It was considered to be a site of authenticity against the morally compromised public sphere, and its integrity was jealously guarded by women and men alike (Verdery 1996). In the late 1990s, the private sphere remained a (reconstituted) refuge for most Russian people, a site of precious and sustaining networks that offset the violence and chaos that were perceived to be "outside" (mafia, crime, corruption, poverty). Although levels of familial violence appear to have increased in the post-Soviet period, most women do not consider it the most pressing problem.[15] Furthermore, as many crisis center workers acknowledge, Russian women who have experienced sexual or domestic violence are commonly mistrustful of attempts from outside to intervene.

Until 1995, crisis centers were marginal offshoots of the Independent Russian Women's Movement, and though they were celebrated in international circles, their work was little understood at home. Despite this lack of fit, in the mid-1990s, the antiviolence campaigns in Russia underwent a qualitative shift. As "violence against women" became an international development issue, more funds were allocated to it and crisis centers moved from being small, rather peripheral offshoots of the women's movement to become third sector heavyweights, a central plank of the independent women's movement and a showpiece of foundation-NGO relations.[16]

The transnational campaigns brought a key resource to Russian women's groups—a model around which to organize. This model is accompanied by skills and methods that can be transferred and taught. For activists, the crisis center model offers a blueprint and a framework. Neat, easy to learn, it has become a kind of do-it-yourself NGO kit. Foundation support has financed the production of easy-to-use materials—brochures, posters, and handbooks, including one titled, *How to Create a Women's Crisis Center*.[17] The Moscow-based network offers trainings, assisted by foundation support. Along with crisis counseling and nondirective listening skills (the hallmark skills of crisis centers), they teach management, NGO development, and public relations.

Russian crisis centers have adopted what they call the "international model" and work to a specific set of standards. Through telephone hotlines and individual consultations, they provide free and confidential legal and psychological counseling to female victims of sexual or domestic violence. Counselors undergo eighty hours of training, run by staff of the most experienced centers with input from feminist psychologists, scholars, and lawyers.

What does all this mean to Russian activists? While I insist on the need to situate my study of Russian crisis centers within this "broader political geography" (Gal and Kligman 2000, 4), I do not mean to suggest that the global blocks out the local or to describe the flow of ideas as unidirectional. Recent scholarship of globalization has argued persuasively against this kind of determinism, and feminist scholars are prominent in the discussion (see, e.g., Gibson-Graham 1996; Grewal and Kaplan 1994). Russian women activists draw on international aid and Western models as resources, translating them as necessary. In the process, projects and campaigns are transformed, not imported statically. How do these "traveling discourses" (Gal and Kligman 2000) arrive, what are the processes of "translation" they undergo (Tsing 1997), and with what do they interact as they are "glocalized"?

In the course of my research in 1995–1997, I found that the notion of crisis center did have a kind of local resonance. Once again, the violence-against-women framing caught on because of its catchall quality. Here, however, the keyword was not violence (*nasilie*) but crisis (*krizis*). One of the things that struck me in the course of my research was the ubiquity of the notion of crisis center (*krizisnyi tsentr*). I came across many women (out of the loop of trainings and unfamiliar with the international model) who expressed their intent to set one up or described their work (unconnected with sexual or domestic violence) to be "something like a crisis center." I came to relate this rhetorical persistence to the fact that the whole of Russian society is perceived to be in crisis—with good cause. In addition to the perception of social and economic breakdown, the Russian crisis is also perceived to be a psychic condition—there is a great deal of talk about the neuroticization of society.

The Perspective from the Provinces: Competing Crises and the Displacement of the Economic

Zhenskii Svet (Women's Light) is a small university-based women's group, dedicated to women's education and consciousness raising. It was founded in the provincial city Tver' in 1991, long before the arrival of Western foundations, in the first wave of independent organizing in Russia. Its founder was Larisa, a professor of history who had written her dissertation on the Western women's movement, one of Russia's few self-identified feminists.[18] One of the reasons I originally made contact with this group was that it claimed to have a crisis center.[19] But I arrived to find that this was not so. While the notion of crisis center did exist within the group, it had not quite taken root. The idea had been introduced to the group in 1992 by some visiting German feminists; the project collapsed, however, when the Germans failed to secure funding, and local interest had since waned. When I asked group members to elaborate about this, they told me that sexual and domestic violence was something they had not really thought much about. It was a terrible thing, but they did not feel any real connection to it. They also insisted that women would not come together around this issue, because it was too private. They could not see how such a project could work in Tver'.

The idea of crisis center, however, had remained in the group, in diffuse forms. Katia was the custodian of one of these crisis center plans. An unemployed woman in her fifties, she attended *Zhenskii Svet* regularly. I met frequently with her during my stay in Tver' in 1997. Katia explained that she was not concerned with dealing with the female victims of sexual violence. She intended her crisis center, or "anti-crisis center" (*anti-krizisnyi tsentr*) as she preferred to call it, to be a service to assist women who encounter economic discrimination (*ekonomicheskaia diskriminatsiia*), or (gendered) discrimination in the workplace. This was a new term to refer to a new phenomenon, since the Soviet regime had an ideological commitment to both full employment and gender equality. She understood that in the United States and western Europe, a crisis center was a service for the victims of sexual and domestic violence but argued that in Russia such a conception did not make sense. She insisted that although sexual violence was indisputably a terrible thing, it was a much less widespread problem than economic violence and discrimination, which touched almost every woman's life.

As I pieced her story together, I came to regard it as a classic survivor's narrative. She had encountered "discrimination" in her own life and now wanted to set up a service to assist women in similar situations. Two years ago before I met her, Katia was pressured to quit her job as a sociological analyst at the Federal Employment Service when initially generous state funding was cut back. Forced to make layoffs, her boss began to exert pressure (*davlenie*) on some members of the staff to leave. To leave, as it were, of their own volition (so the company might avoid paying unemployment benefits). Although both men and women staffed the office, he targeted the women in the group. Katia experienced this treatment as a profound "crisis," as did her female colleagues, who went through the same process. She told me that it was the first time she and her coworkers had had to face the idea of unemployment. She was shocked at the callous disregard of her rights. She was shocked at how her boss, a former *military officer*, she emphasized, had "pressed" her to leave. Agitated by the memory, she told me that the pressure was so intense that one woman had been "on the verge of a heart attack." Katia's account evoked the profoundly destabilizing social dislocation she and her colleagues had experienced at this time. Unemployment was distressing to her not merely because of the financial burden it placed on her but because it was an attack on her dignity, on her very identity, her sense of self. It also cast a blow to her worldview. She was shaken by the fact that a person of education and high social standing (an officer) had behaved in this way.

In many ways, Katia's story is paradigmatic of women's early non-governmental organizing in Russia. Regardless of how they described themselves, of the educational levels of their members, their location or ideological hue, in the early 1990s women's groups were engaged in a common purpose. They were survival mechanisms, set up for and by women who were hard hit by social and economic reform. Involvement in this activity goes beyond a concern with the gendered effects of the market and is frequently driven by a generalized perception of material, moral, and psychological crisis. In their different ways, these organizations have taken on the challenge of creating new forms of social solidarity and togetherness following the collapse of the Soviet collective.

Although Katia's conception of crisis center emphasizes structural factors—economic violence attributable to the market and shock therapy and their gendered effects—hers is neither a straightforwardly "feminist" nor anticapitalist construction. Indeed, she did not address her sense of discrimination toward men as a group or toward the institutions whose policies contributed to it (the International Monetary Fund, or the Russian government). Instead, she addressed herself to the absent, retreating Soviet state. She had been able to find a state agency that had overturned the decision. Although she had not been awarded material compensation, she had received symbolic recognition of the injustice of her dismissal. She intended her crisis center to be a project that would provide similar assistance to local women.

Katia's case perhaps looks idiosyncratic. In many ways, she represents a prior understanding of crisis center, one that preceded the arrival of foundation support. However, I found echoes of her understandings elsewhere. Between 1995 and 1997, before the action research project in Tver', I visited crisis centers in St. Petersburg and several provincial cities. These visits provided alternative insights and left me with quite different impressions of the antiviolence campaigns than those I received in Moscow. Although they formally adopted the crisis center model (the "international standard"), many of these centers had much broader programs in response to local needs. As the director of one provincial crisis center told me, "We go to these Moscow-based seminars, workshops, and conferences, but our agendas are still driven by local concerns." Because these centers are raising the issue of violence against women for the first time, only a relatively small proportion of clients call to discuss it. All the counselors I spoke with confirmed that when they first set up, a wide range of people called their hotlines. Men called as well as women, and, strikingly, a lot of pensioners—in sum, those who felt marginalized and vulnerable. I was told that people called to speak about diverse issues—unemployment, unpaid wages, loneliness, alcoholism, and loss of children to the military service, as well as domestic or sexual violence. As one St. Petersburg–based activist put it, "There is great confusion now, the old system is broken down, but it's not clear what is emerging. People are confused, and there is a great demand for information. They don't know what to ask for, whom to speak to, how to name their problems." Centers have responded to these concerns in different ways; some speak to all callers, others only to female victims of violence. One center in Sergiev-Posad abandoned its women-only focus for a few years in response to local incomprehension.

Counselors in all the centers I visited informed me that women who do call to speak about gendered violence frequently relate it to a range of other materially based issues, such as unemployment, impoverishment, and cramped living space. In response to such calls, counselors focus on the woman in a broader social context, particularly on the family. Activists in provincial cities, where they may provide the only women-oriented services, conclude that it makes no sense to specialize too narrowly. They say it is impossible to separate the problem of domestic or sexual violence from other issues women face. In general, counselors assign a high priority to clients' material problems. In one St. Petersburg center, survivor support groups place great emphasis on practical steps women can take, to the extent that members of some of these groups have gone into business together.

These constructions could work to inform the work of the transnational feminist movement, and these critiques could be the basis for dialogue. The effectiveness of the global women's movement surely rests on its ability to heed local concerns. As Ellen Dorsey (1997, 355) puts it, we need to "carefully tread the line between building common strategies and reflecting the actual concerns and dynamism of the movement on the ground" lest the movement be discredited. There are, however, some serious systemic impediments. First, the logic of grants and funding encourages groups to adopt the themes and terminologies prioritized by donors, making issues that fall outside this rubric unnarratable. Second, NGO staff and donor representatives are frequently not disposed to listen to these commentaries.[20] For both these reasons, crisis centers experience great pressure to conform to the "international model."

Furthermore, I found that the rubric of the crisis center and the technologies that accompanied it brought about significant changes in the ways both staff and their clients formulated the problems facing women, making the articulation of critiques and counter strategies still less likely. In Russia, technologies and methods that are designed to empower women—such as nondirective active listening—ironically work against empowerment insofar as they dissuade clients and counselors from articulating their material concerns. Techniques of nondirective active listening require callers to come to their own solutions. Crisis centers provide information and consultations (on legal issues and social services) but encourage clients to take part in the defense of their rights and make their own decisions. While most centers offer free legal advice, their main message is frequently what not to expect from the state. The director of one center told me, "Their first question is always, 'What will the state do for me [as a battered woman] if I get divorced?' I explain that they have little realistic chance of getting help." In survivor support groups, she works to make women aware of these material and political issues, to recognize that the state is not going to help them, and that the only way forward is to help themselves.

Tver' and *Zhenskii Svet*: Adopting the Western Model

This dynamic became clear to me during my interactions with *Zhenskii Svet*. The action research process that I undertook with members of *Zhenskii Svet* brought the two models of crisis center I have outlined into competition.[21] Katia's "anti-crisis center" for unemployed women was pitched against a "crisis center" for female victims of domestic and sexual violence that accepted the framing of violence against women backed by the transnational campaigns. The latter won out. It won not because it best expressed members' idea of the most important problem facing local women in Tver' but because it was considered most likely to succeed. In crucial ways, as facilitator of the seminar and as a Western outsider with resources to bring to the project, I was the arbiter.[22] The latter model had two advantages. It had broad legitimacy among two key constituencies—Western donor agencies and actors of the local administration—and it was organizationally viable. Both characteristics were consequences of international donor involvement and the success of transnational feminist campaigns.

Through the action research project, I was able to lend my energies to the group as it negotiated the contradictory nongovernmental field. In this context, my status as a Western outsider and my familiarity with donor priorities became a valuable resource that group members were able to deploy. In the course of my fieldwork, I had amassed a great deal of information about women's crisis centers and realized that the network offered great possibilities for provincial women's groups. I shared this information with members of *Zhenskii Svet*.

Some of the women began to see the founding of a crisis center as a way to strengthen and institutionalize some of the more socially oriented programs offered by *Zhenskii Svet*. They saw it as a potential base from which already existing projects could be run and as a place where young women could gain work experience. A key player in this project was Tamara, a doctor and one of the newest and most enthusiastic participants of the group. An assertive, practical woman in her mid-thirties, she had recently moved to Tver' from Siberia with her family when her engineer husband lost his job. She worked part-time at one of the local hospitals, renting office space with another doctor, drawing a meager salary, and offering free seminars in women's health through *Zhenskii Svet*.

When I met her, she was looking for a niche, a place to which she could bring her considerable energies and that would allow her independence. "I'm not afraid of hard work," she told me. "The main thing is that I am committed to what I do." She dreamed of being able to bring about a unity between what she called her hobby (issues of women's health, the women's movement) and her career. The idea of setting up a crisis center appealed to Tamara because it most closely approximated the "concrete social project" she wanted to be involved in. Her own economic vulnerability meant that she was attuned to the plight of women in the city, and she wanted to do something practical to meet their needs. Furthermore, she was persuaded by the issue of gendered violence. As a doctor, she had noticed that many of her female patients had bruises under their clothes. "It was obvious that some of them had violent spouses, but there was no way to talk to them about it," she said.

In summer 1998, with the endorsement of other members of *Zhenskii Svet*, Tamara and I embarked on a preparatory project to set up a crisis center for women in Tver'. Our aims were to learn more about existing services and to locate sources of financial and material support. We met with members of the local administration and staff of the local social security services and traveled to Moscow and several provincial cities to visit and learn from other crisis centers. The strategy was successful. The Tver' project coincided with a specific moment of expansion in the network of crisis centers. It was seeking to reregister itself as a national association and was eager to find more collaborators throughout the Russian Federation. To this end, its sponsors provided start-up funds for new centers and were glad to make the acquaintance of a provincial woman activist, well versed in the tenets of the international women's movement. At the same time, in Tver' local conditions were ripe. Since the mid-1990s, "women's issues" have had political currency in Russia. Throughout the regions of the Russian Federation, officials are now mandated to undertake steps to provide services for women. In this way, *crisis center* has entered the lexicon of government officials and social services personnel and is on the books. We won the support of two key political figures in the city—the mayor (who was preparing for reelection) and the president's representative to the *oblast'* (a female journalist with an insecure political base who had begun to dabble in the "women's movement" to generate support for herself in the city). They were only too happy to make the acquaintance of a community group willing to undertake such an endeavor.

The center set up in fall 1998. Tamara pulled together a group of interested women who were prepared to start work on a voluntary, unpaid basis and led seminars based on the training she had received in Moscow. At the outset of the project, she acknowledged that she saw setting up a crisis center as a pragmatic move. If it took off, it would make a good umbrella project under which already existing projects could continue to run and new ones could be devised. She saw it as a pilot project through which she could discover what local women perceive their real problems to be.

As I followed the crisis center's development between 1998 and 2003 when it closed down, I was able to trace the shifting perceptions of its staff and volunteers. In the first months of its existence, gendered violence was very much on the periphery of the project. The first clients who came to the center were either already personally acquainted in some way with staff members or were chance passersby. These women did not talk about domestic violence but discussed instead a variety of other, mostly materially based problems. When I asked them about their plans for the near future,

Tamara and other staff and volunteers talked about setting up a variety of other projects within the center to meet local women's needs—a "work therapy" club (designed to help local women go into business together and consider economic strategies), a social club, and seminars in cosmetology and women's health. Tamara confided that in some ways she regretted focusing so directly on sexual and domestic violence. She told me, "Women who really experience this will rarely come forward to talk about it—I uncover it in conversations, it lies buried, it is very often a source of grief, but in focusing on it, we scare women away."

She gave a very different account when we met in Boston in February 2000 while she was attending a training course for Russian professionals working on domestic violence. She exhibited increasing self-confidence, both in her own position and in the validity of the crisis center narrative. She told me that much had changed since a telephone had been installed in August 1999. It enabled the center to finally open a hotline for women (*telefon doveriia*), and as soon as the service was advertised the center had been inundated with calls. There was a great appetite in the city for telephone hotlines, and (particularly) for free psychological counseling. She explained that the hotline was open from nine to six every day except weekends and that they received between fifty and seventy calls a month, of which between six and fifteen pertained to domestic violence.

I asked her to tell me about the issues clients raised. She told me that many came to discuss problems in their relationships (*vzaimootnoshenie*) with the people they live with—alcoholism or conflicts over living space after divorce. I asked her how many of these people had experienced domestic violence. She paused to consider and told me that in each case there was an element of domestic violence. However, this term was loosely defined. One woman came to speak of problems with her mother, another about difficult relations with her sister. The rest came to discuss issues with their spouses. Tamara told me that she was surprised that women were willing to come forward and to talk about their problems, however they define them, and that she was surprised too that people do speak about forms of domestic violence. "The need is real," she said.

She had devised an interesting strategy to overcome the problem of women's reluctance to speak of "domestic violence." Center staff have two distinct modes of representing their work. They advertise the hotline as a generalized service, as a hotline for women (*telefon doveriia dlia zhenshchin*), "so we don't scare women away." Beginning in fall 1999, the center ran a couple of support groups, which staff advertised as a "support group for women" (*gruppa podderzhki dlia zhenshchin*), not specifying spousal abuse. When speaking with clients, they avoid terminology that might alienate women; they do not use the terms violence (*nasilie*) or violent behavior (*nasil'stvennoe povedenie*) but speak instead of controlling behavior (*kontroliruiushchee povedenie*). Likewise, they do not refer to the violator (*nasil'nik*) but the offender (*obidchik*). They discuss the myths (*mify*) and prejudices (*predubezhdeniia*) surrounding rape and domestic violence. Meanwhile, they use the language of the campaigns and speak of domestic violence, or violence against women, in their outreach and educational work, for example, when speaking to the media, when lobbying the mayor, and when giving lectures to students of the university, of the police academy, or to lawyers.

Tamara attributes the success of the project to the framing of violence against women. As she put it, "It was important for us to define a specific area of activity in order to achieve this. If we had chosen to deal with violence more broadly, or with economic issues, or with alcoholism as some people suggested, we wouldn't have been able to do it." She told me that the main achievement of the past six months is that the center now has a name, an image (*imadzh*) in the city. She was able to overcome local skepticism precisely because of the international support that the project has won. The symbolic aspect of this support was as important as the material; she had used it as a bargaining chip in negotiations with local power brokers, and it had won her the grudging support of those who were very skeptical about the issue.

As is clear from the account she gave me that day, what appears to have changed most markedly is Tamara's own sense of conviction. Women came with similar problems as previously. But she was more convinced of the efficacy of her project and more tightly socialized into the campaigns. I tried to push her to reflect on these changes. What did these shifts in orientation mean to her? I gained no sense that she was torn by the changes. Rather, she was clearly proud about her work and its success. "We've come a long way," she told me. "There used to be no language for this kind of thing. Now the authorities have been forced to recognize the problem."

Our final conversations about the center revealed a greater degree of ambivalence. When I returned to Tver' in summer 2001, I found Tamara preoccupied with new questions. Although eloquent about the importance of her work, she was alive to its contradictions and eager to discuss the ambivalence of collaboration with donor agencies. We discussed these issues with Natasha, a crisis center colleague from a neighboring city. In the course of our conversation it became clear that the two women were dissatisfied and baffled by foundation policies and felt unheard by foundation representatives. Although they felt that they were doing useful work, they were frustrated that so much time was taken up by bureaucratic activities. What is more, they felt constrained. Grants permit and exclude specific activities, down to the themes of trainings. Natasha explained that agency evaluators had recently visited her center, and it was absolutely clear to her that they were not interested in the content of the center's activities. "They just need pretty numbers, they don't need to hear my thoughts (*raz-myshlenie*) about our work," she said. Further, they were concerned that donors were moving away from supporting the theme of *nasilie* (violence). The new theme, she continued, was *torgovlia liud'mi* (trafficking). Tamara nodded, saying, "We have to be like chameleons to please the foundations. Even if you don't want to take it [trafficking] on, you have to!"

Finally, they had begun to feel a sense of futility about the work they had been encouraged into. They had successfully raised an issue that both felt was real and important, but at the same time, they were aware that it was nested within a host of other concerns. As with the other crisis centers I came across, they found that their clients came to discuss a wide variety of issues. Although they were frequently able to locate (or "uncover") an element of domestic violence in clients' accounts (whether it be verbal or psychological abuse, economic pressure, or actual physical violence carried out by spouses or male relatives), clients most pressingly made reference to material problems that affected both them and their families. Tamara and Natasha's work with women uncovered issues that they felt powerless to address—problems connected with unemployment, unpaid wages, the crisis of living space. "All we can offer is psychological support. It doesn't resolve the main issues," Tamara lamented. "We can't solve the material problems." Natasha agreed, saying, "The global attention to solving women's problems must be the business of the government! Housing, the police, the law—it's too much on our shoulders!"

Indeed, these remarks were to prove prophetic. The crisis center closed in 2003 because of some of the problems these women named. The project lost a crucial local ally when the city mayor suddenly died. His death left the center institutionally vulnerable; staff were unable to defend the center from demands for rent payment from the city legislature. Meanwhile, international funding proved to be a fragile source of support. Center staff were able to secure only modest and sporadic funding from foundations at the best of times, and starting in 2001, these agencies began to redirect their resources to the new hot topic of sex trafficking.

Conclusions

I have tried to convey the local meanings that get screened out by the international renditions of the violence against women campaigns. So what lessons for the transnational women's movement can we draw from this specific case?

While it is important to celebrate the success of the crisis center network in terms of the economic and political opportunities it provides local women, we also need to critically interrogate the success of the campaigns and to be aware of their discursive effects. Within contemporary conditions of globalization, transnational gender politics operates as a mode of power that constitutes some women and some issues as deserving, excluding others (Mindry 2001). Indeed, understanding these effects helps us interpret the skepticism of some of the women involved in the campaigns, such as Nadya, whose comments I began with.

Skepticism about these campaigns testifies to the fact that many people experience these campaigns and similar ones as primitivizing. In the 1990s, "violence against women" became an international development issue, a marker to gauge the "civilization" of states. According to this yardstick, despite the collapse of the political, military, and conceptual boundaries of the Cold War, Russia remains as far away from the West as ever before. In fact, ironically, rather than drawing closer, in the 1990s it slipped backward (from Soviet gender equality to a place of "uncivilized" gender relations). I believe that it was precisely this discursive effect that many of my interlocutors objected to. Furthermore, the framing used by the international campaigns has the ideological effect of obscuring the fact that violence against women is structurally endemic within liberal-democratic capitalist regimes. It is not so much that liberal democratic "civil" society is not violent but that the system allows for the existence (and occasionally encourages the provision) of services to mop it up. Making gender and violence a marker of development obscures a fact that both crisis counselors and their clients know very well—that all forms of violence, including gendered violence, have been exacerbated by structural adjustment, the very liberalizing project that was supposed to bring civility to Russia. No wonder those engaged in the ideological work of these campaigns feel ambivalent about them.

The discursive prominence of terms such as *crisis center* and *violence* and their prioritization exemplifies some troubling aspects of Western democratization aid. The prominence of the issue of violence against women can be read as part of a broader trend, marking a discursive privatization of the social dislocation accompanying transition and a depoliticization of the economic. Stopping up the gaps of the radical free market, services such as crisis centers act as mediators, educating Russian people into the new order. The individualizing, economizing discourses that these centers put out ("self-help," "self-reliance") educate people out of politics, out of expecting anything from the crumbling and retreating state. The winning out of the "international model" marks an abandonment of attempts to tackle structural problems, as my examples from Tver' reveal. Interestingly, both Tamara's and Katia's crisis center projects foreground issues of individual change and development, rather than structural issues, and there is little critical discussion of the path of democratization and development. One of the last things Tamara said to me was that women need to be educated out of the "myth" that domestic violence has material roots. Here, she was making the feminist argument that domestic violence could not be justified as a response to economic hardship. Still, in her ready adoption of this framing, I see her as still taking on the old socialist state and its discredited, materialist ideologies, perhaps not fully aware of the implications of the new ideology that is taking its place. Meanwhile, over time the element of structural critique dropped out of Katia's "anti-crisis" center plan. Whereas formerly she had at least implicitly addressed the state and the illegality of economic discrimination and dismissals, she began to speak only in terms of psychological support. Her new project description was "to afford psychological support to women who are suffering the consequences of loss of work."[23]

This, however, is not the full story. My Tver' case study shows how the model of crisis center was appropriated and embraced and deployed by Russian women activists during the 1990s to various different ends. The women of *Zhenskii Svet*, like many other activists, made a pragmatic, strategic decision to set up a crisis center. They were to some extent coerced into the framing, yet they were able to reappropriate it in key ways. The crisis center met group needs and objectives that preceded the arrival of Western funding. It became an important discursive site where social dislocation and confusion were explored and made sense of, where needs could be defined and named and survival strategies formulated. Like other NGOs, it was a dynamic site in which people negotiate the past and the present. No less significantly, it offered an effective niche, a foothold for those who worked there, contributing to the creation of new forms of solidarity and togetherness. What is more, crisis centers brought nongovernmental women's activists into dialogue with state agencies, contributing to important realignments between spheres.

I regard my colleagues' appropriation of the model as an ambivalent thing—it is part co-optation, part self-justification, and part testimony to a new formulation of gendered violence. Work conducted in the center both embraced and exceeded the gendered violence narrative. In their commentaries I see the germ of a critique and the potential formulation of a collective, or at least less individualistic response to gendered violence that could be useful to us all.

ACKNOWLEDGMENTS

This chapter is based on nineteen months of ethnographic fieldwork conducted in Moscow, Tver', and Pskov between 1995 and 2001; I dedicate it with gratitude to Valentina Uspenskaia and Oktiabrina Cheremovskaia. I am grateful to the Cornell Graduate School, the Einaudi Center for International Studies, and the Cornell University Peace Studies Program for financial support. I would like to thank Elizabeth Armstrong, Nanette Funk, Davydd Greenwood, Nancy Ries, and particularly Michele Rivkin-Fish for their thoughtful and critical engagement with earlier drafts and for their encouragement of these ideas. I would also like to thank the editors of *Signs* and the reviewers for their detailed comments.

NOTES

1. Following anthropological conventions, I use pseudonyms to protect the identity of the women activists I worked with in my research.
2. The official Soviet Women's Committee delegations had connections with some Western feminist activists during the Soviet period. Further, Western feminist texts circulated clandestinely through *samizdat* during the 1970s and 1980s, and there were limited connections between individual dissidents and Western feminist activists.
3. For critical discussions of this topic, see, e.g., Berdahl 1999; Borneman 1992; Verdery 1996; Wedel 1998.
4. Recent feminist scholarship has drawn attention to the gendered effects of democratization and transition, pointing to the ways it has marked the demotion of women as a group in Russia and other postsocialist countries (e.g., Bridger, Kay, and Pinnick 1996; Gal and Kligman 2000; Verdery 1996; Watson 1997).
5. The UN Convention on the Elimination of All Forms of Discrimination against Women (CEDAW), which was adopted in 1979 and entered into force in 1981, makes no mention of violence, rape, abuse, or battery. By mid-1995, however, violence against women had become a "common advocacy position" of the women's movement and the human rights movement (Keck and Sikkink 1998).
6. The Ford Foundation played a significant role in determining patterns of funding and led the way in funding campaigns against violence against women.

While in 1988 major U.S. foundations awarded eleven grants totaling $241,000, in 1993 they made sixty-eight grants totaling $3,247,800 (Keck and Sikkink 1998, 182).

7. See Keck and Sikkink 1998. Sperling, Ferree, and Risman 2001 provides a nuanced account of Russian women's activism in the context of the development of the transnational women's movement, bringing new social movement theory to bear on the changes of the past decade. Their study documents the first phase of Western donor support to Russian women's groups in the early to mid-1990s.

8. Drawing on data from China, Indonesia, and Malaysia, Ong 1996 gives examples of alternative strategies. Gayatri Chakravorty Spivak 1996 presents a similar critique of the Beijing Conference and its colonialist characteristics.

9. Alvarez, Dagnino, and Escobar (1998, 22) introduce the concept of "APSAs" to describe the new service-oriented NGOs that are encouraged into being by international foundations and donor agencies. They regard them as band-aids, palliatives, hopelessly compromised by the role they play in stopping up the gaps of the free market.

10. For discussions of how "NGO-ization" has influenced women's movements, see, e.g., Alvarez 1998; Lang 1997. For a consideration of these issues in the formerly socialist states of central Europe and Eastern Europe and the former Soviet Union, see Abramson 1999; Richter 1999; Snitow, 1999; Sperling 2000.

11. I am grateful to Michele Rivkin-Fish for suggesting the formulation of reprivatization in relation to the international campaigns against domestic violence.

12. Another explanation for this skepticism toward women's groups is that women's organizing was enforced and managed from above by the Soviet state, in a network of official women's departments and councils. Further, feminism was discredited by Bolshevik and Soviet leaders, who labeled it a Western reformist phenomenon (Noonan and Rule 1996, 77).

13. For discussions of state socialist gender arrangements and the corresponding absence of a sense of gender discrimination, see Gal and Kligman 2000; Verdery 1996; Watson 1997.

14. I met many crisis center activists who were keen to establish shelters. They acknowledged, however, that local conditions made it impossible for them to do so. First, it was difficult to obtain premises from local authorities. Second, it was unclear where to relocate women once they had been admitted. While in western Europe and the United States the shelter is a temporary refuge, a stopgap for women and their families before they find their feet, in Russia people have quite literally nowhere to move on to.

15. According to data published in 1995, 14,400 cases of rape were recorded in the Russian Federation in 1993. In the same year, 14,500 women were reported to have been murdered by their husbands or male partners (Attwood 1997, 99).

16. Foundation representatives I spoke with frequently cited the crisis center network as one of the most successful women's NGO projects.

17. The Canadian Embassy funded the publication of the book. According to one of its Russian authors, five thousand copies were distributed to nascent crisis centers and women's NGOs (Zabelina 1996).

18. Its feminist and democratic orientation made the group unusual. It can, however, be considered exemplary of the early clubs and groups founded in academic circles by women familiar with feminist texts and the Western women's movement.

19. I first learned about the group in 1995 from the Network of East-West Women electronic listserv. New women's groups, which had just been hooked up on the Internet, announced and introduced themselves and listed their interests. Groups tended to make broad declarations rather than itemize existing services. This practice was very much of the times, before the standardization associated with NGOs had become widespread.

20. I found that many North American or western European feminists viewed discussions of economic factors as a rationalization for male-perpetrated violence. The standard response was the assertion that rich men also beat their wives. Though of course this statement is true and important, in this context it is extraordinarily dismissive of local concerns and shows little awareness of the extent of economic dislocation in Russia and its devastating effects on the lives of women and their families.

21. In brief, participatory action research (PAR) is a social change methodology involving the participation of a community group in problem posing and solving (Maguire 1987). For helpful discussions of PAR see, e.g., Fals Borda and Rahman 1991; Greenwood and Levin 1998; Maguire 1996.

22. I reflect on my role and the implications of my involvement in this project elsewhere. See Hemment 2000, 2007.

23. During my last trip to the city in 2001, I learned that Katia had been appointed director of the newly founded, government-funded Center for Women and Families.

WORKS CITED

Abramson, David. 1999. A Critical Look at NGOs and Civil Society as Means to an End in Uzbekistan. *Human Organization* 58 (3): 240–50.

Alvarez, Sonia E. 1998. Latin American Feminisms "Go Global": Trends of the 1990s and Challenges for the New Millennium. In *Cultures of Politics, Politics of Cultures*, ed. S. E. Alvarez, E. Dagnino, and A. Escobar, 293–324. Boulder, CO: Westview.

Alvarez, Sonia E., Evelina Dagnino, and Arturo Escobar. 1998. Introd. to *Cultures of Politics, Politics of Cultures*, ed. Alvarez, Dagnino, and Escobar. Boulder, CO: Westview.

Attwood, Lynne. 1997. "She Was Asking for It": Rape and Domestic Violence against Women. In *Post-Soviet Women: From the Baltic to Central Asia*, ed. M. Buckley, 99–118. Cambridge: Cambridge University Press.

Berdahl, Daphne. 1999. *Where the World Ended: Reunification and Identity in the German Borderland.* Berkeley: University of California Press.

Borneman, John. 1992. *Belonging in the Two Berlins: Kinship, State, Nation.* Cambridge: Cambridge University Press.

Bridger, Susan, Rebecca Kay, and Kathryn Pinnick. 1996. *No More Heroines? Russia, Women, and the Market.* New York: Routledge.

Dorsey, Ellen. 1997. The Global Women's Movement: Articulating a New Vision of Global Governance. In *The Politics of Global Governance: International Organizations in an Interdependent World*, ed. P. F. Diehl, 335–58. Boulder, CO: Lynne Rienner.

Escobar, Arturo. 2000. Culture Sits in Places: Anthropological Reflections on Globalization and Subaltern Strategies of Localization. Paper presented at Five Colleges Faculty Symposium on Globalization, Postdevelopment, and Environmentalism, Hampshire College, Amherst, MA, August 19.

Fals Borda, Orlando, and Muhammad Anisur Rahman, eds. 1991. *Action and Knowledge: Breaking the Monopoly with Participatory Action Research.* New York: Apex Press.

Feldman, Shelley. 1997. NGOs and Civil Society: (Un)stated Contradictions. *ANNALS, AAPSS* 554 (Nov.): 46–65.

Gal, Susan, and Gail Kligman. 2000. *The Politics of Gender after Socialism.* Princeton, NJ: Princeton University Press.

Gibson-Graham, J. K. 1996. *The End of Capitalism (As We Knew It): A Feminist Critique of Political Economy.* Cambridge: Blackwell.

Greenwood, Davydd J., and Morten Levin. 1998. *Introduction to Action Research: Social Research for Social Change.* Thousand Oaks, CA: Sage.

Grewal, Inderpal, and Caren Kaplan. 1994. *Scattered Hegemonies: Postmodernity and Transnational Feminist Practices.* Minneapolis: University of Minnesota Press.

Hemment, Julie. 2000. Gender, NGOs, and the Third Sector in Russia: An Ethnography of Russian Civil Responsibilities. PhD diss., Cornell University.

———. 2007. *Empowering Women in Russia: Activism, Aid, and NGOs.* Bloomington: Indiana University Press.

Kamat, Sangeeta. 2002. *Development Hegemony: NGOs and the State in India.* New York: Oxford University Press.

Keck, Margaret E., and Kathryn Sikkink. 1998. *Activists beyond Borders: Advocacy Networks in International Politics.* Ithaca, NY: Cornell University Press.

Lang, Sabine. 1997. The NGOization of Feminism. In *Transitions, Environments, Translations: Feminisms in International Politics*, ed. J. W. Scott, C. Kaplan, and D. Keates, 101–20. New York: Routledge.

Maguire, Patricia. 1987. *Doing Participatory Research: A Feminist Approach.* Amherst: University of Massachusetts Center for International Education.

————. 1996. Considering More Feminist Participatory Research: What Has Congruency Got to Do with It? *Qualitative Inquiry* 2 (1): 106–18.

Mindry, Deborah. 2001. Nongovernmental Organizations, "Grassroots," and the Politics of Virtue. *Signs* 26 (4): 1187–1212.

Noonan, Norma C., and Wilma Rule, eds. 1996. *Russian Women in Politics and Society*. Westport, CT: Greenwood Press.

Ong, Aihwa. 1996. Strategic Sisterhood or Sisters in Solidarity? Questions of Communitarianism and Citizenship in Asia. *Indiana Journal of Global Legal Studies* 4 (1): 107–35.

Paley, Julia. 2001. *Marketing Democracy: Power and Social Movements in Post-Dictatorship Chile*. Berkeley: University of California Press.

Richter, James. 1999. Citizens or Professionals? Evaluating Western Assistance to Russian Women's Organizations. Report prepared for the Carnegie Corporation.

Snitow, Ann. 1999. Cautionary Tales. *Proceedings of the 93rd Annual Meetings of the American Society of International Law*, 35–42.

Sperling, Valerie. 2000. *Organizing Women in Contemporary Russia: Engendering Transition*. Cambridge: Cambridge University Press.

Sperling, Valerie, Myra Marx Ferree, and Barbara Risman. 2001. Constructing Global Feminism: Transnational Advocacy Networks and Russian Women's Activism. *Signs* 26 (4): 1155–86.

Spivak, Gayatri Chakravorty. 1996. "Woman" as Theatre: United Nations Conference on Women, Beijing 1995. *Radical Philosophy* 75 (Jan.–Feb.): 2–4.

Tsing, Anna Lowenhaupt. 1997. Transitions as Translations. In *Transitions, Environments, Translations: Feminisms in International Politics*. J. W. Scott, C. Kaplan, and D. Keates, eds. New York: Routledge.

Verdery, Katherine. 1996. *What Was Socialism, and What Comes Next?* Princeton, NJ: Princeton University Press.

Watson, Peggy. 1997. Civil Society and the Politics of Difference in Eastern Europe. In *Transitions, Environments, Translations: Feminisms in International Politics*, ed. J. W. Scott, C. Kaplan, and D. Keates, 21–29. New York: Routledge.

Wedel, Janine. 1998. *Collision and Collusion: The Strange Case of Western Aid to Eastern Europe, 1989–1998*. New York: St. Martin's Press.

Zabelina, Tat'iana. 1996. Sexual Violence towards Women. In *Gender, Generation, and Identity in Contemporary Russia*, ed. H. Pilkington, 169–86. New York: Routledge.

11

Memorializing Murder, Speaking Back to the State

Belinda Leach

Memorials to women murdered by men have materialized on the Canadian landscape over the past several years, brought into being by groups that usually include relatives, friends, and antiviolence activists.[1] Some of these memorials blend gently into the landscape. Others startle when one stumbles upon them unexpectedly (Cultural Memory Group 2006). A few of these were dedicated before fourteen women were murdered at l'École Polytechnique in Montreal on December 6, 1989, because they were women, in the killer's own words. Many invoke that act even as they commemorate a friend, sister, mother, daughter, coworker, or simply a member of the same community, whose death at the hands of a man has shaken those around them. These memorials have often become rallying points where the local feminist community holds noisy Take Back the Night gatherings and reflective December 6 vigils (Bold, Knowles, and Leach 2002).

In this chapter I consider the relationship between the Canadian state and violence against women, and the intervention into that relationship of memorials to murdered women constructed through the efforts of frontline antiviolence workers.[2] As in many other countries, in Canada memorials are most commonly erected to celebrate the heroic acts of men who died serving the country. Murdered women—the underside of state-sanctioned violence—are usually mourned quietly and markers noting their deaths disappear in vast cemeteries or do not exist at all. Unlike the former kinds of memorials that appear to function largely as "scriptural tombs," intended to keep the dead dead (de Certeau 1988), memorials to femicide have an activist and forward-looking intent, seeking to keep memory alive and change the future (Bold, Knowles, and Leach 2003).[3] I argue that through creating memorials and memorializing practices, frontline workers provide an alternative to culturally sanctioned ways of remembering murdered women. In the process, they communicate the nature and extent of gender-based violence against women to a larger public, and back to the state itself. Yet, they do this in a highly contested context in which frontline workers must step cautiously around hegemonic constructions of family grief and state responsibility.

The chapter conceptualizes the everyday violence that women frequently experience as a manifestation of the embeddedness of gendered violence in state and social institutions. It traces the relationship between the Canadian feminist antiviolence movement and the state through events and state responses over the past three decades, paying particular attention to the paradox that, for the feminist antiviolence community, the state is both part of the problem and part of the longed-for solution. Drawing on local ethnographic fieldwork with a Canadian women's shelter organization, I examine how frontline antiviolence workers relentlessly contest how "the rendering of physical hurt" (Riches 1991, 295) is represented. In so doing, these workers—paid staff and unpaid volunteers working for a local feminist shelter organization—confront hegemonic constructions of violence against women that undermine a shared acceptance of its moral repugnance, while simultaneously diminishing access to the resources of the state to assist them in their work. The chapter shows how, through the construction of a local memorial to a woman murdered by her male partner, as well as other ongoing memorializing practices, frontline workers and their organizations offer an alternative construction of violence against women to the hegemonic version the state presents through its policies and legislation. I conclude by considering the risks involved in these actions as funding programs increasingly insist on gender-neutral "victim" services and programming and penalize organizations for what is deemed "political" advocacy.

Anthropologies of Violence

While anthropology has made a significant contribution to the study of political and state violence and its experience and resistance in everyday life, much of this attention has focused on repressive states (Asad 1992; Nagengast 1994). There is little concern for these issues in the context of states governed by what are taken to be nonviolent regimes. In contrast to obviously violent environments, the study of violence within a state like Canada requires a conceptualization that encourages analytical attention to some of the hidden sites of violence. These sites include what

Scheper-Hughes (1992) identifies as specific configurations of policy, rhetoric, institutions, and politics. These configurations provide a useful framework for examining how violence against women is embedded in Canadian society through social institutions and cultural conceptions. As Linda Green (1999, 7) shows in her own work, such social institutions and conceptions are then "reproduced locally and revealed in everyday life." Kleinman, Das, and Lock (1997) extend Scheper-Hughes's idea to consider how everyday violences are frequently exacerbated—if unintentionally—by the responses of institutions and social policy.

Mainstream studies of violence against women and policy attempts to address it are impeded by common conceptualizations that rely on simple binaries. Kleinman, Das, and Lock (1997, 227) observe that within scholarship: "current taxonomies of violence: public vs. domestic, ordinary as against extreme political violence—are inadequate to understand either the uses of violence in the social world or the multiplicity of its effects in experiences of suffering, collective and individual." Such reductions moreover minimize the significance of the issue and obscure the fact that violence against women is systemic. Two widespread ideas in particular invade popular perceptions of the issue, fueled by often ill-considered media contributions. The first is that the batterings or killings of women by their partners are "private" issues, and the second is that the killings of women by strangers are the work of deranged and socially disconnected individuals.

Harvey and Gow (1994) have claimed that in Anglo-American contexts violence is culturally identified as transgressive. As I demonstrate in what follows, only in recent years has violence against women been considered transgressive in Canadian society, and that judgment continues to be tenuous and contested. In this context frontline antiviolence workers struggle to keep violence against women in the public eye, to make it visible and show that it is pervasive, through their everyday and memorializing practices.

Violence against Women and Gendered State Violence

When feminists work together to establish memorials to murdered women, they intervene in and attempt to disrupt a hegemonic discourse that separates everyday male violence from the sanctioned violence of the state. States' claims that only they may exercise force legitimately constitute social categories of who may use violence and against whom. Within states, certain kinds of conflicts are minimized as "law and order" problems, which may nonetheless warrant violent intervention. Amita Baviskar (2001) has argued that one of the tasks of social movements is to make visible the violence that underlies the social contract and can be mobilized at the will of the state. Feminist analysts have argued that gendered (and racialized) violence is intimately connected to other more clearly sanctioned forms of violence (Kelly 2000). This analysis makes explicit the links among intimate partner violence, colonialism, nationalism, and militarism and implicates the state in sustaining patriarchal domestic relations through its exercise of violence in different venues.

Sherene Razack (1998), for example, has highlighted the intersections between practices of colonialism and patriarchy in her discussion of (white) men's coming of age in faraway places, where a common part of the colonial experience for men was their engagement in sexual activities with "local" women, blind to the power imbalance multiplied by colonialism and patriarchy, even in liaisons construed as consensual. Andrea Smith (2005, 23) pursues a similar line of argument, linking colonial, race, and gender oppression by arguing that "patriarchal gender violence is the process by which colonizers inscribe hierarchy and domination on the bodies of the colonized."[4] Smith insists on expanding the conceptualization of sexual violence to show how environmental racism, residential school policies, forced sterilization and medical experimentation, and spiritual appropriation all operate as violence in support of the state's genocidal agenda for native peoples in the Americas.

Smith extends the well-established feminist argument that the binary distinguishing violence carried out in private spaces from violence carried out in public spaces fails to capture links among forms of violence, and especially the ways that private "domestic" acts and public "random" ones are connected to violence occurring in police stations and military establishments and that occurring in more conventionally identified conflict zones. Cynthia Enloe has long argued for recognizing the connections among militarization, neo-imperialism, war, and coerced sexual relations (paid for or not), focusing much of her attention on U.S. imperialism in Southeast Asia and its aftermath (Enloe 1988, 1990, 1993). Liz Kelly (2000, 47) argues that it is impossible to make a clear distinction between peace and war for women (and for many men, too), since the violence of armed conflict always articulates with gender relations, and militarism constructs a brutalized form of masculinity played out in private and public spheres. The veracity of this argument became all too clear as reports emerged from U.S. military bases of several murders of women by their husbands, soldiers recently returned from active duty in Afghanistan and Iraq (Smith 2005).

Enloe's and Kelly's arguments are further confirmed when we consider the ways rape is used as a weapon of the state, against its own as well as "other" citizens. Historical research has shown that in all parts of the world conflicts have included the rape of enemy women (Jacobs, Jacobson, and Marchbank 2000), but even in a less obviously charged context, custodial rape is common. Violence against women is usually dissociated from other institutionalized forms of violence, but as the state deploys its power, gendered and racialized/racist violence is common. The issue is not only that this violence is perpetrated by state representatives but that it is also ignored and implicitly condoned by the state. The treatment of the disappearance of aboriginal women in Vancouver and along the so-called Highway of Tears in British Columbia, a situation recently raised by the United Nations in talks with Canada as a serious concern, attests to this point. In these cases entrenched gendered and racialized categorizations render aboriginal women undeserving of the state's full protection and furthermore, as Smith (2005, 10) points out, as inherently violable by state or civilian men. Referring to the United States, Angela Davis (2000) asks, "Can a state that is thoroughly infused with racism, male dominance, class-bias, and homophobia and that constructs itself in and through violence act to minimize violence in the lives of women?" With these words, Davis captures the paradox of the feminist movement's (and individual women's) relationship to a state that abuses its power in misogynist acts (and abuses of minority populations), yet is simultaneously the only actor with sufficiently broad power to make sustainable, legally binding, and enforceable change.

Violence against Women and the Canadian State

Feminist memorializers address their statements not simply to members of the public who encounter a memorial but also to the state, making claims on the resources of the state to address the issue. States, however, are not monolithic, and clearly different states fashion and tolerate different gender regimes. Within these regimes, gender relations are supported and reinforced by specific policies, and with greater or lesser capacity to wield control over citizens. The Canadian state is produced day by day through a variety of mechanisms that attempt to unify disparate groups over a large and diverse geographic area. The hegemonic Canadian national narrative celebrates the (ethnic, religious, linguistic) difference that underlies political and symbolic coherence through the "myth of the Canadian mosaic," institutionalized in an official policy of multiculturalism (Moynagh 2002, 104). Eva Mackey (2002, 9) argues that a persistent and key theme in the Canadian national myth is that "Canada is marginal to and victimized by various forms of colonialism." Constructed as a feminized victim suffering at the hands of external others (first Britain, now the United States), Canadian identity is fictionalized as homogeneous and unified, able to transcend the internal difference that constitutes it but always in need of protection. This fiction has the effect of denying the state's capacity to "victimize internal others on the basis of race, culture, gender, or class" (Mackey 2002, 12). The process of constructing this national narrative, as Moynagh (2002, 97) argues, stitches "historical sutures that close out stories of racial terror and sexual injustice"—such as the history of slavery in Canada and the ongoing treatment of First Nations people, and the ways both of these are particularly gendered—even as it simultaneously celebrates difference.

Although the hegemonic Canadian national narrative celebrates unity and coherence emerging from diversity, Mackey (2002, 16–19) argues that in practice the national project involves more "flexible strategies" that manage cultural diversity internally and can account for inclusions and erasures on a situational basis. Thus, strategies gradually shift and can exploit the dangers and opportunities contained in ambiguous situations. Mackey draws on Asad's (1993, 17) notion that dominant power has "worked best through differentiating and classifying practices" that in Canada are institutionalized in what is constructed as a liberal and tolerant state.

The Canadian state has historically "managed" the position of women within it through a form of social patriarchy that later became characteristic of welfare states. Policies were designed primarily to stabilize the family such that women could (barely) sustain both paid and unpaid work roles (Leach and Yates 2008; Ursel 1992). Women internalized the persistent contradiction and coped individually in their own homes with particular partners. Within this patriarchal familial model, violence by men against women partners was considered a private matter, of little interest to the courts, or indeed anyone else.

The management of women's issues shifted in the early 1970s after the Royal Commission on the Status of Women was forced on a reluctant government by pressure from thirty-two national women's groups (LaMarsh 1968).[5] Following the commission's recommendations, the federal Women's Program was established as a branch of the Secretary of State, which appointed feminists from outside government to run the program and provided operational grants to women's organizations (Schreader 1990, 197), including shelters and rape crisis centers. Public funding then supported activism and services around issues involving violence against women. This work, which was a central piece of the work of the feminist movement in the 1970s in Canada, included the establishment and maintenance of shelters (often, as in the city of Guelph, in small, barely financed premises) and rape crisis centers. Through the 1970s and 1980s much of the antiviolence work consisted of local initiatives. But there were successes at the national and provincial scales, such as the introduction of mandatory-charge legislation, that resulted from the work of equality-seeking women's groups.[6] Sustained feminist demands for increased state attention to the issue—to change the justice system and improve funding for shelters and other programs, as well as to recognize that violence is tied to women's subordinate position—accompanied unprecedented attention to and analysis of several well-publicized incidents of violence against women, culminating in the killings at l'École Polytechnique in Montreal on December 6, 1989.[7]

Catalyzed by these events, the government established the Canadian Panel on Violence Against Women, whose 1993 report, *Changing the Landscape*, formed the basis for reforms of the Canadian system and for some in Europe as well (Hague, Kelly, and Mullender 2001). Through the 1990s, a host of other federal initiatives were put in place along with provincial action plans and numerous smaller studies of the issue.[8] The federal Family Violence Initiative was established in 1988, the year before the Montreal killings, with the investment of $176 million over eight years for work on "domestic violence, familial child abuse and elder abuse" (Hague, Kelly, and Mullender 2001, 32). The title "Family Violence" for this initiative, which has been identified as a mainstream approach to antiviolence work, raised a further issue for feminist activists, who have repeatedly sought to ensure that violence against women is explicitly named and not obscured behind the terms *domestic* or *family*. This again speaks to the paradox for feminists and to the ways in which the feminist movement engages with the state and its institutions.

Canada, unlike many other countries, has had a relatively long history of direct funding from the federal government (and from provincial funds as well) to feminist social agencies, with much more limited support for these issues deriving from private sources. As detailed earlier, a considerable portion of state support was redirected to antiviolence initiatives in the late 1980s and early 1990s. While state support for feminist initiatives might appear to have been a success, Gillian Walker (1992) has argued that these initiatives drew the feminist antiviolence movement into the restrictive discourses of the state in problematic ways. Speaking of the women's movement in the 1970s, Walker highlights the shifts in language that took place within the feminist antiviolence movement and in its negotiations with the state. She argues that "our thinking came to be organized so that the state, through its social problem apparatus, could be induced, shamed or pressured to respond" (336). While feminists objected to the undifferentiated term *family* violence because they argued it worked against women's interests, bureaucrats argued that this term permitted them to "'slip women in,' in circumstances where wife battering itself would have been 'too contentious an issue'" (322). Changes in the legal code, for example, from "rape" to "sexual assault," allowed charges to be laid more easily but removed a powerful tool for naming this specific form of violence against women. These moves, as Walker shows, situated violence against women within a particular set of institutional relations, allowing activists and policy makers "to define the problem in ways that linked specific aspects to particular institutions and agencies within the government" (324). Walker analyzes the implications of using the term *violence*, arguing that in a context where the state claims the right to the legitimate use of "force," the term *violence* carries ideological weight (328), doing ideological work to reinforce the state's legitimacy. Walker fears, however, that through such terminological moves, women's protest is absorbed into the state's institutional structures, with the loss of its political potential.

Over the past forty years in Canada, violence against women has been recast as a serious social issue requiring the dedication of state resources, and the state has come to accept some responsibility for bringing about change. Much of this change has taken place as a result of the sustained efforts of the feminist community, which come vividly into focus when especially violent incidents targeting women take place. I now turn to one example of such efforts, where a woman's murder became the catalyst for a particular form of activism.

Memorializing Murder

Two years after the violence that targeted women in Montreal, Marianne Goulden was killed by her partner at her home in Guelph, in front of her young daughter. Marianne had left a former abusive partner, becoming one of the first residents of the residential shelter facility established by

Guelph-Wellington Women in Crisis (WIC). After a time, she became a volunteer and then a staff person with the organization. Her death hit the organization very hard. Marianne's long relationship with WIC had been cemented by the naming of the shelter after her—Marianne's Place. At the time of Marianne's death, WIC was preparing to occupy a new shelter, having fought a losing battle to rebuild on the site of the original shelter, deemed unsuitable for new development because of its close proximity to a river. When the new location had been secured, the organization asked Guelph City Council to designate the former shelter site as a park dedicated to Marianne.

All the adjacent land on both sides of the river and across the road was already part of a riverside park system. Yet it still took considerable work on the part of board members and staff of WIC to persuade City Council to dedicate the park to Marianne. WIC staff felt fortunate to be able to draw on the support of a board member who was a well-known and respected community leader, and they were convinced that without his influence, Marianne's Park (as it came to be known) would never have been created. In some ways, City Council had few options, since it had already established that the land could not be developed. Yet WIC staff heard that getting the approval required that favors be called in. As a veteran staff person said, "Those were also the days when we had to apply to City Council to have them announce Take Back the Night and allow the march," and "every time you went . . . it would always be with your fingers crossed hoping that they were going to do it that year."

At the same time, WIC staff were struggling to get the necessary permits to expand the new building acquired for the shelter. As Justine, the executive director at the time recalls, "We started to build anyway." The contractor "dug the footings and poured them and he just said 'stop me' to the city." She continued: "Getting that little hunk of land named Marianne's Park was not a straightforward thing; it was almost as hard as getting the friggin' building permit for the new shelter." Fighting City Hall's Planning Department on two fronts, making presentations to committees, and addressing what was perceived to be a very conservative council regarding a feminist issue was in some ways simply business-as-usual for a feminist service organization.

Justine also recalls that "at a certain point we did pull out the sympathy card around Marianne." "At the time," she added, "City Council was not exactly really open to a lot of violence against women stuff." She remembers that within City Council and the community more broadly there was shock that there had been a murder in Guelph and contempt for the man who had murdered Marianne. So pitching a dedication to Marianne, rather than to "the violence against women thing," seemed the pragmatic route to take: "If you could just get it approved, then we could have Take Back the Night there, and you could have the December 6 vigil there, and other events."

Joan, who followed Justine as executive director of WIC, saw a different motivation in the approval, even if it remained unspoken: "At the time of this, violence was really becoming very apparent to the whole city; . . . there was lots of other work done across the province and the country around violence against women and I think it gave them a way not to feel so guilty about doing stuff."

While the pitch to City Council focused on an individual community member and her contributions to the city, within the feminist community the space "felt like sacred ground," partly because the original shelter had been there, and even more "because she was there for so long, and so much had happened and so much history." Another staff person said, "I think that the park is about violence against women and the power of women's work, what women working together can achieve." The dedication of the park, on December 6, 1993, memorialized Marianne and the organization's own history in that place.

Vigils to remember the events of December 6, 1989, were held that year, and on every December 6 since, at hundreds of sites across Canada. In Guelph, they were held first in the Unitarian church, then at the University, and then downtown. With the dedication of Marianne's Park, the local feminist community acquired a site for the event that connected local incidents of violence—and most explicitly, Marianne's murder—with the murders of the women in Montreal.[9] Yet the commemorative plaque to Marianne that sits in the park references Montreal, and through that, broader issues of violence against women, only obliquely through the date of dedication. The plaque's wording was worked out jointly by one of Marianne's daughters and a WIC staff person. That person said she had seen her role as a facilitator, adding, "and the fact that it wasn't political is completely reflective of the process that was happening there in that I wanted to help the family move where they could with it and present their mother the way they wanted to." For this person, who had known Marianne and her family very well, "she was a lot more than a victim . . . [and] her surviving was more important than his act of violence and her collusion in his violence."

In the WIC newsletter announcing that the park had been established, the link was more explicitly made: "With this dedication it is our hope that the community will never forget the many women who have and will lose their lives to violence until it is no longer acceptable."

In the decade following the park's dedication, Take Back the Night rallies and December 6 vigils were always held there.[10] In contrast to the process WIC staff engaged in to ensure the dedication, where violence against women as a systemic problem was downplayed and Marianne's contribution as a community member was made the focus, these events are far more explicitly political. At both, the names of dead women are read. At Take Back the Night rallies and marches, women noisily reclaim streets where they feel unsafe to walk alone at night, sometimes visiting specific sites where women have been subjected to violence. At December 6 vigils the names of the fourteen women murdered in Montreal are read, as well as the names of all the women killed in Ontario during the past year, often with details of how they died and the names of the children who died with them. At both events, women's testimonials of their own experiences of violence are made a focus. A WIC staff person explained:

> What we really worked towards was involving survivors who were the age of the Montreal women and who can talk about their lives and what's unfolded, the fact of being survivors. So they can talk very directly about the horror. [But also] this is what was lost: look at this dynamite woman, and this is what is lost. How to do this work in making violence against women as close to the right size as possible in people's minds is really, really challenging, in how you do that in a pretty garden.

To address critics who have argued that December 6 vigils focus on white, middle-class women, commemorative activities, including those in Guelph, have become deliberately more inclusive in terms of race and class.[11] In recent years, these events have included presentations about women living with conflict in places such as Afghanistan, Darfur, and the former Yugoslavia. These are often presented by women who came as refugees from those places to Canada.

Yet even as the scope of the events has expanded to include a broader conceptualization of violence against women, early December always brings national debates over how long the day should continue to be commemorated and local ones over how women murdered by men in the community should be remembered. Every year newspaper columns suggest that it is time to allow the December 6 murdered women to "rest in peace," and sometimes the young feminists hired to put the events together express discomfort about discussing the details of recent deaths of women.

This response causes much dismay among more seasoned antiviolence workers engaged in a relentless struggle to make visible the everydayness of violence against women through telling their individual stories whenever there is the opportunity for making the news or catching the ear of a policy maker.[12]

When new memorials to murdered women are established, aside from the constant struggles waged with local authorities to get permissions, disputes frequently emerge over whether to state explicitly that this woman was murdered (Cultural Memory Group 2006). As a veteran WIC staff person explained:

> Do they want to celebrate the life, or is it more denial around this woman [who] died, she was murdered. We're doing this kind of thing [frontline antiviolence work] but it's too hard to go there all the time. . . . When we named the shelter for Marianne it was for celebration of who she was and the miracles she had performed in her life; . . . that's where I'm wanting to go as well, and not into violence against women in quite that way.

Another staff person, who feels strongly that the circumstances of the murders be more explicit, said, "[Often]we have to sneak it in." And, she added, referring to the plaque in Marianne's Park, "we didn't do a very good job sneaking it in."

Speaking Back to the State

The everydayness of violence against women renders it largely unconsidered as a public issue, often until an especially shocking event brings it out from the private spaces and into the media and the courts. Frontline antiviolence workers spend their days working with survivors and their nights trying to suppress the stories they have heard so that they can sleep. They put a lot of energy into finding ways to keep the issue alive in the public eye, struggling against hegemonic constructions that persist in viewing violence against women as a relatively minor crime, to insist that all violences against women be considered morally repugnant. The two strategies they use reinforce and complement each other. Naming violence against women as often and as publicly as possible, and doing so through the stories of those who have suffered it—told either by women themselves, or by those who survive—has become a standard practice. In this strategy, speaking plainly about the actual physical violence and attaching that violence to actual named women and children renders the physical hurt unambiguously intolerable, countering state and popular strategies that are more likely to refer to "unspeakable acts," by actually speaking them. In this way, violence against women is repeatedly inserted into media and policy discourses, and debates that threaten to disappear are kept alive. Violence against women is then represented as widespread *and* horrific, individually experienced *and* collectively incumbent.

Establishing memorials to women murdered by men is a complementary strategy to that everyday work, providing physical reminders of women's experiences of violence. After their initial construction, memorial sites require little to sustain their intervention into hegemonic constructions of violence against women, but their silent power can be mobilized and activated when a site becomes the setting for rallies and vigils. Individually, each site communicates a slightly different aspect of the issue. Some commemorate minority women explicitly. Others began with ominously empty space for future inscriptions, which only too quickly fill up (Cultural Memory Group 2006, 154).

Both frontline worker strategies, then, offer an alternative construction of gendered violence to the weak but hegemonic version that the state condones. This alternative redefines the meanings of those who have died and presents possibilities for an alternative subjectivity for survivors. Using this double-edged political strategy, frontline workers point to individual instances of women's murder (this woman died, on this day, in this place) and insistently draw attention to the systemic nature of gender-based violence.

Conclusion

The systemic nature of violence against women is increasingly represented at events through references to state-sanctioned violence—the wars in Afghanistan and Iraq and civil conflicts elsewhere—through which women are brutalized. These references allude to the role of the Canadian state in sustaining militarized environments and neocolonial relations that shape women's lived experiences. Yet despite its increasingly active role in military combat operations, and in contrast to the prevalent idea of Canada as a world peacemaker, the Canadian state continues to view itself as characterized by fairness and progressive ideas (Mackey 2002). In certain ways that view can be substantiated. In 1993, Canada established the legal right for women to claim refugee status on the basis of gender persecution, which frequently involves gendered violence. Canada is the first country to take this action, which is a significant legal achievement. Yet, as Razack (1995, 46) shows, such refugee claims are most likely to be successful when women are leaving a country that is constructed in Canada as "dysfunctional and exceptionally patriarchal," while overlooking the often violent forms that patriarchy takes within Canadian borders.

This position is consistent with the state's domestic policy shift in the past few years, making major cuts to funding for women's equality initiatives on the stated basis that in Canada women have achieved equality and thus government funding should be redirected to gender neutral programs, such as "victim" services, which channel funds away from feminist shelters and sexual assault programs.[13] Since the mid-1980s, public financial support for a range of equality initiatives at the federal level in Canada has declined and narrowed through changes in funding policies and mechanisms and, more recently, through direct cuts to the Women's Program. At the provincial level, funding agreements for shelters and sexual assault centers took on new stipulations in the 1990s. In Ontario, a punitive conservative government made clear that to qualify for funding, feminist organizations were not to engage in what was considered "political" advocacy. If they did so, they risked losing their funding to provide critical services to abused women. With these recent developments, the feminist movement's dependence on the state for funding support has proven to be ambiguous. With a velvet fist, state policies increasingly circumscribe the work of activists.

The relationship between state institutions and violence against women is critical. Andrea Smith and Sherene Razack insist that we understand the ways in which sexual violence is a key mechanism for sustaining patriarchy, white supremacy, and capitalism. These operate "in and through each other" (Razack 1998, 339) to secure white, middle-class elites. Smith (2005, 166) argues that in this context state funding for antiviolence activism and services does nothing more than manage and control dissent by "incorporating it into the state apparatus." Why would we expect that real material resources would be committed to dismantle the systems of domination that secure hegemonic masculinity and elites? Why would the revolution be funded by the very forces it seeks to overthrow (Incite! Women of Color Against Violence 2006)? Despite Schreader's (1990) appealing argument that state funding for feminist work signaled success for the women's movement in Canada, the erosion of such funding over the past twenty years and the containment of women's protests undermine that claim.

The umbrella organization that represents women's shelters in Ontario voiced its concerns about the cold climate in which shelters increasingly operate:

> Some shelters worry about being too publicly outspoken on issues, fearing it might jeopardize the partnerships they've worked hard to build with powerful community systems. Some have concerns about loss of fundraising potential, and even public funding, if they appear to be "too political" or seem critical of public policy, especially if there are few allies in their area. Added to these pressures are the lack of time/resources to do their work. We hear about the frantic efforts of shelters to provide direct services, participate in coordination and collaborative community projects, as well as to organize fundraising and awareness events. (OAITH 2007, 6)

Despite these pressures, frontline workers continue their sustained efforts to fight against violence against women using all the tools—cultural, economic, and political—available to them. They work with survivors of violence individually, they educate collectively, and they intervene in public debates to disrupt the hegemonic constructions that impede the social justice agenda. Speaking back to the state is still critically necessary yet ever more difficult.

ACKNOWLEDGMENTS

This chapter derives from a collaborative research project with Guelph-Wellington Women in Crisis, funded by a strategic research grant from the Social Sciences and Humanities Research Council of Canada. Many of the ideas expressed here emerged from intellectual exchange with my academic colleagues in this project, Christine Bold and Ric Knowles, for which I thank them. The other members of the Marianne's Park research team, Sly Castaldi, Jodie McConnell, and Lisa Schincariol, have also generously contributed invaluable time, energy, and ideas to the broader project, without which none of this work could have taken place.

NOTES

1. The Cultural Memory Group has identified sixty-two such memorials in Canada.
2. In Canada seventy-five women were known to have been murdered by a current or former partner in 2004 (Statistics Canada 2006). More than 28,000 incidents of women assaulted by their spouses were reported to police in 2000, probably about a third of the actual cases of assault against a female partner. In 1999–2000, 57,000 women and 39,000 children were admitted to Canada's 448 shel-

ters for abused women, and every day over a thousand women and children are turned away from shelters, mainly because they are full. In 2000, 23,352 women were victims of reported sexual assaults, estimated to be about 6 percent of actual incidents (Ontario Women's Directorate 1995). While these numbers cross age, race, and class distinctions, the combination of racist and sexist attitudes toward First Nations women (Amnesty International 2004) and racialized women makes these groups of women are more vulnerable than others.

3. A vast literature on memorials, monuments, and memorializing has emerged over the past several years, and their role in facilitating societal remembrance and forgetting. See, e.g., Connerton 1989; Young 1992. For the analysis of gender and memorializing, see Hirsch and Smith 2002; Schirmer 1994, and with specific reference to memorializing violence against women, see Rosenberg 2003.

4. McGilligray and Comaskey (1999) also make this link between violent colonial histories and the treatment of First Nations peoples in Canada, examining the relationships among intimate violence, aboriginal women, and the justice system, although their focus is on reform of the justice system.

5. Judy LaMarsh, then minister of national health and welfare, who first presented the idea of a Royal Commission to Prime Minister Lester Pearson in 1963, recalled these details, referring to a comparable initiative of the Kennedy administration in the United States.

6. Mandatory-charge legislation requires that charges be made in domestic violence situations even when police at the scene are not able to establish an arrestable offense. Feminist critics have countered that this policy often results in failure to arrest, leaving women vulnerable to further attack.

7. An example of a highly analyzed and well-publicized incident of violence against a woman was the rape of "Jane Doe" in her Toronto apartment in 1986 by the "balcony rapist." She assisted the police in their investigations that led to the arrest and conviction of the accused. She then initiated a civil suit against the Toronto police for negligence and violation of her rights under the Charter of Rights. The central issue in her suit was that the police chose not to alert women about the danger of a rapist in their neighborhood. Rather, they used women as bait in their bid to catch the rapist in the act of rape and more likely ensure his conviction. Madame Justice Jean MacFarland's ruling clearly criticized the pervasive attitudes of the Toronto police toward women and rape: "The conduct of this investigation and the failure to warn, in particular, was motivated and informed by the adherence to rape myths as well as sexist stereotypical reasoning about rape, about women and about women who are raped. The plaintiff therefore has been discriminated against by reason of her gender and as a result the plaintiff's rights to equal protection and equal benefit of the law were compromised." (MacFarland decision 1998 excerpted at *www.owjn.org/archive/jane.htm.*)

8. Other federal initiatives in the 1990s included the establishment of five federally funded research centers on violence against women across the country; law reforms that included increased protection for complainants in rape cases, "pro-

charge" policies that encourage the police to lay charges in wife assault cases, and expanded police training; giving the police power to remove firearms from domestic premises; and expanded protections through civil laws, such as emergency intervention orders to permit an immediate restraining order, giving sole occupancy of a house to an abused woman, or removing the perpetrator from a residence (Hague, Kelly, and Mullender 2001).

9. The federal government named December 6 the National Day of Remembrance and Action on Violence Against Women. Many have subsequently argued that this resolution has allowed the government to appear to have acted on the issue, while little has changed.

10. In 2000 another park, just across the river from Marianne's Park, was dedicated to the memory of the fourteen women who died in Montreal on December 6, 1989. Accompanied by considerable debate, the December 6 vigil was moved there. See Bold, Knowles, and Leach 2002 for a discussion of this move and its implications.

11. In at least one case, the University of Toronto Women's Centre decided not to continue to hold the vigil. "The event tends to focus everyone's attention on fourteen young white women," the center's Gillian Morton said. "It affects such a small constituency—we need to take into account women who are left off the list as victims of violence."

12. The stakes involved in naming violence in a local (Canadian) context are discussed in George 2000.

13. The Conservative government of Stephen Harper, elected to a minority in 2006, eliminated "equality" from the mandate of Status of Women Canada, slashed its operational budget, resulting in the loss of 61 out of 131 positions, the closure of 12 out of 16 regional offices, and the elimination of the Independent Policy Research Fund, the Court Challenges Program, and many other programs. The Harper government has also reneged on important commitments to build a national child care program, resulting in cuts of $1.2 billion annually to provinces and territories for child care services.

WORKS CITED

Amnesty International. 2004. *Stolen Sisters: A Human Rights Response to Discrimination and Violence against Indigenous Women in Canada*. Amnesty International.

Asad, Talal. 1992. Conscripts of Western Civilization. In *Civilization in Crisis: Anthropological Perspectives*, ed. C. W. Gailey, 333–51. Gainesville: University of Florida Press.

———. 1993. *Genealogies of Religion: Discipline and Reasons of Power in Christianity and Islam*. Baltimore: Johns Hopkins University Press.

Baviskar, Amita. 2001. Written on the Body, Written on the Land: Violence and Environmental Struggles in Central India. In *Violent Environments*, ed. N. L. Peluso and M. Watts, 354–79. Ithaca, NY: Cornell University Press.

Bold, Christine, Ric Knowles, and Belinda Leach. 2002. Feminist Memorializing and Cultural Counter-Memory: The Case of Marianne's Park. *Signs* 28 (1): 125–48.

———. 2003. How Might a Women's Monument Be Different? *Essays on Canadian Writing* 80:17–35.

Connerton, Paul. 1989. *How Societies Remember.* Cambridge: Cambridge University Press.

Cultural Memory Group. 2006. *Remembering Women Murdered by Men: Memorials across Canada.* Toronto: Sumach Press.

Davis, Angela. 2000. The Color of Violence against Women. *Colorlines,* Fall, no. 10.

De Certeau, Michel. 1988. *The Writing of History.* New York: Columbia University Press.

Enloe, Cynthia. 1988. *Does Khaki Become You? The Militarization of Women's Lives.* San Francisco: Pandora Press / Harper Collins.

———. 1990. *Bananas, Beaches, and Bases: Making Feminist Sense of International Politics.* Berkeley: University of California Press.

———. 1993. *The Morning After: Sexual Politics at the End of the Cold War.* Berkeley: University of California Press.

George, Glynis. 2000. *This Rock Where We Stand: An Ethnography of Women's Activism in Newfoundland.* Toronto: University of Toronto Press.

Green, Linda. 1999. *Fear as a Way of Life: Mayan Widows in Rural Guatemala.* New York: Columbia University Press.

Hague, Gill, Liz Kelly, and Audrey Mullender. 2001. *Challenging Violence against Women: The Canadian Experience.* Bristol, UK: Policy Press.

Harvey, Penelope, and Peter Gow, eds. 1994. *Sex and Violence: Issues in Representation and Experience.* New York: Routledge.

Hirsch, Marianne, and Valerie Smith. 2002. Feminism and Cultural Memory: An Introduction. *Signs* 28 (1):1–19.

Incite! Women of Color Against Violence, ed. 2006. *The Color of Violence: The Incite! Anthology.* Cambridge, MA: South End Press.

Jacobs, Susie, Ruth Jacobson, and Jennifer Marchbank, eds. 2000. *States of Conflict: Gender, Violence, and Resistance.* London: Zed Books.

Kelly, Liz. 2000. Wars against Women: Sexual Violence, Sexual Politics, and the Militarized State. In *States of Conflict: Gender, Violence, and Resistance,* ed. S. Jacobs, R. Jacobson, and J. Marchbank, 45–65. London: Zed Books.

Kleinman, Arthur, Veena Das, and Margaret M. Lock, eds. 1997. *Social Suffering.* Berkeley: University of California Press.

LaMarsh, Judy. 1968. *Memories of a Bird in a Gilded Cage.* Toronto: McClelland and Stewart.

Leach, Belinda, and Charlotte Yates. 2008. Gendering Social Cohesion. In *Solidarity First: Workers and Social Cohesion in Canada,* 21–37. Vancouver: University of British Columbia Press.

Mackey, Eva. 2002. *The House of Difference: Cultural Politics and National Identity in Canada*. Toronto: University of Toronto Press.

McGilligray, Anne, and Brenda Comaskey. 1999. *Black Eyes All the Time: Intimate Violence, Aboriginal Women, and the Justice System*. Toronto: University of Toronto Press.

Moynagh, Maureen. 2002. "This History's Only Good for Anger": Gender and Cultural Memory in Beatrice Chancy. *Signs* 28 (1): 97–124.

Nagengast, Carole. 1994. Violence, Terror, and the Crisis of the State. *Annual Review of Anthropology* 23:109–36.

Ontario Association of Interval and Transition Houses (OAITH). 2007. *Year in Review*. Toronto: OAITH.

Ontario Women's Directorate. 1995. *Dispelling the Myths*. Toronto: Ontario Women's Directorate.

Razack, Sherene. 1995. Domestic Violence as Gender Persecution: Policing the Borders of Nation, Race, and Gender. *Canadian Journal of Women and the Law* 8 (1): 46–88.

———. 1998. Race, Space, and Prostitution: The Making of the Bourgeois Subject. *Canadian Journal of Women and the Law* 10 (2): 338–79.

Riches, David. 1991. Aggression, War, Violence: Space/Time and Paradigm. *Man* 26 (2): 281–97.

Rosenberg, Sharon. 2003. Neither Forgotten nor Fully Remembered: Tracing an Ambivalent Public Memory on the 10th Anniversary of the Montreal Massacre. *Feminist Theory* 4 (1): 5–27.

Scheper-Hughes, Nancy. 1992. *Death without Weeping: The Violence of Everyday Life in Brazil*. Berkeley: University of California Press

Schirmer, Jennifer. 1994. The Claiming of Space and the Body Politic within National-Security States: The Plaza De Mayo Madres and the Greenham Common Women. In *Remapping Memory: The Politics of TimeSpace*, ed. J. Boyarin, 185–220. Minneapolis: University of Minnesota Press.

Schreader, Alicia. 1990. The State-Funded Women's Movement: A Case of Two Political Agendas. In *Community Organization and the Canadian State*, ed. R. Ng, G. Wlaker and J. Muller, 184–99. Toronto: Garamond.

Smith, Andrea. 2005. *Conquest: Sexual Violence and American Indian Genocide*. Cambridge, MA: South End Press.

Statistics Canada. 2006. *Violence against Women in Canada . . . by the Numbers*. Ottawa: Statistics Canada.

Ursel, Jane. 1992. *Private Lives, Public Policy: One Hundred Years of State Intervention in the Family*. Toronto: Women's Press.

Young, James E. 1992. The Counter-Monument: Memory against Itself in Germany Today. *Critical Inquiry* 18 (2): 267–96.

Walker, Gillian. 1992. *Family Violence and the Women's Movement: The Conceptual Politics of Struggle*. Toronto: University of Toronto Press.

12

Laliti, Compassionate Savior: The Hidden Archaeology of Founding a Shelter

Jamila Bargach

In the Berber dialect spoken in the southern part of Morocco, the word *laliti* combines two concepts: rescue, in the sense of rain saving the earth—and by extension people—from the devastating consequences of drought; and compassion.[1] Laliti is also given as a first name to girls. I distinctly remember how I simply fell in love with the intonation, the singing rhythm of low-low-high of the syllables, and I became enamored even more when I came to understand its rich meaning. I even decided to name my daughter Lalita, but destiny chose otherwise. Then I proposed the name Laliti to a committee of the Moroccan nongovernmental organization (NGO) that received funds from a Swiss donor to open a domestic violence shelter in Morocco. The NGO in question was short of staff and I had offered my services to build the shelter free of charge. I was astonished that they so easily trusted me after I had volunteered for a mere two months in their adult education section. I thought their acceptance was a sign of trust that I could not possibly let down.

Violence against women has been a taboo topic in Morocco for decades. The first official antiviolence campaign initiated and launched by NGOs took place as recently as 1989. The NGO efforts led finally to an official plan and document issued by the state in 2003 called *The Strategy for Fighting against Violence against Women*. This document constituted a victory in the feminist struggle because in the document the state recognizes gender-based violence as a violation of rights and not merely a "private" issue, as had been so commonly believed. This document offers many progressive ideas in the struggle to free the country of gender-based violence, and it lays out a strategy that proposes to translate these ideas into action. Of these, I would like to single out the document's emphasis on the necessity for the creation of shelters as an important link in a chain of services all intended to fight against violence. "The strategy," however, remained a dead letter. The historic amendments to the Moroccan family laws in 2004 attracted all the attention and the efforts of feminist NGOs to the extent that the fight for a law against violence lost preeminence, or at least did so at that time.[2] Historically, some NGO activists claimed that since the old family law, Moudawana, was itself an agent of symbolic as well as structural violence against women, their struggle against violence had in effect never stopped. When in 2006 a new antiviolence law project was launched and proposed to the secretary general of the government in 2007 by the Ministry of Social Development, most established feminist associations exerted a lot of pressure and the text was withdrawn. The intention of these NGOs was to open up and widen the scope of the debate primarily between themselves and the government so that more progressive clauses and resolutions would finally be presented to the parliament. As I write this chapter, the situation concerning this new law is still at a standstill, though the collective of NGOs has been and continues to hold meetings to discuss and draft the memorandum they aim to present to the government.

There are today in Morocco seven shelters all run by local NGOs, operating with international funds. In addition, there are two shelters run by Christian missionaries. Four of the seven shelters specialize in helping unwed mothers, whose existence is a thorny social problem itself, while the other three grew organically from legal orientation centers operated by NGOs that offer their services free of charge to women seeking legal advice about such matters as divorce, custody, alimony, and violence. In fact, feminist organizations have been the first in Morocco to offer complete shelter services to female victims of gender-based violence because the Moroccan government fails to do so. The need became apparent when the staff of many orientation centers started housing more and more women who were running away from abuse in their own homes and in the offices of the NGOs, but offering one's house could be only a temporary solution. Despite a decade of progressive political changes, there still is no state-run shelter in Morocco and the debate between feminist associations and state representatives over the form of the law to fight violence against women has stalled. What the Moroccan government's response will be to the necessity of creating and responsibly managing these institutions is yet to be known.

Working in the Idealist's Bubble

I return now to Laliti, where I was given the task to turn the idea into a reality, to turn an empty building into a safe space for women and their children. As I read and reread the project, I was taken by the nobility of the mission, by the intricacies of the proposed internal organization, and by the way the arguments claim that this shelter constitutes the necessary brick in building the road to liberating women of all classes and all walks of life from violence and domination. It speaks a language that I strongly believe in and have fought for as an individual and contributed to in collective venues. I was unaware at the time, however, that the grant had been awarded to a person who had left and severed her ties with the NGO. I learned a few years later that she left because of intense and ugly internal fighting for the leadership of the organization. Since the project was still funded but there was no one to carry it through, the secretary general (SG) of the NGO—the one who won the internal war—asked me to carry this mission. She was aware of my position as an anthropologist with expertise on issues of marginality and questions of rights. Years later I realized that despite the SG's utter ignorance of what a shelter is really about, it was out of the question for her to let the funding go and miss an occasion to be in the spotlight, a beacon of the feminist movement in Morocco.

Thus began my hybrid identity as anthropologist cum frontline worker. I began working, but then where does one start? There were no blueprints to follow, no maps to orient me. So I visited the only shelter already running up in Rabat (at the time) and that was, as Laliti would later be, run by an NGO. I also visited the shelters run by Christian missions and then went to the library for a reading spree on the issues of gender-based violence, children and violence, and working with victims of violence and abuse, as well as on the history and experiences of shelters throughout the world and similar structures through different historical epochs. Soon, however, the NGO called me and put an end to my academic enthusiasm. "This is not a book you are writing; just rent a house and find someone to help you run it," I was told. I thought the call was rude and quite unprofessional but then reasoned that it had to do with the pragmatic approach of an NGO accustomed to political tactics and subterfuge, to the "end justifies the means," and that perhaps I was too caught up in academia, far from a matter-of-fact dealing with things. Time would prove just how wrong I was.

After I was called to order, I realized that funding agencies work with statistics, deadlines, and reports. I had to hasten the process by unwillingly emerging from the library. I tried to put ads in the papers to start hiring the staff, including an administrative assistant, a social worker, and a psychologist who would act as a consultant and possibly a mentor. The NGO discouraged me and refused to pay the advertising fee, since their habit was to check first in their known entourage. I let myself once again be persuaded, but I was lucky, because I hired three people, two of whom proved and continue to be absolutely committed professionals, one with experience and two willing to learn, willing to embark on the adventure. We set up work, and the task was more than daunting. Again, where does one start? So we sat and studied the project. We revised my notes from the library and from my visits, and we decided that we could not have a shelter without the physical building itself. We visited about ten houses and finally chose one that was seventeen miles from the city, covering a two-acre property with a garden, its own source of water, and a truly beautiful landscape. Once the building was securely rented, our enthusiasm soared, leaving us feeling as though we were runners in a marathon and that we were winning the race. We began planning for the setup of the house. Downstairs there was one large dormitory with a bathroom, a room reserved for day care, a very large living-room area with a small enclosed space for learning activities for the women, a large kitchen, and food storage. Upstairs we planned another dormitory, a smaller room with two beds for wounded women needing special treatment, the infirmary, one room for the sleeping staff, and two offices for us. We exploited every little corner in the house and hoped to use the garden to produce our own vegetables and even flowers.

What do we do when we rent a house? We furnish it. Thus, we sat down and selected furniture and thought about sheets for beds, towels, a stove, toilet deodorants, pots and pans, games for children, desks and chairs, and dozens of other details. We went to the traditional markets and to huge modern stores. We chose, we bargained, and we put things in consignment. Then the differences started taking shape between the kernel of what was to become the hired professional staff of Laliti and the feminist NGO that was, with the exception of a dozen poorly salaried staff, largely run and staffed by activists. Why do we need to have "so much stuff in this shelter?" I was repeatedly asked. "Couldn't they just do with what's available?" Surely, but then nothing was there. After so much arguing back and forth—a sort of sterile exchange between an ideology deeply grounded in an adversarial stance and a practice attempting to reach an established goal for which it was hired—we did reach consensus. We were finally able to secure money for half of the furnishings we wanted, but we had to fulfill the remaining needs through donations from individuals or established firms and businesses. It was certainly difficult, since we had no history to present to these potential donors. In the end, however, this effort proved worthwhile because it allowed us to build some important relations with the business world.

After two months, we felt that the house had the basic necessities to be operational, and we focused then on planning what to do with the women once they came to the shelter. We were given funds to set up a shelter for twenty beds, fifteen for women residing between two and six months and five beds for emergency cases of one or two nights. The women would usually come with their children and we decided to accept children up to age five, because six years old is the official age to join the public education system. We had neither the means nor the potential at this early stage of the planning to accommodate school-aged children.

With the same enthusiasm, the three of us continued meeting way past paid hours and on weekends to resolve the numerous unanswered questions. The argument we shared and all believed in was that while Laliti was to give shelter to women running away from domestic violence and abuse, it also had the mission of transforming these women from abused and suffering individuals to empowered women able to stand on their feet, face up to their torturers, and walk on the path of self-sufficiency with dignity. We constructed this space as a transformative one: How are we going to get the women into the shelter? What are our criteria for selection? How are we going to advertise these criteria and to whom? How are we to deal with the authorities regarding clause 496 in the penal code that turns us into an unlawful institution?[3] How are the women going to be occupied once in the shelter? Should the mothers stay with the children in the day-care facility we created or not? How should the collaboration with the psychologist and the lawyer be carried out in freeing the women from the circle of violence? Our questions were endless but, as we learned later, despite our best intentions, our best efforts at finding answers, and our overflowing enthusiasm, only hands-on experience would allow us to work out adequate solutions or compromises appropriate to each case.

While we were legally part of the NGO, we were given the semblance of "semi-autonomy" in internal management matters. At the same time, we still had to continually negotiate all sorts of issues with the NGO, though the emphasis was by and large on the material aspects, since they were the only ones allowed to sign the checks. This situation created tension, and we were subjected to a lot of pressure. Our constant pestering, as they called it, depleted us of needed energy and created a very negative, even hostile atmosphere. We became women living with violence, the only difference being that we did not share the same physical building with our torturer. Nonetheless, we believed zealously in our mission, which was fed constantly by a pure form of idealism. Out of our personal experiences we set up a "haven," a house that was at the same time public and private, which sought to transform the suffering and the pain of the women into productive fodder for a better tomorrow. I guess our sentiments were not much different from those that animated socialists or liberation movements as they organized and ascended to power. Of course, we were naïve. Sometimes we realized that we were, and other times we were so deeply enmeshed in the mission that we continued our efforts unabated. I think our major error was to set up this shelter without really considering the women themselves, their histories, and their embodied experiences.

After four months of intensive preparation—and because of the mounting pressure from the NGO, which threatened to not pay the salaries of the staff (as I continued to be an unpaid volunteer)—we finally and officially, though reluctantly, opened. It was a strange feeling. We were elated as we opened to receive our first case of domestic violence. We all experienced an awkward feeling, but the power of denial worked wonders. When we spoke about it that very morning, we decided we simply had to accept it as part of what animated us, but in hindsight I realize that for all of us "violence" was still an abstract category. Though we had read and met some women in the Legal Orientation Center run by the NGO, violence was a passing story, an assemblage of events, of actions and reaction, but not really an embodied experience we shared of life's complexities and its everyday ups and downs.

The Legal Orientation Center called, and we had our first case. We were still waiting to get a car so I went to town to pick up the woman in question with her two children, a five-year-old boy and an eight-year-old girl. With the experience we have accumulated, we know now that this first case was an extremely difficult one, in a category we identify today as five stars. First of all, this woman's husband was a policeman, who could act with impunity. She had lived for over ten years with domestic abuse, and she was deeply caught in the violence cycle. She also was incapable of cooperating or engaging in a conversation, extremely self-absorbed, and totally negligent of her children; some of these behavioral patterns were a direct consequence of her violent life. The second case came the next day, also a woman with two children who had run away with only the clothes on her back after her husband and mother-in-law tried to kill her. We had to take her to the hospital, treat her wounds, and give her special accommodations because the first woman was very hostile about sharing the large dormitory where we had put her. This second woman, like the first, was totally ensnared in the violence cycle. But she was gentle and cooperative, if somewhat introverted; her children resembled her, though the only reality they had ever known was violence. After the third case came in—a young woman with two boys running away from terrible abuse by her partner—we started experiencing serious discipline issues. The children of the first woman, who were extremely rowdy and undisciplined, started beating the other children. Their mother refused to cooperate in the household maintenance as she had agreed to do when she first came in. She argued that her social status, her class position, and her position as the wife of a policeman set her apart from the other two women, who were used to manual labor and who came from lower social classes.

The First Deluding Element Seeps into the Idealist Bubble

I found myself thinking: How could victims of violence be so difficult and uncooperative in a space that was set up specifically for them? How could these women who bore the marks of years of physical beatings and psychological torture and who had run away looking for shelter, for protection, be so unbending, so aggressive, and so hostile toward those who were there to do the professional job of rehabilitating them? Yes, I know these are naïve questions that are usually covered in a Psychology 101 class, but it was a hard blow for the team to come face-to-face with the reality that planning on paper for hypothetical women was much easier and more rewarding than facing these women, complex human beings like all of us, and having to argue that within the shelter there are rules that have to be followed. We never thought there could be resistance.

The final straw came from our first beneficiary. The woman thought she had waited too long to take her turn in the only shower we had in the shelter and physically attacked the second resident, the shy, gentle woman who probably never imagined she would experience such fury in a place that had offered her sanctuary. Four of us came running down the stairs to stop the attack and immediately ordered the perpetrator to pack up and leave. We were certainly inexperienced but that was our bottom line. She had used violence in a place set up precisely to fight it. She left and went directly to the NGO headquarters to complain about us.

The SG of the NGO called me and admonished us for sending a poor victim of violence out of the only place where she could be protected from it. She called us incompetent and a shame to all institutions. Only after I explained what had happened did she adjust her tone. I used the occasion to insist that we needed a psychologist to frame our work and truly lead the team, because none of us had a clinician's experience, which, we were learning, was essential to building a rehabilitation center. While looking for a psychologist willing to work with us under the tight restrictions set up by the NGO, we continued receiving beneficiaries. In our selection among the potential beneficiaries that the Legal Orientation Center proposed to us, we were extremely careful not to choose women with uncontrollable tempers (though we knew we could not possibly know for sure) because we felt we lacked the means to deal with them. For example, when ten women seeking shelter applied, we would accept only four.

Then the "famous" case of Fatiha came. The controversy this case involved was, for me, the final piece of the puzzle that allowed me to clearly understand the relationship that was evolving between Laliti and the NGO, on one hand, and the kind of ethical approach that needs to ground the work within a shelter, on the other. As Fatiha was later to tell us before leaving the center, their landlord evicted her and her husband because they were over a year late with their rent, and thus they planned that while he went away to somehow gather money, she would pretend to have been beaten and come to the center, where she and her three children would have all the essentials for survival. She was lucky we chose her to come to the center, but once settled, she started arguing with the administration about the guidelines that all the beneficiaries needed to respect. We assumed her behavior was the consequence of violence, and therefore we were firm but understanding. Although she refused adamantly to press charges against a husband she constantly described as being monstrous, we could not influence or force her to do so because we were not supposed to tell the women what to do. Our policy with the women is not to interfere with their decisions but simply to orient them. At that time, three months after receiving our first beneficiary, a wonderful psychologist joined us for two days a week—one day for the beneficiaries and one day with the administration helping us set up the center. When Fatiha refused to see her, we started having doubts. Usually, the women need to talk, and they jump at the chance to see the psychologist. So we called her. As Fatiha came upstairs to our office, she must have felt something was awry because when we confronted her with her unconventional behavior for a battered woman, she simply and easily, with no second thoughts about being a liar and a cheat, revealed her scam.

The Bubble of Idealism Starts Showing Seams

The SG and her assistant descended that same afternoon on Laliti. The SG accused us of choosing only easy cases, saying that she was aware of all that we did and did not do and that she knew especially of our cowardice. Her accusation sent me into a fury—how dare she judge us in such a manner? What about the perjury of Fatiha? What about honesty and all the other positive moral values? What about our dedication because of our belief in a cause, in a mission? "Well, there is no perjury from Fatiha; she simply suffers from economic violence and her place is in Laliti." Silence. A moment of stupefaction. The psychologist, my assistant, the social worker, and I stared unbelievingly, stupefied even, at the SG as she began pouring out a logorrhea, delivered in a high pitch and a single breath, about what economic violence is and how it operates and that it is the global-capitalist economy that turned all these women into alienated victims, robbing them of their agency, even of the possibility of facing up to and articulating their real needs. Her words were spoken as the good ideologue she was, surely with conviction, but I had penetrated the smoke screen and could see how she needed to keep the upper hand in all matters and decisions.

There was no point in arguing with the SG. I felt depleted after shouting earlier with her, and we all just stood there in this hot, closed office, listening to, what I constructed later to be, a delirious approach to violence. Once things calmed a bit, the psychologist ventured to wedge in one essential idea: that we had priorities concerning physical violence and that we needed to respect the values in which we rooted our work. Yet, we could definitely not win with the SG. She pulled out the card of the funding agency and the statistics that justified their donation. We countered by speaking about quality, and she answered that quantity does not discount quality. We stayed like this for a while, trading words, but not conversing. There was really nothing to say. The next day, Fatiha was sent away. The SG understood that Laliti's administration had a mind of its own, and she retaliated by retaining or delaying funds for running the shelter. My disillusion with the NGO was immense. I had misgivings about some of the beneficiaries, but I continued to believe in a world free of domestic violence. "What next then?" my internal monologue ran. "Can disillusion be productive? Is it possible to disembody 'violence,' to turn it into an abstraction, a free-floating sign not connected to bodies or contexts?" Today I realize that this was the break after which the return was hard, if not impossible. My bubble of idealism was full of pinholes. My enthusiasm was slowly being undermined by doubt about the real value of the work being done and by my anxiety and fear about having become so involved that I could not extricate myself from a very messy situation. Then I realized that the NGO's stance is the easy one; it is easy in the sense that it identifies an "antagonist block" (whether it is a person, a state, a firm or business, a set of customs, or a society as a whole) and then goes after it. As a matter of fact, the NGO agenda and its activities are, to a large extent, defined by this external entity. In the case of a shelter, however, who is the "antagonist"? It is the "system" that lives in each one of us as "agents," as carriers and reproducers of these elements and this culture. This is so much more difficult to counter. Who sets up the agenda and how can we go about changing things then?

While reading the notes I have kept from this period, I relive the feeling of uneasiness I experienced that week. I was full of questions. I could not simply discard the activism of the NGO, since it was their passion that compelled me to volunteer with them in the first place. I also could not hold all the beneficiaries responsible for the dishonesty of a few. And finally, what did I really think I was doing when I embarked on this adventure? That was the same fated week when, as the director of the Laliti shelter, I was confronted yet again with some serious disciplinary issues. We had accepted to the house a beneficiary with her three little girls because she just needed time to find a way to accommodate her new condition. She did have a loving husband, but he had killed someone in a fight. She wanted to stay in the city to go and visit him but did not want to go live with her family or her in-laws. The psychologist evaluated her case and warned us to be careful with her because of "emotional instability," but we figured that this instability was due to her extremely precarious living conditions. The tensions, however, kept mounting. She was extremely territorial, arguing for hours about her share in the household chores. She refused to eat what we all ate, started bringing in food for her girls (strictly forbidden in the shelter because it creates terrible jealousies between already fragile children), and overall acted in an unethical manner. We gave her a first warning. A second and then a third followed by the end of the week. It was my job to announce this third warning after which she simply had to vacate the shelter. After six months of operating this shelter, after having been coached by the psychologist, and after having had so many moments of belief and disillusion, I had to be the "official" and tell this woman to leave. I had to put on a mask and decree like an almighty ruler, "You need to leave because the security of the shelter is more important than the security of one individual." My feet transported me in front of her. I violated the protocol for situations like this.

My bubble of idealism exploded like a bomb, sending shreds, shingles, and odd pieces all across the two-acre property, reverberating throughout the shelter, bringing all to a sudden halt. My voice, not me, was shouting, "You leave here!" My heart was looking at the girls, especially the youngest one, who played with my own daughter, who often came with me to Laliti. I hated this voice, the voice of authority, the voice of the community, the voice of the righteous norms. The staff and beneficiaries all stopped their activities, formed a circle, and just stared at this woman screaming, "Clear the place!"

My memory fails me after that, but my assistant later explained to me that the staff hurried me upstairs and helped me lie down. They proceeded with the exit protocol with the woman. I realized that I had just made a terrible and unprofessional mistake. I lost my temper, and I was not supposed to do that. I acted in a violent manner rather than being firm but calm. I have replayed this scene hundreds of times in my head since it happened, and I recognize my responsibility. At the same time, the situation reached the limit of what I could bear.

Maintaining Hope, Realistically

Since this incident, I have worked hard to set up staff retreats with volunteer professionals to discuss how to live with witnesses and stories of violence, how to develop a "professional" attitude without losing one's human compassion, and how to keep separate the realm of work and the privacy of one's life. While the work at the front lines is about inviting oneself into the private lives of others, it is also about making clear distinctions about what belongs where. After three years of juggling my teaching load and my work as director of the Laliti shelter, I slowly withdrew from the shelter.

This has been one of the most intense lessons in my life and one that has taught me about the pitfalls of the idealism that animated me throughout this adventure. I realize that despite all the academic texts that I taught in my seminar about utopia I simply and willingly fell into its trap, experiencing how individuals become simple atoms giving life to an idea, like a communal utopia, a phalanstery.

The Laliti shelter has housed over three hundred women with their children. While many of them did return to their husbands, they were transformed individuals. The ones that have chosen divorce or separation have indeed gone through a process of empowerment and broken the circle of violence successfully. For the main Moroccan religious holidays, many of the women come back to gather, talk, socialize, drink tea, and eat cookies. Then, I realize that there is something to the word *Laliti*. And there is something about a saving compassion.

NOTES

1. Laliti is a variation of the real name of the shelter. I have changed it to protect the identity of those taking part in this adventure.
2. These amendments raised the age of marriage for young women, allowed them to contract a marriage without the father or the legal guardian, prohibited unilateral divorce, and allowed women to ask for a divorce. In all these changes, there are, of course, areas of gray. See Bargach 2005a and 2005b,
3. Despite the amendments of the Penal Code in 2003, clause 496 was kept. For associations this clause embodies the discriminatory nature of the code and for them opening a shelter amounts to an act of civil disobedience. Authorities are notified that the shelter is open and, as there is an increasing awareness of violence, "business" runs smoothly though the shelters are in effect unlawful.

WORKS CITED

Bargach, Jamila. 2005a. An Ambiguous Discourse of Rights: The 2004 Family Law Reform in Morocco. *Hawwa: Journal of Women in the Middle East and the Islamic World* 3 (2): 245–66.

———. 2005b. "Wall Hit Me": Urbanites on the Margin. *Muslim World Journal of Human Rights* 2 (1): article 8.

Contributors

M. Cristina Alcalde is an assistant professor in the Gender and Women's Studies Department at the University of Kentucky. Her research focuses on domestic violence, gender, and race in Peru and among Latinas and Latinos in the United States. Her book, *The Woman in the Violence: Gender, Poverty, and Resistance in Peru*, was published in 2010 by Vanderbilt University Press.

Sharman L. Babior holds a PhD in anthropology from the University of California, Los Angeles, where she has taught courses in anthropology and women's studies since 1994. Her primary research examines women and gender, family and social organization, domestic and sexual violence, the contemporary status of women in Japan and cross-culturally, and human rights issues.

Jamila Bargach holds a PhD in anthropology from Rice University. She is the director of academic programs for Dar Si-Hmad in Sidi Ifni, Morocco. She has taught at the École Nationale d'Architecture in Rabat, and in 2010–2011 she held the Campbell Fellowship for Women Scholar-Practitioners from Developing Nations. Her first book, *Orphans of Islam: Family, Abandonment, and Secret Adoption in Morocco*, was published by Rowman and Littlefield in 2002. She is currently completing a book on unwed mothers in Morocco.

Stephanie J. Brommer is on the faculty at City University of Seattle, where she teaches sociocultural anthropology and communications and also manages the online communications undergraduate degree program. Her current research focuses on domestic violence representations in music videos. A former newspaper reporter, she received her PhD in sociocultural anthropology from the University of California at Santa Barbara, her MS in journalism from Northwestern University, and her BA in French language and in semiotics at Brown University.

Cyleste C. Collins is a research assistant professor in the Mandel School of Applied Social Sciences and faculty associate at the Center on Urban Poverty and Community Development at Case Western Reserve University. She earned her MSW and PhD in social work from the University of Alabama in 2005. Her research is focused on understanding psychosocial processes in a cultural context. She has research and practice experience in such areas as domestic violence, homelessness, substance abuse, child abuse and neglect, and perceptions of discrimination.

Hillary J. Haldane is an assistant professor of anthropology at Quinnipiac University in Hamden, Connecticut. Her research focuses on comparative indigeneity, gender-based violence, and the instrumental use of "culture" in institutional settings and government policies. Her ethnographic research on the front line of gender-based violence has appeared in *Practicing Anthropology* and *Global Public Health*.

Julie Hemment is an associate professor in the Department of Anthropology at the University of Massachusetts, Amherst. She has published on topics of gender, postsocialism, and NGOs and civil society. Her current research investigates the restructuring of social welfare provision in Russia by examining provincial projects to promote youth voluntarism.

Uwe Jacobs has been working with Survivors International for the past fifteen years. He is a clinical neuropsychologist and a psychotherapist. He is an expert on the psychological and neuropsychological assessment of asylum seekers and has written and published guidelines on this topic. He is the recipient of the 2009 Community Health Leaders Award from the Robert Wood Johnson Foundation.

Lynn Kwiatkowski is a cultural anthropologist in the Department of Anthropology at Colorado State University. Her research focuses on medical anthropology, gender violence, political violence, hunger, and critical development studies. She has carried out ethnographic fieldwork in Vietnam, the Philippines, and the United States and is the author of *Struggling with Development: The Politics of Hunger and Gender in the Philippines* (Westview, 1998).

Belinda Leach is a professor of anthropology at the University of Guelph. Her research investigates gender, livelihoods, and feminist organizations in Canada and has been published in *Critique of Anthropology, Identities, Focaal: Journal of Global and Historical Anthropology*, and *Signs*. She is coeditor with Winnie Lem of *Culture, Economy, Power: Anthropology as Critique, Anthropology as Praxis* (State University of New York Press, 2002), and co-author with Tony Winson of *Contingent Work, Disrupted Lives: Labour and Community in the New Rural Economy* (University of Toronto Press, 2002). She is currently a co-editor of *Identities: Global Studies in Culture and Power.*

Roxane Richter is a doctoral candidate at the University of Witwatersrand in Johannesburg, South Africa, and president of the U.S.-based nonprofit World Missions Possible, an organization dedicated to providing free medical care and aid in dozens of impoverished and disaster-stricken nations. She has extensive experience as an emergency medical technician in national and international disaster aid and emergency medical services. Her research focuses on women's health care and justice challenges in refugee disasters.

Kim Shively is an assistant professor of anthropology at Kutztown University of Pennsylvania, where she specializes in gender and religion in the Middle East. She received her MTS from Harvard Divinity School and her PhD from Brandeis University. Her research has focused on women and religion in Turkey, including a two-year research project on domestic violence and women's shelters in Izmir, Turkey. She is currently preparing a book titled *Sharp Edge of the Sword: Religious Lives in Secular Turkey* for the Society for the Anthropology of Religion book series published by Palgrave Macmillan.

Jennifer R. Wies is an assistant professor of anthropology at Eastern Kentucky University. She completed a PhD in anthropology at the University of Kentucky with an emphasis on applied and medical anthropology. Her research focuses on those who labor with vulnerable populations, such as victims of gender-based violence, people with HIV/AIDS, children, and college women. She has published her work in journals such as *Global Public Health* and *Human Organization*, as well as in the edited collection *Empowering Women in Higher Education and Student Affairs: Theory, Research, Narratives, and Practice from Feminist Perspectives* (Stylus, 2011).

Index